Yielding To God's Clarion CALL

BISHOP R.S WALKER
MINISTRIES

Yielding To God's Clarion Call

by Bishop Rodney S. Walker, I.

Yielding To God's Clarion Call

To purchase additional books, Manuals, DVDs, CDs, EBooks, and other products:
www.bishoprswalkerproducts.com

Published by
Another Touch of Glory Press
Bishop RS Walker Ministries
2760 Crain Highway
Waldorf, Maryland 20601

Voice (301-843-9267) or (877-200-8967) - Fax (240-585-7093)
www.bishoprswalker.com
admin@bishoprswalker.com

Cover Design by
HCI Media
Kelly Putman, Jr.

DEDICATION

This book is dedicated to my lovely wife, Pastor Betty A. Walker. She has been an extraordinary blessing to me and provides tremendous support with all of my writing projects. Her encouragement and assistance, in every area of preparation, is greatly appreciated. Thank you Betty! I could not do this without you.

ACKNOWLEDGEMENTS

Thank You... To my son, Rodrick Walker, for your contribution in developing the format for this book.

Elder Carla Aultmon and Elder Tracy Morgan, for your contributions with editing this publication.

To Elder Cynthia V. White for your support and assistance in preparing this book for publication. I appreciate your willingness to meet the challenges necessary to prepare this product for printing and distribution.

To my son, Rodney S. Walker, Jr., for your constant support and contribution to this project.

To Elder Vicki Browning for your continued assistance in the office during the times I am writing as you block problems that may occur from me. Thank God for your tremendous gift of problem solving.

To my daughter-in-law, Natasha Walker, for all the care and support she gives to my son, Rodrick, as he works overtime, in many cases from home, to complete these projects.

Many thanks to Kelly and Patryce Putman for their care, support and production of the cover on this tremendous work.

To all of my students at Bishop R. S. Walker Ministries School of the Prophets for the great questions and demand you cultivate which assist in developing me as a Prophet.

Your ideas and suggestions contributed immensely to the birthing of this project. It is good to have all of you as part of the team. I am confident that good things will come from our joint efforts. There is no way I could get this project completed by my efforts alone. Thank you, again, for a job well done.

CONTENTS

Chapter 1

UNDERSTANDING TODAY'S PROPHET

$\mathcal{A}$ lot of people understand who they are in the prophetic, but the problem normally comes when they don't have a good enough foundation in the word to be able to defend their office to other people who don't really believe in apostles and prophets in this day. What God has led me to do is to really dig in the word and get a foundation for the office of the prophet so that we will know that it exists, how long it will exist, how we can know whether or not we are prophets, and how we know to what degree we will manifest that particular office.

When it comes down to the prophetic and the office of the prophet, it is more than just prophesying. We have to go beyond just giving someone a prophecy, beyond just encouraging people. It goes into such a deep place that we have to identify what we are designed to do--levels of maturity, levels of endurance, and levels of manifestations--we have to understand all of this so that we will be able to manifest what we are supposed to manifest in the season when we are supposed to manifest that thing.

Another thing that we cover in this class is teaching prophets and prophetic people how to go in the word and study it from a different standpoint and be able to go beyond the page. We must be able to go deep into the word, where we will be able to identify seasons and times, identify moments of impartation and moments where God is demanding a manifestation, and be able to give a message or an utterance in the prophetic. How do we really know what to share and what time to share that? How do we identify whether someone is in the season where he or she can receive this particular word? Is this the season in which to give this particular word? All of these things we have to share by way of the prophetic.

THE IMPORTANCE OF SEASONS AND TIMES

God demands that prophets understand seasons and times. Then, when we go into a particular region, it is imperative that we know the principalities and powers that govern those regions. There is a fight that takes place against prophets, those that have a word for a particular area. We have to fight because of the utterance that we are to give a particular area at a specified time. Many of us are going to have to fight a battle because of the utterance that we are purposed to give for that region at a specified time. If we do not understand that, then we do not understand our warfare. When we come to understand our assignment for that particular region, we will understand our warfare, and we will be ready for the battles to come.

This is important because the battles are designed to stop the voice of God for that area. There are things that are not going to take place in this particular time if there is not an utterance. God puts the words in a prophet's mouth for that region, and God's expectation is for that prophet (male or female) to verbalize that thing in the atmosphere and in the hearing of that particular person so that there will be manifestation for that person. One of the problems that we encounter is that when the prophet speaks, many times the prophet has not come into a revelation and understanding who he or she is. But when we come into this understanding, we walk in a different anointing.

There is an anointing that is on us, and there is an anointing in us. The anointing that comes upon us changes according to season and the assignments in that season. Anointing is upon us for a season to do particular things, but the anointing that is within does not change--it grows. Many of us do not excel in the things of God because we do not identify what anointing comes upon us in what season. Remember, as our season changes, so does our anointing; as our time changes, so does our anointing. There is an anointing on us and an anointing within us. The anointing that is within us does not change--it only grows; but the anointing that comes on us comes on us to do a particular thing for that season.

When we understand what season we are in, then we also begin to identify why there is change in mood swings and our attitude. These things change because God is preparing us for the people whom we are going to encounter in this next season. When we understand this, we begin to walk in the anointing that is upon us for this next season.

An example of this can be found in Luke 4:18-21: "*The Spirit of the Lord is upon me, because he hath anointed me to preach the gospel to the poor; he hath sent me to heal the brokenhearted, to preach deliverance to the captives, and recovering of sight to the blind, to set at liberty them that are bruised, To preach the acceptable year of the Lord. And he closed the book, and he gave it again to the minister, and sat down. And the eyes of all them that were in the synagogue were fastened on him. And he began to say unto them, This day is this scripture fulfilled in your ears.*" (KJV)

Notice that Jesus did not come right out and say this; it was a little while before he declared this. He came into a particular place, found His place in the book, and announced what was on Him and why it was on Him. Notice what Jesus said: *"The spirit of the Lord is upon me, because He has anointed me."* And then He goes on to explain in verses 18-21 why the anointing was on Him. The people that you are going to encounter are going to have to know what anointing is on you so that they can know how to receive from you. If you know what anointing is on you but people do not know how to receive from you, then we have lost the battle. So people have to know what anointing is on you and what they can expect.

WHAT DOES YOUR PRESENCE MEAN?

As prophets and prophetic people, we have to know what our presence means. When you come into a particular place, what does your presence mean as a prophet or as a prophetic person? Remember, we deal with the prophetic in four different areas: basic prophetic, gifting, prophetic ministry, the office of the prophet. In any one of these categories, what does your presence mean when you come into a particular arena or a particular city? It becomes imperative that you understand exactly what your presence means. Now remember, God said in Psalms 105:15: *"Do not touch my anointed ones; do my prophets no harm."* (NIV) Why would God say that? It is because of how He views you. He views you as His anointed, as His mouthpiece, and as His very physical presence that has come into the room or has stepped into a city. When Jesus walked into a city, He understood that nobody was going to die or stay dead in the city.

God said to me recently that one of the reasons that His people are not getting the manifestations that He desires that they get is that they do not know who they are. They do not know that they are His anointed. They do not understand that they are the very presence of God when they come into a place. They don't understand that when they showed up, God showed up in them.

God uses several different levels of revelation to help you understand what your presence means as a prophet. In one level of revelation, God is expecting some man or some woman to reveal to you some of the hidden secrets or hidden mysteries that God has spoken to him or her; this is your receiving revelation based on flesh and blood. Another level of revelation is when God has challenged you, when you get information by the Spirit of God and you are hearing God in your spirit speak to you. And the third level of revelation is when your ear is to the mouth of God. That is the level that God expects from prophets. Every time God opens His mouth, He expects those who walk in the office of the prophet to hear Him. God expects that when He voices something in the earth, all prophets hear Him, regardless of the region they are in, regardless of the level of the prophetic that they walk in. God has that expectation. He starts to echo that word through every known region. God is expecting us, as His people, to make that deposit in other people.

One reason that we do not grow in revelation is that we are not sharing the revelation that we have received to people in our region according to their season and time. When we step into someone's presence, we have to understand what season the person is in. We do not have any excuse for not knowing. We do not have to go off and pray; God will just reveal that to you. According to Amos 3:7, "**Surely the Lord GOD will do nothing, but he revealeth his secret unto his servants the prophets.**" (KJV) God will reveal His secrets to everyone that walks in the office of the prophet.

When it comes down to walking in that office of the prophet, God now begins to reveal demands and begins to pull you out into particular areas and pull information out of you in order to bring you into that next place. He brings you into a place that causes something inside of you to open up as never before. At this time there is an arena of information that is now ready to come to you.

THE CONFIDENTIALITY TEST

One of the greatest tests that prophets will encounter is the test of confidentiality. When you are a prophet, God opens up people's files to you. He reveals to you people's information, and this is one of the greatest tests that prophets have to pass. God does not gossip, and He expects prophets to come up to His standard of being confidential before He opens people's files to us in a great way. Gossip is the enemy's way of disqualifying you for the next level in the prophetic. The devil cannot shut you down; when you are flowing in the prophetic, there is no way the Devil can shut you down. The only way he can shut you down is to get you disqualified. Gossip is unauthorized information: this is information that you are not authorized to carry.

If gossip is information that certain people are not authorized to carry, that means that I cannot share that information. If you are not authorized to have the information, I may not be able to give that information to you. I may be able to carry certain information, but you may not be authorized to have that information. When God sees that you have passed that test, He will open anybody's file to you. What God reveals He intends to heal. The only reason that He shares information with you is because He intends to use you to heal that person who is the reason that He gives you someone's information.

Remember, I said that there is an anointing on you that changes from season to season, from time to time. God does not share information with you as a prophet or a prophetic person if He is not going to pour the anointing on you to heal people. Prior to doing that, He is going to put an anointing on you to make sure that you are able to carry that out. God is never depending on your ability to get someone healed. God is always going to provide an anointing to come on you to get it done. Remember, the anointing that is on you never comes to reveal information, but the anointing in you is the anointing that causes you to grasp information and understand. The anointing that is on you is on you for you to carry out a particular assignment, but the anointing is in you so that you can gather information and understand. First John puts it this way: you have unction from God and you know all things; in other words you have an anointing from the Holy One, and you know all things. You find that in KJV, 1 John 2:20: "*But ye have an unction from the Holy One, and ye know all things*" or in NIV, *1 John 2:20: "But you have an anointing from the Holy One, and all of you know the truth."* This means that you have an anointing to know all things; therefore, when you need information, you get it at that specific moment.

One of the things that will cut you out from having the information you need is making the statement "I don't know"; you should never bring that word out of your mouth, particularly if you are a prophet. Learn to change that word to "I will find out." Because you have an unction from the Holy One, in other words an anointing from the Holy One, the Holy One that lives in you will bring to the surface the information that you need at the time when you need it. If you learn to get "I don't know" out of your vocabulary, I guarantee that you will never approach a situation that you do not have information for. For every situation that you approach, you will have the information because you have an unction-1 John 2:20 But ye have an unction from the Holy One, and ye know all things KJV-in other words, an anointing from the Holy One--and you will know all things. It does take some level of boldness to declare that, because we have traditionally taken pride in stating the fact that we do not know everything. Do you realize that Jesus never positioned Himself like that? Jesus always had an answer. As a matter of fact, it says this in the word--be ready to give every man an answer, whoever asketh of thee, be always ready to give an answer, notice in 1 Peter 3:15, "*But sanctify the Lord God in your hearts: and be ready always to give an answer to every man that asketh you a reason of the hope that is in you with meekness and fear:*" (KJV) How can God demand this of us if we do not have an answer at the specific moment that we need it?

One of the first things that we are going to have to identify is the relationship that we have with God. This is a great challenge for many of us. When we come into the revelation of understanding of relationship with God, we should be willing to step out on faith even when we do not have all of the information when we first step out. We should also understand that if we do not have the information that we need to have when we need it, we make God look bad, and God is not going to let that happen. He tells us what He expects in 1 Peter 3:15. We have to stretch ourselves to the fullest measure possible when we do not have all the information that we need the first moment that we step out.

THE OBEDIENCE TEST

As a prophet, one of my toughest assignments was to step out there not having all the information before I stepped, because in my mind I did not know that I had the information. I had no evidence in my mind of having all of the information that I needed. The walk of a prophet is a faith walk. Most people who are intellectuals have a difficult challenge with this because they can't go out on one word. They have to have all of their ducks lined up in a row before they will step out.

Remember that God said to Abram, I want you to go south to a place that I will tell you about. If Abram had been an intellectual person, he would never have left home. Why? Because God had not given him all of the information, he did not have all of the travel information about his destination. When you are walking as a prophet, God is not going to give you all of the information in advance. Notice what God said to Abram in Genesis 12:1: *"Now the LORD had said unto Abram, Get thee out of thy country, and from thy kindred, and from thy father's house, unto a land that I will shew thee:"* (KJV) God gave him a bit of information to let him know what direction he was going, and this gave Abram a fraction of comfort. Abram left not having all of the information about where he was going because God told him I will show you where you are going later. Even though Abram left home, he did not completely obey God, because he was to leave all of his kindred and from his father's house. Abram was to take only his wife and possessions, but he felt some level of responsibility to Lot and he took Lot also.

That meant that God was going to have to take care of Lot. Now God could not tell Abram where he was going until after He got rid of Lot. Now here was the challenge: God never told Abram that He was not going to tell him where he was going until He got rid of Lot. God does not repeat instructions unless you are walking in full obedience. If God ever repeats instructions to you, then you should shout hallelujah because that is not the norm for God. Some of us are waiting on God to give us more instructions, but because we have never fully obeyed the instructions that we have already been given, we are not going to receive additional or repeated instructions from God. God will let you walk years in partial obedience and never tell you again what He originally said. Therefore, He did not say to Abram, "I told you to take only those that you are responsible for (your wife and your possessions)."

We are not going to get fullness of the blessing that God promised until we walk in complete obedience. I understand what Abram must have been feeling, but he still had to obey God. The only thing that caused Abram and Lot to separate was a disgruntled argument between Abram's herdsmen and Lot's herdsmen. At the point of their separation, Abram was now walking in the fullness of the obedience to the first instructions that God had given him. Once that separation happened, God talked to

Abram about where he was going. Abram could not have an effective encounter with Melchizedek until he got rid of Lot. Remember Genesis 14:18-20: "*Then Melchizedek king of Salem brought out bread and wine. He was priest of God Most High, and he blessed Abram, saying, 'Blessed be Abram by God Most High, Creator of heaven and earth. And blessed be God Most High, who delivered your enemies into your hand.' Then Abram gave him a tenth of everything.*" (NIV) The purpose of Melchizedek was to come and bless Abram. That could not happen until Abram walked in full obedience.

THE IMPORTANCE OF KNOWING YOUR PROPHETIC ASSIGNMENT

Now take a look at 1 Corinthians 12:27-30: "*Now ye are the body of Christ, and members in particular. And God hath set some in the church, first apostles, secondarily prophets, thirdly teachers, after that miracles, then gifts of healings, helps, governments, diversities of tongues. Are all apostles? are all prophets? are all teachers? are all workers of miracles? Have all the gifts of healing? do all speak with tongues? do all interpret?*" (KJV) Notice what this scripture says, in verse 28, "*And God has appointed these in the church: first apostles, second prophets, third teachers, after that miracles, then gifts of healings, helps, administrations, varieties of tongues.*" (NKJV)

God has appointed these offices in the church. God did this. He set first apostles, secondarily prophets, thirdly teachers. Now by way of the prophet, God set you in the church so that you would carry out a particular assignment. There will be no real release of anointing until you become totally persuaded that God has set you in the church. The real anointing cannot show up until we know exactly why we are in the church where we are. I know exactly why I am where I am in "God Is In Control Church." I am there to carry out a prophetic assignment. My assignment there has everything to do with bringing people into purpose. God would have never set me there if He did not want me to do that. So as long as people need to identify their purpose and need to come into destiny, I am needed. When people stop coming, needing to identify their purpose and to come into their destiny, I am no longer needed there and my assignment is finished.

THE IMPORTANCE OF BEING A GOOD STEWART OF WORDS

According to Ephesians 4:7: "*But unto every one of us is given grace according to the measure of the gift of Christ.*" (KJV) So the gift that is on you determines your level of grace. We are not talking about the saving grace of Jesus. We are talking about the empowering substance that is on us. Every one of us has been given this empowering grace for a specific reason. One word for gift is charismata and comes from the word charisma; this gift is smeared on you. The other word for gift is doma; this passage is talking about doma. This gift is connected to the office. As long as you stay connected to your office, a level of empowering comes on you; this gift is called doma, and it is what is being talked about in Ephesians 4:7 because it is dealing with your office. The empowering grace gift on the office is anointing, grace, and favor. All of these are on the office. Most of us do not use the fullness of our office; we do not realize how much is on that office. Some of us who are called as prophets never step into the office because we are afraid of it. There is nothing to be afraid of; it is only something to be admired. Why? Grace--that empowering substance, doma--allows us to face any giant, and with the mantle that is on your life, you can annihilate it. You are going to be able to take that giant down by way of your mouth because you are the mouthpiece of God. You are able to take anything down with your words. One of the weapons of a prophet is his mouth. If the devil can get you to use your mouth wrong, he can use your mouth against you.

Take a look at this example in 1 Kings 17:1: *"And Elijah the Tishbite, who was of the inhabitants of Gilead, said unto Ahab, As the LORD God of Israel liveth, before whom I stand, there shall not be dew nor rain these years, but according to my word."* (KJV) Do you realize that this prophet is walking in serious confidence? He says that there is not going to be neither dew nor rain except at his word. This means, as a prophet of God you can walk into any situation and declare what is going to be according to your word. This does not happen just because you are a child of God. It happens because there is a mantle on your life. As a prophet of God, there is a mantle on your office. The prophet of God is able to say that there is not going to be rain until I say.

Now according to 1 Kings 17:7-9: *"And it came to pass after a while, that the brook dried up, because there had been no rain in the land. And the word of the LORD came unto him, saying, Arise, get thee to Zarephath, which belongeth to Zidon, and dwell there: behold, I have commanded a widow woman there to sustain thee".* (KJV) The brook has dried up, and this is a manifestation of the accuracy of Elijah's word, because the river is flowing and the only way that the river will continue to flow is if rain comes. But it is not just Ahab who is affected. Someone else is affected in the city other than Elijah and Ahab. There is a widow woman who is being affected. The raven is feeding Elijah, so he does not need to be fed. Now God sends Elijah to the widow and says that He has commanded her to feed him, but God does not tell the widow woman anything about what He said to Elijah.

Can there be a command of God and you not know it? Yes, because the widow woman does not know that God had commanded her to do that. Elijah now tests her by asking her for water to see if she heard what he heard. After that he asks her for a little cake. He finds out that he heard what God said but she did not hear. Elijah now has to persuade the widow to take care of the man of God when she does not have anything. Now the prophet has to convince the widow to give him what he asked. How are you going to persuade someone to give you something when he or she doesn't have anything to give? Can you do that? Yes, you can when the anointing is on you. Once she obeys him, it is not over yet, because now he has to manifest for her what she needs. It is not over until she receives.

Another example is the woman who built a room onto her house for the man of God. This is found in 2 Kings 4:15-20: "*And he said, Call her. And when he had called her, she stood in the door. And he said, About this season, according to the time of life, thou shalt embrace a son. And she said, Nay, my lord, thou man of God, do not lie unto thine handmaid. And the woman conceived, and bare a son at that season that Elisha had said unto her, according to the time of life. And when the child was grown, it fell on a day, that he went out to his father to the reapers. And he said unto his father, My head, my head. And he said to a lad, Carry him to his mother. And when he had taken him, and brought him to his mother, he sat on her knees till noon, and then died.*" (KJV) When the child died, she did not go to her husband, and she did not go to God. She went to see the man of God; she took her son to the prophet. She was expecting a manifestation from the prophet concerning the life of her son. When she got to the prophet she did not say anything. We see this in 2 Kings 4:26: Run now, I pray thee, to meet her, and say unto her, Is it well with thee? is it well with thy husband? is it well with the child? And she answered, It is well .KJV Notice he asked three questions and she gave the same answer. It is well with me. It is well with my husband.

And he asked about her son she said, "it is well". She would not allow her words to be in disagreement with the prophet's words that had already been said in verse 16. Some things you cannot say, just to keep your confession right. Even though she said it is well, the prophet knew something was wrong. When he identified what the problem was, he knew the son was dead and said God has withheld it from me. He was talking about a problem that he did not know was happening.

In 2 Kings 4:27: "*And when she came to the man of God to the hill, she caught him by the feet: but Gehazi came near to thrust her away. And the man of God said, Let her alone; for her soul is vexed within her: and the LORD hath hid it from me, and hath not told me*". KJV That brings me into a great revelation. He was totally amazed that something happened in his region and he did not know about it, because God has said in Amos 3:7:….. "*Surely the Lord GOD will do nothing , but he revealeth his secret unto his servants the prophets.*" (KJV) If you are a prophet, nothing should happen in your region without your knowing about it.

REGIONAL INFORMATION SHOULD BE AVAILABLE TO PROPHETS

This is the account of the woman's story in 2 Kings 4:28: "*Then she said, Did I desire a son of my lord? did I not say, Do not deceive me?*" (KJV) She was expecting her son to live, and that is what the prophet did. He raised him from the dead. This is an amazing revelation to me that nothing should happen in your region without your knowing about it. When something happens in your region, you should know about it. When something happens in your family, you should know about it.

One of my personal examples of this is that of my nephew. This particular nephew was living in the fast lane, and every time he got into trouble, I would know about it. I would tell him of my dreams about him. One time I was praying after a particular dream, and when I told him, he told me that he was running and someone was shooting and the bullet passed him and hit the person who he was with in the foot. And I said, man, you are going to have to quit and come out of this type of life. Another time when I told him about my dream, he stayed in his house for awhile until that was over. This went on for years. Finally, I had a dream that I was running after him. Someone had put him in a truck, but I could not catch the truck. I ran with everything that was in me, but I could not catch the truck.

I went looking for him but I could not find him. I called, but I was not able to get him. He returned my call, but I missed his call, and the next day I received the word that someone had put him in his truck and shot him about 14 times, and then I understood my dream. This time you won't catch him, all the other times you saved him, but this time you won't be able to save him. I shared that to say that something like that could not happen and I not know about it because that was in my region. Nothing should happen in my region and I not know about it, not have my ear to the mouth of God. There are particular things that God is going to reveal to us in this our time, and we are going to have to be sensitive to what God is saying and make sure that we are running after God with every thing that we have.

TAPPING INTO DIVINE REVELATION

God put the apostle, prophet, evangelist, pastor and teacher in the earth for a specific reason. That reason is to keep the devil from kicking the church around. The revelation that Jesus is talking about in Matthew 16 is that revelation that Peter received from the Father. This is the level of revelation that prophets and prophetic people should be receiving, and this is another level of revelation where we are walking in the revelation that Jesus walked. This is revelation that we need to walk in God in order to defeat the devil. God has you seated in a place where you should have victory every day. One of the reasons that we do not walk in victory is that we do not know our position. The rock is a level of revelation that Peter accessed from the Father.

This level of revelation that I am talking about can be found in Matthew 16:13-19: "*When Jesus came into the coasts of Caesarea Philippi, he asked his disciples, saying, Whom do men say that I the Son of man am? And they said, Some say that thou art John the Baptist: some, Elias; and others, Jeremias, or one of the prophets. He saith* unto them, *But whom say ye that I am? And Simon Peter answered and said, Thou art the Christ, the Son of the living God. And Jesus answered and said unto him, Blessed art thou, Simon Barjona: for flesh and blood hath not revealed it unto thee, but my Father which is in heaven. And I say also unto thee, That thou art Peter, and upon this rock I will build my church; and the gates of hell shall not prevail against it. And I will give unto thee the keys of the kingdom of heaven: and whatsoever thou shalt bind on earth shall be bound in heaven: and whatsoever thou shalt loose on earth shall be loosed in heaven.*" (KJV)

Jesus was talking only to Peter; we see that in verse 18. All of the disciples were there at the same time with Peter and Jesus, but Jesus was talking about the one that came up with the revelation. Peter received the benefit of walking in a place that he had not manifested yet. He was getting information before they received the Holy Spirit. They did not receive the Holy Spirit until Acts chapter 2. The Holy Spirit came to them all in Acts 2:1-4: "*And when the day of Pentecost was fully come, they were all with one accord in one place. And suddenly there came a sound from heaven as of a rushing mighty wind, and it filled all the house where they were sitting. And there appeared unto them cloven tongues like as of fire, and it sat upon each of them And they were all filled with the Holy Ghost, and began to speak with other tongues, as the Spirit gave them utterance.*" (KJV) So Peter received this before time.

THE THREE LEVELS OF THE HOLY SPIRIT

As prophets and prophetic people, you have to go to another level of the Holy Spirit. There are three levels of the Holy Spirit that you experience in your life. The first level is mentioned in Acts 2:38: "*Then Peter said unto them, Repent, and be baptized every one of you in the name of Jesus Christ for the remission of sins, and ye shall receive the gift of the Holy Ghost.*" (KJV) Most of us operate in the body of Christ just as people who have received the Holy Spirit. When you have received the Holy Spirit, you have Him by measure, and you have just enough of the Holy Spirit to speak in tongues and do signs and wonders. With this measure of the Holy Spirit, you can do everything that God told you to do, because the Holy Spirit is all you need and He was given to us on the day of Pentecost. Level two is being filled with Him, and level three is being filled with the Holy Spirit without measure. Both of these are found in John 3:30-34: "*He must increase, but I must decrease. He that cometh from above is above all: he that is of the earth is earthly, and speaketh of the earth: he that cometh from heaven is above all. And what he hath seen and heard, that he testifieth; and no man receiveth his testimony. He that hath received his testimony hath set to his seal that God is true. For he whom God hath sent speaketh the words of God: for God giveth not the Spirit by measure unto him.*" (KJV) This is prophetic word that we need to get in on because most of us have received the Holy Spirit and are satisfied.

Being filled with the Holy Spirit is not enough for prophets; they need to have the Holy Spirit without measure. Most of us have received the Holy Spirit, and now we are satisfied, but that is not enough of Him. Notice in verse 34 John mentions that he whom God has sent speaks the words of God and God gives him the Spirit of God without measure. What is receiving the Holy Spirit without measure? It is receiving Him where it cannot be measured. In verse 31 John mentions that Jesus comes from above and is above all, and that is where we must get our revelation. We are seated in heavenly places in Christ Jesus, who is seated on the right hand of the Father. This means that we are from above and are above all because those that come from heaven are above all, but those that are of the earth are earthly and speak of the earth. Therefore, we must get our revelation just as Jesus did, having the Holy Spirit without measure. Now we need to figure out where we are, because if we have one-fourth Holy Spirit, then we have three-fourths flesh. Therefore, we need to be filled with the Holy Spirit and also to have Him without measure.

How do we become filled with the Holy Spirit without measure? We do that by speaking in tongues at our every opportunity. The way you build up yourself is by praying always in the Spirit, and we see that in Jude 20: *"But ye, beloved, building up yourselves on your most holy faith, praying in the Holy Ghost."* (KJV) Even when you are in your office at work, you can do this quietly. The more you talk with Him, the more you get filled up with Him. This is not a time for praying in intercession, because when you are praying in intercession, you are in a session for someone you may not even know. Pray in the Spirit early in the morning because this is the time for you to fill yourself with the Holy Spirit. When you pray in the Spirit in intercession, you are pouring out, not taking in.

Remember who we are. We are the ones who took the place of the Devil, which is why he does not like us. He was recognized as the anointed Cherub, the one that covered, the one who led the worship. Who are we really, as a prophetic person or a prophet? We are created in the image of God, and we are fellowship partners with God. God loves fellowship. God wants us to experience fellowship with Him when He comes down and when we go up and fellowship with Him. How are we going to go up? We are able to do that because we are seated in heavenly places with Christ, as seen in Colossians 3:1-2: *"Since, then, you have been raised with Christ, set your hearts on things above, where Christ is seated at the right hand of God. 2 Set your minds on things above, not on earthly things."* (NIV) and you are above all. This is the reason God has to have you with the Holy Spirit without measure. As a prophetic person or a prophet, you must have an open door policy with God, the awesome privilege to barge into your office anytime He gets ready. That is what I have with God. I can go into Him anytime I get ready, and He can barge into my life anytime He gets ready. I give God permission to interrupt me anytime He wants.

AUTHORITY, ORDER AND STRUCTURE

God wants prophetic people and prophets to bring authority, order, and structure. When God sends you into a situation, it is going to be void and without form. God wants us to change things the way He did in Genesis 1:3. "*And God said, "Let there be light," and there was light.*" (NIV) Light came by His saying, and that is what we must do, we must speak to things, situations, circumstances etc. When God asks us to carry out a particular assignment, we do not want to do it because of the way the people act in that situation. These people or situations are without form and void and without order. God sends us in at the beginning of something so that we can bring form and order to those particular situations. Many of us tell God that we are not able to bring order and structure because we need that in our own lives and that is why we become the first partakers by setting ourselves in order by speaking the words that bring order to our lives. Stop declaring that your life is out of order.

Speak what you desire. For example, if you are a person who bounces checks, then speak to that situation and say that you are not going to do that anymore and change some things. Another example is that of a single man looking for a wife. God is not necessarily going to send you a person exactly according to what you have in your mind; therefore, you must speak to what you desire and keep on saying that. We must start speaking to things.

I do that by speaking to the things that I want to change. One example of this that I am currently practicing is speaking to the parking lot at my church to fill the empty spaces with new members for the church. That section is now filled, so I am speaking to the other portions of the parking lot. For many years my children did not have peace, so I started speaking the word of God on them. I spoke Isaiah 54:13-14: "*And all thy children shall be taught of the LORD; and great shall be the peace of thy children. In righteousness shalt thou be established: thou shalt be far from oppression; for thou shalt not fear: and from terror; for it shall not come near thee.*" (KJV) I did that until that manifested in the lives of my children. Do not verbalize statements declaring that your children are stupid. Speak only what God says about your children, not what you see. If you need a new car, you get that the same way God got the new earth. How did God get a new earth? He spoke it. All of that power and authority are in your office. Use what is in your office.

Matthew 16:18: "*. . .upon this Rock I will build my church...*" was Jesus' prophetic proclamation of the New Testament church. Jesus preached, taught and demonstrated the power of the Gospel of the Kingdom of God as portrayed by Matthew. He presented the spiritual and heavenly kingdom that could only be entered into by repentance and faith. The Kingdom of God was given to a nation that would bring forth the fruits thereof, thus the background is set for the building of His church.

Ephesians 4 depicts the gifts given by Jesus. It is through these gifts that Jesus establishes the structure of church leadership.   Ephesians 4 gives an exhortation of the privileges and responsibilities of the Christian through unity and love. It also includes an explanation of how "the body" would be led and the means by which it would function and mature. Properly termed the "ascension gifts" (ministry), they are commonly referred to as the "five-fold ministry." The foundational purposes for these gifts are also described in Ephesians 4:12-13 For the perfecting of the saints, for the work of the ministry, for the edifying of the body of Christ: 13 Till we all come in the unity of the faith, and of the knowledge of the Son of God, unto a perfect man, unto the measure of the stature of the fulness of Christ: KJV.

The apostle Paul prophetically reveals in Ephesians 4:8 that everything the body of Christ would need to grow and mature was established by Jesus: "....*When he ascended up on high, he led captivity captive, and he gave gifts unto men*" As we examine specifically the gift of the prophet, we will identify his purpose, responsibilities, and the duration that he will exist in the church.

The "ascension gifts" brought authority, order, and structure to the church. The apostle Paul further depicts the ranking responsibility in the order of the apostle, prophet, evangelist, pastor and teacher. "*And he gave some, apostles; and some prophets; and some, evangelists; and some pastors and teachers.*" (Ephesians 4:11 KJV)

THE PURPOSE OF THIS PROGRAM

This program is designed to identify and bring clarity of understanding to the ranking authority, positions, roles and responsibilities of the prophetic ministry and how the prophet contributes to:

1. The perfecting of the saints,
2. The work of the ministry, and;
3. The edification (building up) of the "Body of Christ."

The word of God also shows us the duration that these gifts would be with us:

1. till we all come into the unity of the faith,
2. and of the knowledge of the Son of God;
3. unto a perfect man;
4. unto the measure of the stature of the fullness of Christ.

In today's church, the prophets have not fulfilled their role and purpose. Without the prophet active in his role in today's church, the church has become less effective than she would have been if the order and plan of God for the church had been followed through.

The role of the prophet is essential to bringing certain aspects of God's word and order to the body of Christ. They must show the way, even in their times of testing.

Among the reasons for the prophet are:

1. So that we do not continue to be children tossed to and fro
2. So that we are not carried about with every wind of doctrine (teaching) as Ephesians 4:15 says: "***But speaking the truth in love, may grow up into Him in all things, which is the Head even Christ.***" (Ephesians 4:15) KJV

THE WORLD BEFORE ADAM

Why has God selected you to operate in the prophetic, and what is your place in God? Many of us, as prophets and prophetic people, are not producing at the level that God wants us to produce at, and the reason that we don't is because we do not know who we really are, nor do we understand why God has selected us and why the enemy hates us. I am convinced that in times past we only thought we knew who we are, but once you read this, you will know who you are and why the enemy hates you so much.

Let's start with Genesis 1:1-2: "***In the beginning God created the Heaven and the earth. And the earth was without form, and void; and darkness was upon the face of the deep. And the Spirit of God moved upon the face of the waters.***" (KJV) From this passage we can see that in the beginning, God created the heaven and the earth. This is the period before time. This is the period before history. This was the time of the cavemen and dinosaurs, etc. In the beginning, God did, then billions of years passed. When we notice that the earth was without form and void and the darkness was upon the face of the deep, we know that this condition is not beautiful, nor is it perfect. Does God create things in that condition? Let's find out from Ecclesiastes 3:11: "***He hath made every thing beautiful in his time: also he hath set the world in their heart, so that no man can find out the work that God maketh from the beginning to the end.***" (KJV)

Notice that this passage lets us know that God had made everything beautiful. Everything that God makes is beautiful. You are beautiful because everything that God makes is beautiful. When He created the earth, it was beautiful. The earth was a marvelously beautiful place when God created it. In the beginning God did it; He created the heaven and the earth, then billions of years passed. We actually call this period the prehistoric period, we call the creatures prehistoric, we call the people prehistoric (cavemen and -women). This is the period before history, and the Bible talks about it.

This is largely missed in the church, but if prophets and prophetic people miss this, we miss an important portion of how we are supposed to operate, and it is called "creating".

As prophets and prophetic people, we have to get away from the thinking that the best that we can do is to prophesy. In the School of the Prophets, we do not even teach you to prophesy. If you can understand this, prophecy is not a problem. Understanding of this will cause us to stop prophesying to people to get new cars and spouses, because all you have to do is straighten up your life and you can get a car or a spouse. You do not need a prophecy to get those. Now also from Ecclesiastes 3:11: "........*also he hath set the world in their heart, so that no man can find out the work that God maketh from the beginning to the end.*" (KJV) we see that God has set the world in their heart so that nobody can find out the work that He made from the beginning to the end. Nobody can find this out; God does not reveal everything so that everybody can understand. God understood that many would not understand this, so this particular phase of creation God planted in the heart so that it was not clear otherwise. This is the reason that scientists are still trying to figure it out. Now in Genesis 1:1-3: "*In the beginning God created the Heaven and the earth. And the earth was without form, and void; and darkness was upon the face of the deep. And the Spirit of God moved upon the face of the waters. 3 And God said, Let there be light: and there was light.*" (KJV) In verse 3, God said let there be light, and we have considered that the word "let" was a word of creation. But the problem is that we are dealing with a whole world that had been destroyed. Therefore, the word "let" was a word of permission, because this was a restoration, not a creation.

The prophetic challenge for us is to quit prophesying to people without knowledge. It is one thing for us to speak a creative word into your life and bring about something that has never been. It is another thing for us to speak a word of permission to something that is being blocked or stopped. For example, if you receive a word of prophecy concerning wealth and you neglect to tithe, there is a whole world of financial blessing that shuts down to you. Now the very second that you get that in order, a prophet can say to you, Let there be wealth, and now it opens up. The prophet did not create that; he permitted it. But he or she cannot permit it until everything is in proper alignment. There may be many prophecies that prophets have prophesied to people that have not come to pass. Prophecy after prophecy may come, but nothing is going to happen if the floodgates are closed because of a violation somewhere. So the word "let" is not a word of creation--it is a word of permission. There are prophecies that have been given to people that have not come to pass because there is a violation in place somewhere. No matter how many prophets prophesy to you of wealth, it will not come to pass as long as you are in violation of the tithe.

Now let us look at the place where we cross over into the place of creation, because

Genesis 1:3 is a place of restoration, not the place of creation. More than likely you have never heard creation talked about; you have only heard restoration talked about. Would you agree that when God creates something it is created perfect? We see that is true in Psalms 18:30: "*As for God, his way is perfect: the word of the LORD is tried: he is a buckler to all those that trust in him.*" (KJV) God's way is perfect; now, as a prophet, you are to create it perfect, and you should not stop short of what is perfection. Do you realize how many of us have no problem with imperfection, and the reason for that is because imperfection keeps the pressure off us? When God has created a thing and it comes in violation, He does not need to recreate it.

He just permits it once the violation has been corrected. If it is in violation, it only needs permission, not creation. Many times we are trying to get many things to work, and they are not about to work because they are in violation. Things that are in violation are without form (no shape, no order to them), void, empty (God created this, so it cannot be empty, because God created everything beautiful; therefore, this is the restoration, not the creation), and darkness is upon them--that means that they lack order, and when there is no order, God is not in it.

Now let's take a look at Job to get to the next step. Now, remember that Job is not in its proper chronological order in the Bible. This becomes a major problem. Job was on the earth during Adam's day. Job had some information that we needed to know about the creation. Because this book is located around the book of Psalms, we think that is when he was on the earth, and we don't look for creation information in the book of Job. But Job was in Adam's day, and he has some information about creation. Now as prophets of God, if we start with the restoration, we cannot serve our real purpose of creation. Take a look at Job 9:1-10. Verses 1-4 read: "*Then Job answered and said, I know it is so of a truth: but how should man be just with God? If he will contend with him, he cannot answer him one of a thousand. He is wise in heart, and mighty in strength: who hath hardened himself against him, and hath prospered?*"KJV Now when we understand that Job was just talking without knowledge at this time, God gets involved with what he is saying, and God's rebuke of him gave us some valuable information about creation. Job's rebuke became our fortune of knowledge. Continue with verse 5: "*Which removeth the mountains, and they know not: which overturneth them in his anger.*" What mountains? This goes back to a time of destruction of the world that was.

Remembering that God creates everything beautiful and perfect and when we go back to Genesis 1:2 and read about the earth being without form and void and darkness was upon it, we know now this is not beautiful. If this God that we serve creates things perfect, there must have been mountains at the actual time of creation. We know that this was not creation because God creates everything perfect, so the earth had to have had some mountains. If you have ever seen mountains, you know how beautiful they are, so there had to be some mountains there at the creation; now we see in verse 5 that there were mountains there, but God overturned them when He became angry. It is not easy to get God upset, but when He gets angry, He can destroy some things. Continuing with verse 6: "*Which shaketh the earth out of her place, and the pillars thereof tremble.*"

We have a difficulty here because God did not shake the earth out of its place after Adam. It was never shaken out of its place after Adam, so when was it shaken? This happened before history. Now God comes down, and out of his anger, He begins to walk and shakes the earth out of its place. The pillars that upheld the earth begin to crumble. Now what pillars were these? Take a look at verse 7: "*Which commandeth the sun, and it riseth not; and sealeth up the stars.*" The word "let" in the book of Genesis is a word of permission. When did the sun stop rising after Adam? It has not. Now this lets us know that the word "let" is a word of permission. These events happened in prehistoric time. When God tells the sun not to shine, it won't shine until He comes back on the scene and says "let," giving it permission to shine again. Now we have to understand that God has already told the earth what to permit and what not to permit, so when we are in violation of these things, there are certain things that just cannot happen.

In this same verse, God told the stars not to shine, He sealed them up so that no light came from them. Now this is the interpretation that darkness was upon it, pure darkness. The sun is not shining, and the stars are sealed, and there is no light to be seen. Now we have the darkness upon the deep, and there was nothing to be seen. Now, as God is looking at His creation, the time that is called the "dateless past" we see in verses 8-10: "*Which alone spreadeth out the heavens, and treadeth upon the waves of the sea. Which maketh Arcturus, Orion, and Pleiades, and the chambers of the south. Which doeth great things past finding out; yea, and wonders without number.*" This was the time period that He was going to blot out, but He wanted to make sure that His people would know what had happened. Now in the beginning God created the heaven and the earth. The word "beginning" is Hebrew word that means "dateless past." God wanted His people to have information that other people do not have. Understand that scientists have the same bible that we have, but they don't have the information that God wanted us to have. This should encourage you to know that you have information that the scientists do not have.

This helps me to be the prophet that God has really called me to be, and it gives me a glimpse of an understanding as to how to function. Take a look at Jeremiah 4:23-28: "*I beheld the earth, and, lo, it was without form, and void; and the heavens, and they had no light.*" This (verse 23) confirms Genesis; the words beheld or behold means "to see", but how did he see something that has no form? Jeremiah is giving us an understanding of the vision that he had, and Jeremiah is saying that I beheld (saw) the earth and then it was not, I saw the heavens and then it was no light (the lights went out).

When you go outside and see the stars shining, that is the first heaven, and all of the lights are on and they have continued to shine since Adam. Verse 24 continues: "*I beheld the mountains, and, lo, they trembled, and all the hills moved lightly.*" Jeremiah is saying here, I literally saw that the mountains and the hills were there, and then they trembled and were no more, and the hills moved back lightly. Where did they go (move to)? They moved back into the waters and were no more. This gives us a glimpse of what time period these events occurred. In verse 25: "*I beheld, and, lo, there was no man, and all the birds of the heavens were fled.*" Now Jeremiah is saying that I looked and all of these things were, and then I saw that there was no man and all the birds of the heavens (left) were gone.

Now at what point after Adam did all the birds leave? This has not happened since Adam, certainly not in Noah's flood, because the Bible says that they were still here and Noah had some birds with him. So that did not happen after Adam's day. It was in the time of the dateless past. Verse 26 reads: "*I beheld, and, lo, the fruitful place was a wilderness, and all the cities thereof were broken down at the presence of the LORD, and by his fierce anger.*" Jeremiah is saying here that he saw a fruitful place and then it became wilderness. Now Genesis 1:2 says that the earth was without form and void and darkness was upon it.

What is he talking about? There was a fruitful place, and then he saw the earth, a wilderness. Genesis 1:2 does not talk about the earth being a fruitful place. Then Jeremiah says he saw all of the cities, and then he saw that they were broken down. What cities? And when were they broken down? He saw all the cities that were there and then the cities were broken down. When after Adam were the cities broken down? All of this happened at the presence of the Lord and by His anger. Now do you realize why Abraham asked God not to be angry with him? During the time pleading for the righteous in Sodom and Gomorrah, he kept saying God, "do not be angry with me". Abraham understood God's anger. God showed up.

Now, when something does not function according to God's order, He comes down and destroys it and starts over and puts it in order. Why did God do all of this? It was because the earth was not functioning according to the order He desired and He was angry. In His anger He told the sun not to shine, He sealed the stars and did not allow them to shine, He crumbled the mountains and the hills and they moved into the waters, He made the fruitful place a wilderness and broke down all of the cities. And then God said the whole land shall be desolate, but I will not make a full end to it. Why would God not bring it to a full end? It is because He was not done with it yet. In the process of doing all of this, God made the whole land desolate but did not make a full end of it.

We see this in verse 27: "*For thus hath the LORD said, The whole land shall be deso-late; yet will I not make a full end.*" Now we see that the Lord said that He will make the land desolate yet He will not bring it to a full end. This is important for us to understand. We should never discount what God said that He is going to do in our lives. Because if God says something to you, He has every intention of fulfilling that thing. He might bring it to desolation, but He will not let you die. He will not bring it to a full end.

Now God says in verse 28: "*For this shall the earth mourn, and the heavens above be black: because I have spoken it, I have purposed it, and will not repent, neither will I turn back from it.*" God will not change His mind about you. As prophets, we have to maintain this mindset. We have to understand what God is saying about someone and know that if He, God, will not change His mind, neither can we. We are only supposed to say what God is saying about people. If God is saying that He is going to bless them, then we have to say that regardless of what we see on their lives right now. This means that God might bring them to desolation before fulfillment comes. He may have to wipe some friends out of their lives before fulfillment comes, He may have to get some family members away from them before fulfillment comes, but fulfillment is on its way and it will come.

Now let's follow this further in Isaiah 24:1: "*Behold, the LORD maketh the earth empty, and maketh it waste, and turneth it upside down, and scattereth abroad the inhabitants thereof.*" Now take a look at this. God makes the earth empty and makes it waste and turns it upside down. What happened? Now what happens when God turns the earth upside down? Since the earth is two-thirds water, what happens when God turns it upside down? The whole thing is flooded out and scattered the inhabitants. What inhabitants? Verse 1 says that the earth was empty, so what inhabitants are being spoken of here? There were no people, no birds are here, and nothing that is living with a body is in the earth at that time. Now the only things that were left in the earth were demons. God knew that they would not die, so when He turned the earth upside down, all of the demons scattered. The demon spirits were the inhabitants. Do you want to know why you are having the challenges that you are having? It is because demons were scattered abroad now they are everywhere.

Now let us get more information about the creation from Job's rebuke. We find this in Job 38:1-30: "*Then the LORD answered Job out of the whirlwind, and said, Who is this that darkeneth counsel by words without knowledge?*" God is rebuking Job at this point. And in the next verse, God demanded an answer from Job. "*Gird up now thy loins like a man; for I will demand of thee, and answer thou me. Where wast thou when I laid the foundations of the earth? declare, if thou hast understanding.*" When did God lay the foundation? "*Who hath laid the measures thereof, if thou knowest? or who hath stretched the line upon it? Whereupon are the foundations thereof fastened?*"

*or who laid the corner stone thereof; When the morning stars (the stars are the angels of God) sang together, and all the sons of God shouted for joy?"*KJV Now He is talking about the sons of God, not us, but the angels. This is when they went into praise. When did all of this happen? God is asking Job about the laying of the foundations of the earth. Now are you able to understand the time period of these events?

Now if we look closely at verse 8: *"Or who shut up the sea with doors, when it brake forth, as if it had issued out of the womb?" When did God do this?* Verses 9-12 continue, *"When I made the cloud the garment thereof, and thick darkness a swaddling band for it, And brake up for it my decreed place, and set bars and doors, And said, Hitherto shalt thou come, but no further: and here shall thy proud waves be stayed? Hast thou commanded the morning since thy days; and caused the dayspring to know his place;"* When did this happen? Verse 13 reads: *"That it might take hold of the ends of the earth, that the wicked might be shaken out of it?"* When were the wicked shaken out of the earth? Not since Adam. Verses 14-25 continue: *"It is turned as clay to the seal; and they stand as a garment. And from the wicked their light is withholden, and the high arm shall be broken. Hast thou entered into the springs of the sea? or hast thou walked in the search of the depth? Have the gates of death been opened unto thee? or hast thou seen the doors of the shadow of death? Hast thou perceived the breadth of the earth? declare if thou knowest it all. Where is the way where light dwelleth? and as for darkness, where is the place thereof, That thou shouldest take it to the bound thereof, and that thou shouldest know the paths to the house thereof? Knowest thou it, because thou wast then born? or because the number of thy days is great? Hast thou entered into the treasures of the snow? or hast thou seen the treasures of the hail, Which I have reserved against the time of trouble, against the day of battle and war? By what way is the light parted, which scattereth the east wind upon the earth? Who hath divided a watercourse for the overflowing of waters, or a way for the lightning of thunder;"*

Now can I submit to you that when God turned the earth upside down, He brought in such fierce temperatures that everything froze. This is why scientists were able to find things. God froze things, and when the temperature is raised, everything will melt. This was the wisdom of God, because once the melting started, a water course was needed so that the melting water would have a course to follow. Verse 26 reads: *"To cause it to rain on the earth, where no man is; on the wilderness, wherein there is no man;"* Now we see rain, but no man is here. It had never rained in history, after Adam, but it did in the prehistoric time. This is not Noah's rain, because there was no rain after Adam until Noah. We see all of this in Genesis; this is work of restoration. Verses 27-30 continue: *"To satisfy the desolate and waste ground; and to cause the bud of the tender herb to spring forth? Hath the rain a father? or who hath begotten the drops of dew? Out of whose womb came the ice? and the hoary frost of heaven, who hath gendered it? The waters are hid as with a stone, and the face of the deep is frozen."*

Now we see that the water was hard (hid as with a stone), and the face of the deep was frozen. Now in Genesis 1:2: darkness was upon the face of the deep, but the face of the deep was frozen. When God turned it upside down, He froze it. Everything was frozen; something had to keep this until God was ready to allow it to melt; now this was the time period of the restoration of the earth. If we understand every bit of this, we now have a word of creation in our mouth where we would declare a thing and watch it become.

Now we move to Psalms 104 and see what else happened at the period of restoration. Psalms 104:1-25 begins: *"Bless the LORD, O my soul. O LORD my God, thou art very great; thou art clothed with honour and majesty. Who coverest thyself with light as with a garment: who stretchest out the heavens like a curtain: Who layeth the beams of his chambers in the waters: who maketh the clouds his chariot: who walketh upon the wings of the wind: Who maketh his angels spirits; his ministers a flaming fire: Who laid the foundations of the earth, that it should not be removed for ever. Thou coveredst it with the deep as with a garment: the waters stood above the mountains."*

This is the period of restoration, and in the next verse we see God rebuking the waters. "At thy rebuke they fled; at the voice of thy thunder they hasted away." Now at what point did God rebuke the waters? That was Genesis 1:8; the waters abated. They just moved away. How did the waters know where to go? God had set a water course and the waters knew where to go, and God had set boundaries that they may not pass over and they turn not again to cover the earth. We see all of this in the following verses. *"They go up by the mountains; they go down by the valleys unto the place which thou hast founded for them. Thou hast set a bound that they may not pass over; that they turn not again to cover the earth. He sendeth the springs into the valleys, which run among the hills."*KJV

Now we are to find out why God brought His creation to desolation and discover God's reasons for restoration of His original creation. We start in Isaiah 14:12: *"How art thou fallen from heaven, O Lucifer, son of the morning! how art thou cut down to the ground, which didst weaken the nations!"* KJV This is what I was trying to get to. Lucifer was the reason that all of this happened, from creation in Genesis 1:1, then billions of years passed by, a prehistoric time that we call the dateless past that we have been talking about. After God created the earth, Lucifer was in charge of the earth, and he was the reason that God destroyed everything. Lucifer was the reason for it all because he weakened the nations. What nations? There were nations that were here during prehistoric time, prehistoric men.

Remember, all of this was before history. How did he get to weaken the nations unless he had a voice to speak to them? Lucifer weakened the nations; he had a voice to the prehistoric people, he was a prophet preaching to the prehistoric nations. That is the reason that he does not like prophets. He tries to discredit every prophet that he can and lead them away from God, just as he led one-third of the angels away from God. How do you think that he was able to lead one-third of the angels that God created away from God? Lucifer was also a priest. We see that in Ezekiel 28:14-18, specifically in verse 18. Also in verses 14-17 we see God speaking to Lucifer about His displeasure with all the evil that was found in him and how wonderful He had created him.

Ezekiel 28:14-18 reads: "*Thou art the anointed cherub that covereth; and I have set thee so: thou wast upon the holy mountain of God; thou hast walked up and down in the midst of the stones of fire. Thou wast perfect in thy ways from the day that thou wast created, till iniquity was found in thee. By the multitude of thy merchandise they have filled the midst of thee with violence, and thou hast sinned: therefore I will cast thee as profane out of the mountain of God: and I will destroy thee, O covering cherub, from the midst of the stones of fire. Thine heart was lifted up because of thy beauty, thou hast corrupted thy wisdom by reason of thy brightness: I will cast thee to the ground, I will lay thee before kings, that they may behold thee. Thou hast defiled thy sanctuaries by the multitude of thine iniquities, by the iniquity of thy traffick; therefore will I bring forth a fire from the midst of thee, it shall devour thee, and I will bring thee to ashes upon the earth in the sight of all them that behold thee.*" (KJV) Now we see here that God is saying to Lucifer, You have polluted or defiled your sanctuaries. You cannot pollute your sanctuaries unless you are a priest. Lucifer was also a priest, and that is why he hates priests and tries to discredit all of the priests that he can and lead them away from God.

How was Lucifer (who became Satan) in position to be prophet, priest and king? He was fourth in line behind the Father, the Son and the Holy Spirit. He was not in the Godhead, but he was the chief ranking official over the angels. Notice in the passage above, Ezekiel 24:14-18, the conversation that God is having with him concerning this. In addition, he wanted to exalt his throne above the stars of the earth. God had fashioned Lucifer in such a way that he led worship as a prophet, he led people, as a priest where he had a throne, and therefore he was king.

Now God reminds him of wanting to exalt his throne, and we can find that in Isaiah 14:13-16, specifically in verse 13. God talks about Lucifer's desire to exalt his throne above the stars of God, which is an indication that his throne was beneath the stars and it was in the earth. When Jesus was revealed in the four gospels, he was revealed as prophet, priest and king, and he had to do what he did because God needs man to be manifested as prophet, priest and king with the power to cover the earth. Adam failed at that, but Jesus had to do what He did as prophet, priest and king. Now the plans in Lucifer's heart were exposed in Isaiah 14: 13-16: "*For thou hast said in thine heart, I will ascend into heaven, I will exalt my throne above the stars of God:*" What throne? His throne was in the earth, and only kings have a throne. "*I will sit also upon the mount of the congregation, in the sides of the north:"* What congregation? *"I will ascend above the heights of the clouds; I will be like the most High."* Now God says to Lucifer, *"Yet thou shalt be brought down to hell, to the sides of the pit. They that see thee shall narrowly look upon thee, and consider thee, saying....,"* Now we see that they (the demons in that place; that were already demoted), and now they see that Satan has lost his position of prophet, priest and king: say to Satan, Are you now become like us? Isaiah 14:10:

All of them will [tauntingly] say to you, Have you also become weak as we are? Have you become like us? (AMP)

It is as if they were surprised that he was the one who led them to hell and the pits. Lucifer was in a position above all angels, including the angels that were led away from God and as a result of that became demons. That is why he had opportunity to lead them away from God. Demons did not exist; until Lucifer led them away from God, they were all angels. They go on to say to Satan: Are you the one who caused all of this trouble? Are you like one of us? They are not talking about us (God's people) because we are seated in heavenly places with Christ Jesus. They are talking about Satan. Verse 16 continues as the demons say to Satan: *".......Is this the man that made the earth to tremble, that did shake kingdoms?"*(KJV)

That is why Satan hates you and me. Jesus has given us the example of how prophets and prophetic people are to operate as prophets, priest and kings. We are in the earth to carry out a very important assignment. We should be able now to go hard after the things that God desires that we do. We are to take things that are void and without form and add our part to make that thing perfect. We are to restore some things, understanding that we must get rid of the violations of God's order in the earth and bring things back into God's order. If darkness is upon a thing, then God is not in that, and since the earth is the work of the Lord, then it must be beautiful and perfect and this is the way God really is.

Whatever God is going to do, it must be perfect. Often we stop just short of perfection. We should realize that when Genesis 1:2 talks about the earth being void and without form, it is not perfect, and there was something that was very wrong with the earth since God creates things beautiful and perfect. In our thinking, we must move up in the level of our understanding and operate as God and do things according to His way. When we look at Genesis 1:2, we know that the earth was not perfect in that state. God wants us to know how to do in the earth what He did and also to understand why Satan hates us and why certain demons are out to destroy us or cause us to stop short of what we are designed to accomplish in the earth. I believe that now we are enlightened and understand why God has made us so powerful in the earth.

Many of us, as prophets and prophetic people, will begin producing at the level that God wants us to produce. We must stop trying to be like God and become as God. God is perfect in His way, and if we are like God we can religiously be trying to be perfect, we can be like God without having His Spirit. But you cannot be as God without having the Spirit of God. We must endeavor to be as God to hear and operate by the Spirit of God. Now with this understanding we can begin to grow up to be the sons of God that Paul is talking about in Ephesians 4:15, growing up into Christ in all things, which He is the head. "*But speaking the truth in love may grow up into Him in all things, which is the Head even Christ.*" (Ephesians 4:15) KJV

UNDERSTANDING CHRIST IN HIS ELEMENT

As we carry out the work of His ministry, we are secretly or privately hidden in Him. Do you believe that you serve a just God? Have you ever done something wrong and it seemed that God did not see? You knew that you did something wrong, and the devil should have come after you, but he did not. You are mysteriously and secretly hidden in Christ. This is found in Colossians 3:2-3: "*Set your minds on things above, not on earthly things. For you died, and your life is now hidden with Christ in God.*" (NIV) and also in Job 1:6-10: "*Now there was a day when the sons of God came to present themselves before the LORD, and Satan came also among them. And the LORD said unto Satan, Whence comest thou? Then Satan answered the LORD, and said, From going to and fro in the earth, and from walking up and down in it. And the LORD said unto Satan, Hast thou considered my servant Job, that there is none like him in the earth, a perfect and an upright man, one that feareth God, and escheweth evil? Then Satan answered the LORD, and said, Doth Job fear God for nought? Hast not thou made an hedge about him, and about his house, and about all that he hath on every side? thou hast blessed the work of his hands, and his substance is increased in the land.*" (KJV)

Noticed what Satan did when he saw the sons of God as they gathered to present themselves to God, for the sons knew the exact moment that they should meet God. Remember that angels are not just sitting around doing nothing; they are on earth, so when Satan saw them beaming up to meet God, Satan came also among them. How did Satan get in on this meeting? It is because Satan is not in hell. He is going to and fro through the earth looking for you and me, but we are mysteriously hidden in Him and Satan cannot see us. When Satan saw the sons of God beaming up for the meeting, he went also to the second heaven, where he has access because the meeting was in the second heaven. Satan does not have access to the third heaven. How did Satan get to Job? Job 3:23-26 explains: "*Why is light given to a man whose way is hid, and whom God hath hedged in? For my sighing cometh before I eat, and my roarings are poured out like the waters. For the thing which I greatly feared is come upon me, and that which I was afraid of is come unto me. I was not in safety, neither had I rest, neither was I quiet; yet trouble came."* (KJV)

God did not turn Job over to Satan. He had him hidden and hedged in, and Satan could not see him, but Job was afraid and that thing that he feared came upon him. We must deal with our fears. The doorway to get to Job was opened by Job because he feared. Now look at what God said to Satan in Job 1:12: *"And the LORD said unto Satan, Behold, all that he hath is in thy power; only upon himself put not forth thine hand. So Satan went forth from the presence of the LORD."* (KJV) God said to Satan, "Behold," and this word simply means look. Unless God tells Satan to look, you are not exposed to Satan. You are mysteriously hidden in God. If you understand this, then you will never wonder again why some people seem to do wrong and get away with that action.

It is because they are mysteriously hidden by God, but at some point He does remove the hedge and say, "Look," and at that point they will be seen. This is not a license to sin or to do wrong, because at some point God opens the hedge. No matter where you go or where you are, Satan cannot see you do wrong unless God says, "Look." Do you realize why you cannot see angels today? It is because God has not told you to look. If God ever tells you to look, something supernaturally happens to your eyes and you will be able to see them.

As a prophet, you are walking in a particular office, and it has nothing to do with gender. I do not believe in the word "prophetess" because that is just an apology for being female. When this word is being used in the Bible, it is to let you know the prophet that is being talked about is female; she is nevertheless a prophet. The office is prophet, apostle, pastor etc. When people use words like pastorette or apostletess, they are trying to get women to apologize for being female. The offices have no gender attached; you are in the office of pastor, male or female. You are in the office of apostle, male or female.

When you operate in the ascension gift that God has given you, this is what is called the "Mysteries of Christ." Why? Because as we carry out the work of His ministry, we are (mysteriously or secretly) hidden in Him. Jesus' great end and design in giving gifts unto men were intended for the well-being of His church. All of the ascension gifts were given for a certain period of time. That period of time is identified by the word "until," which indicates continuance. The church has not yet come into unity and maturity. Therefore, the church is still in need of the ascension gift ministry.

Key Point: "Until" the church comes into unity and maturity, there will always be the need for the ascension gifts.

The "body" is divided because of denominations. This is one reason why only part of the fulfillment has come to pass. We need all of the ascension gifts and we are one nation unto God and one body of Christ. 1 Peter 2:9 calls us a generation, not many generations. A royal priesthood, not many priesthoods and one holy nation.

But you are a chosen generation, a royal priesthood, an holy nation. (I Peter 2:9)

The word specifically says that you are to "give" diligence to make your calling and election sure: for if ye do these things, ye shall never fall... 2 Peter 1:10: Wherefore the rather, brethren, give diligence to make your calling and election sure: for if ye do these things, ye shall never fall:KJV In addition with all of our getting, we must get understanding Proverbs 4:7 Wisdom is the principal thing; therefore get wisdom: and with all thy getting get understanding . KJV. Our next chapter will give us an understanding of what a prophet is.

Chapter 2

WHEN THE PROPHET IS IN HIS/HER OFFICE

*T*he prophet is a person whom God has chosen for the purpose of revealing His mind to the body of Christ or the church. Before they were called prophets, they were called "seers" and had the same functions as the Old Testament prophets.

Beforetime in Israel, when a man went to inquire of God, thus he spake, come, and let us go to the seer: for he that is now called a prophet was beforetime called a seer. (I Samuel 9:9)

The prophet is called to be the "mouthpiece" or one who speaks on behalf of God. As prophets, we must purpose in ourselves to quickly understand the gravity of who we are, what our role is, and that there will continually be many challenges to this position, both naturally and spiritually.

He said unto him, I am a prophet also as thou art; and an angel spake unto me by the word of the Lord, saying, Bring him back with thee into thine house, that he may eat bread and drink water. But he lied unto him. (I Kings 13:18)

The prophet must also understand the reality that his enemy, Satan, will produce other voices in an attempt to enter in and distort the voice of God. Voices that are not of God will lead into false prophecy.

Key Point: Understand Satan's job is to distort the voice of God.

JESUS' MINISTRY

During the period when Jesus walked the earth and throughout the remainder of the New Testament, God never said to anyone, "Go and Kill." Killing is not in the plan of

God any longer. The reason for this is that after the Old Testament, God's work in the earth was complete, and the door of the earth was open for the introduction of Jesus' ministry to begin, as presented in the four gospels of the New Testament.

Jesus now sits at the right hand of the Father. In Acts 2 and through a portion of the book of Revelation, the Holy Spirit stood up. The Holy Spirit is standing in His role and responsibility to guide and teach today.

THE MOUTHPIECE OF GOD

The deceiver, Satan, desires to distort the real voice of God. Since the prophet is God's mouthpiece, Satan wants to deceive him and cause him to be in error. Give the word, but only say what God is saying, not what He seems to be saying.

Key Point: When we understand and accept that prophets are the "mouthpieces" of God, we will clearly understand the reason Satan would attempt to cause us to hear other voices.

If the mouthpiece has been proved, tried, tested, and is fine-tuned in hearing accurately from God, there will be no opportunity for deception in prophesying God's word. The prophet is responsible for the nation he is in. We will learn that the prophet is also responsible for turning the direction of the town, city, country, nation and the church to which he has been assigned. The prophet is one that must interpret what God is saying to the location (the town, city, country, nation, and church) wherein God has placed him.

Consider what God thinks of His word. Remember He said He would exalt His word above His name. As you think about that, do you realize how important it is to be proven, tried and tested as a prophet?

The prophet, as well as the apostle, is one who is made "a spectacle" (I Corinthians 4:9). The prophet is one who walks alone. If you cannot deal with loneliness, then you do not want to be a prophet. The prophet is one of the most disliked persons that exist. If you cannot deal with being disliked, you must consider whether you are truly called to be a prophet. The word says that we are fools for Christ. If a person is not willing to look like a fool, he is not ready to be a prophet.

Key Point: If you are truly called to be a prophet, then stay in training, pray, and come into the reality of your role. If God said you're strong enough, THEN YOU ARE. DO NOT PLAY WITH YOUR CALLING. Many people duck in and out of their call according to what they feel. The Bible says in I Corinthians 15:58 (AMP), "Therefore, my beloved brethren, be firm (steadfast), immovable, always abounding in the work of the Lord (always being superior, excelling, doing more than enough in the service of the Lord), knowing and being continually aware that your labor in the Lord is not futile (it is never wasted or to no purpose)."

THE PROPHETIC PERSPECTIVE OF THE GOD-HEAD

Let us understand the dispensations and who was working in each one. A dispensation is an era of time during which man is tested in respect to obedience to some definite revelation of God's will.

1. Genesis to Malachi

From Genesis to Malachi, ultimately it was God doing what needed to be done:

In the beginning God created the heavens and the earth. (Genesis 1:1)

God speaks or prophesies everything into existence.

And God said, Let there be . . . (Genesis 1:3)

God, Himself, prophesied regarding the hatred between the seed of the serpent and the seed of the woman.

And I will put enmity between thee and the woman, and between thy seed and her seed; it shall bruise thy head, and thou shalt bruise his heel. (Genesis 3:15)

And God said unto Noah, The end of all flesh is come before me; for the earth is filled with violence through them; and behold I will destroy them with the earth. (Genesis 6:13)

TYPE OF CHRIST

In the Old Testament, we find two significant things that God did until a type of Christ would come on the earth. That type of Christ was the prophet Moses. In Numbers 14:11-16, we read the account of the dialogue between God and Moses regarding Israel's rebellion against God.

God would have destroyed the Israelites and begun a new nation through Moses. But, Moses interceded on behalf of the children of Israel, saying to God, "You cannot do that, lest the enemy accuse you of not being able to bring the people out." The first thing that we see that God did was to destroy. Secondly, He created and began a process of replenishing in the earth.

THE NATURE OF GOD

The second significant act was shown in the nature of God. We see in the Old Testament that God's nature was not only to create but also to destroy. This act was carried out in Genesis 6:7, 23. The nature of our holy God's love could not be compromised by the acceptance of mankind's sin.

As we observe the Old Testament prophets, we see that they moved in levels or degrees of prophecy. The anointing would come upon them as God chose to use them. These men and women were wholly separated unto God. He would choose and raise them as His prophets to reveal His mind to the people, the leaders, and/or the nation.

Key Point: The ministry of the Old Testament prophets was always to show the true spiritual meaning behind the strict letter of the law.

The office of the Old Testament prophets was considered to be somewhat higher than that of the New Testament prophet. There were many similarities between their titles and functions. All Old Testament prophets were forerunners, pointing to the pattern prophet, Jesus Christ.

2. THE GOSPELS

The Gospels are the introduction to the Redeemer, Jesus the Christ. The word said that Jesus came to seek and save the lost, not to destroy them (Luke 19:10). It must be clearly understood that the purpose and nature from which Jesus was operating was to bring into the earth salvation for a lost and dying world. The word "salvation" comes from a Greek word that means "deliverance." Throughout the period Christ moved upon the earth, He was deliberately focused on His mission and goals: first, to redeem; second, to deliver; third, to reveal the grace of God; and fourth, to establish His church.

We have entered a new covenant because of our Redeemer, Jesus. Jesus made a way for us when situations seemed hopeless, 2 Corinthians 5:17: "*...old things are passed away; behold all things are become new.*" It is because of the new covenant that we now embrace the New Testament.

The New Testament prophet came along with that new covenant.

THE HOLY SPIRIT

The Holy Spirit came to sustain us and to stop us from continued falling. The Holy Spirit was purposed to bring forth the fullness of all that God intended. It is important to know that the Holy Spirit has come to bring the balance. Remember in Matthew 28:19: the other side of the revelation is that the fullness of the Godhead is demanded to be shown ... "***baptizing them in the name of the Father and of the Son, and of the Holy Ghost.***" The very next verse says, "teaching them." Let's talk about that word "baptize." The word "baptize" comes from a Greek word that means to immerse or to dip, to take totally under. Therefore, if the word says to baptize them in the name of the Father, we must take them totally under in who the Father is. Who is he? He is both creator and destroyer. God never stepped outside of His purpose and nature. That is why the earth was without form and void, and darkness was upon the face of the deep. For the same reason, Noah was told to build an ark because the destroyer had to do His work and recreate. This time God would start over with Noah. He started over with Adam. What did Adam and Noah have in common? They both were told to replenish the earth.

However, the job of the Holy Spirit is to guide us in all things. John 16:13: But when he, the Spirit of truth, comes, he will guide you into all truth. He will not speak on his own; he will speak only what he hears, and he will tell you what is yet to come. NIV says that the Holy Spirit will give the prophet the needed balance in order to enter the fullness of that which is inside of us. Colossians 2:9 says: "***For in Him (Jesus) dwelleth all the fullness of the Godhead bodily.***" *v.10 "and ye are complete in Him . . ."*KJV The Bible further says that we are in Him and He is in us. Therefore, the fullness of the Father, Son and Holy Spirit is in us. The Holy Spirit sustains us within the boundaries, and He balances us. We have the ability to create and destroy, to redeem through the ministry of reconciliation, and to sustain through love, grace and mercy. The fullness is in us. Yet, the Holy Spirit teaches us what to do and when to do it as prophets.

Chapter 3

PROPHETS AT THE NEXT LEVEL

Understanding Dispensations

We must understand dispensation. Let us take a look at the book of Job. Even though it is before Psalms, it is not after Adam. When I looked at his age and realized that he was living longer than God had said that man would live at that time, I asked God about this situation. Then I realized that I was looking at Job in the wrong dispensation. He lived during Adam's time, not David's. When you hear or read something in a particular dispensation, then you have to understand how things operated in that particular situation.

God will train you in the operation of God the Father (to create and destroy), God the Son (to save and redeem), and God the Holy Spirit (to maintain what had been saved and redeemed). We can understand which one is in operation according to the particular dispensation.

You go from anointing to anointing to do what you have to do in life. If you are married, you are anointed to be married; if you are single, you are anointed to be single. You have to operate in what you have been given first. You cannot come to church and not have used the anointing you have to take care of your family.

When you understand dispensations you will know how God wants you to operate in His fullness. God will tell you to do something that you cannot do, and He will also tell you to do some strange things. You have to hear what God said, then you have to obey, even if it seems strange to you. God told me to do some strange things while training me to hear His voice and to know His heart. At that time, I do know that I was operating in pride. Now when God tells you to do something strange, you cannot operate in pride. God will have you say some things to someone that are so strange that you may have to close your eyes and just say what God is saying.

THE PLACE OF PERFECTION

There is a place that you have to depart from if you are ever going to operate effectively. The place that we have to leave is found in Hebrews 5:13-14: "*For every one that useth milk is unskilful in the word of righteousness: for he is a babe. But strong meat belongeth to them that are of full age, even those who by reason of use have their senses exercised to discern both good and evil.*" (KJV) Notice that this passage is talking about the elementary truths of God, and this is the room where most of us live. Remember when this manuscript was originally done, it was not separated by chapter and verse. There was no punctuation. This passage flows into Hebrews 6:1-6. Now in verse one: *Therefore leaving the principles of the doctrine of Christ, let us go on unto perfection;.......*KJV, we notice the word "therefore", and whenever we see the word "therefore," we must understand what it is there for. "Therefore" is there because of the two verses at the end of chapter 5, meaning therefore or for that reason let us go on. The room in which we have existed for this past period is the room of the principles of the doctrine of Christ; however, many of us do not understand what some of these doctrines mean. We don't know what they are. For instance, what is the doctrine of the resurrection of the dead? What is the doctrine of eternal judgment? Do we know what that means? When we begin to understand how much we do not know, we understand that we do not qualify for leaving. We cannot leave this room until we understand these doctrines and principles.

The next room is the place of perfection. Many in the body of Christ do not believe that this next room exists. Many pastors do not believe, and they think that it does not exist, and that is why many of us do not press to go to the next room. Then why would God tell us to be perfect even as our Father which in heaven is perfect? It is because there is another place that exists that we have not been familiarized with. This place in the next room is found in Hebrews 6:4-6. Once you enter into this room, this is what will be working all of the time. In verses 4-6 God said: "*For it is impossible for those who were once enlightened, and have tasted of the heavenly gift, and were made partakers of the Holy Ghost, And have tasted the good word of God, and the powers of the world to come, If they shall fall away, to renew them again unto repentance; seeing they crucify to themselves the Son of God afresh, and put him to an open shame.*" (KJV) That is the reason Satan, Lucifer himself, could never come back into a right standing with God. It was impossible because he experienced all of this and then fell away. All of the angels that were with God experienced this also, so when they followed Satan and fell away, it was impossible to renew them. I kept putting emphasis on and in the above passage because you are never positioned to fall away and never be renewed again if you only have one or two of these working. You have to have them all working all of the time. When you have all of these working all of the time, this means that you have come into the next room (the next place in God) where all of them were working all of the time.

Remember what Paul said in 2 Corinthians 12:2: "*I knew a man in Christ above four-teen years ago, (whether in the body, I cannot tell; or whether out of the body, I cannot tell: God knoweth;) such an one caught up to the third heaven.*" (KJV), this is the place we are trying to get into this next room with God.

Hebrews 4:4-6 normally scares some people, but fear not because we have to realize that we have not come into this room where we live. We have not come into this yet. But if we would just leave, it is possible to come into this room.

There are particular things that you can't be stuck with, and you have to understand that you must make a decision to depart from particular relationships, churches, ministries, assignments or people that you associate with if you are going to operate effectively in this next room. We must be willing to release anything. We cannot be so attached to things that we would not be willing to let them go especially if God requires it of us. We must get rid of all carnality around us wherever it is found.

When God deals with the prophet, God does not speak according to time. He always goes beyond time. We have to bring people into the next room, because if we do not, they are not going to make it in the dispensation of the kingdom.

PROPHETS MUST UNDERSTAND DISPENSATIONS IN ORDER TO WALK IN THE FULLNESS.

We must be kingdom minded in order to move across dispensations. Remember Elijah earned a place in the seventh dispensation based on his obedience. Elijah was one of the prophets who were in the dispensation of Law, the fifth dispensation. So how does he show up in the seventh dispensation? Only God can do this! How did he do that? He exited the earth and did not die. He is one of the two people who did that. He was raptured out. He did not die, so he has to come back and die because it is appointed unto man once to die, and then undergo judgment. We find this in Hebrews 9:27: "*And as it is appointed unto men once to die, but after this the judgment:*" (KJV)

UNDERSTANDING THE PURPOSE OF THE FIVE-FOLD MINISTRY GIFTS

Embrace the understanding that when Jesus Christ established the church, He did that with the understanding that there was going to be a five-fold ministry. As we begin to understand the flow of the ministry that was established in the church, we will come to a rich understanding of how important our position is in the body of Christ and where we are supposed to be within the body of Christ geographically or positionally. When we examine this, we begin to understand where each of us fits in the body of Christ and what we are supposed to do.

Now Jesus goes on to say to Peter in Matthew 16:17-18: *"And Jesus answered and said unto him, Blessed art thou, Simon Barjona: for flesh and blood hath not revealed it unto thee, but my Father which is in heaven. And I say also unto thee, That thou art Peter, and upon this rock I will build my church; and the gates of hell shall not prevail against it."* (KJV) The rock that he was talking about was a level of revelation that Peter has which did not come from flesh and blood but from God in heaven. The rock is the apostolic prophetic ministry that the gates of hell cannot prevail against it. He was dealing with the apostolic and prophetic ministry, the structure of the five-fold ministry that is designed to have a level of revelation where Jesus will have to say to us, *"Flesh and blood did not reveal this to you but my Father which is in heaven."* Now if we are called as an apostle, prophet, evangelist, pastor or teacher, then we are a part of what Jesus was talking about. Let's look in Ephesians 4:7-13. *"But unto every one of us is given grace according to the measure of the gift of Christ. Wherefore he saith, When he ascended up on high, he led captivity captive, and gave gifts unto men. (Now that he ascended, what is it but that he also descended first into the lower parts of the earth? He that descended is the same also that ascended up far above all heavens, that he might fill all things). And he gave some, apostles; and some, prophets; and some, evangelists; and some, pastors and teachers; For the perfecting of the saints, for the work of the ministry, for the edifying of the body of Christ: Till we all come in the unity of the faith, and of the knowledge of the Son of God, unto a perfect man, unto the measure of the stature of the fulness of Christ:"* (KJV)

God is going to use this rock, this apostolic prophetic ministry, to build the church, and the gates of hell shall not prevail against it. Therefore, it is imperative that we understand that our position is designed to be a part of that which God is going to use in order to build the church. In order to stop the gates of hell from prevailing against the church, you and I must make sure that we are in position. We have to literally lie under the spout where our oil is designed to come out. We cannot be just anywhere. We must be where God desired us to be at the time that He desires that we be there.

As members of an apostolic or prophetic house, we are designed to come into a level of revelation (Matthew 16), and if we are not coming into that level of revelation, then we have not made the right hookup. If you are called as an apostle, prophet, evangelist, pastor or teacher and you are not in the geographical location where God told you to be at the time He has desired you to be there; then there is a major portion that is designed to happen that is not happening right now because your part is not in place. This is one of the reasons we cannot doubt God, because if God say that we are a prophet or one of the other four offices, we must understand that and embrace that so that God can do some of the things that He desires to do.

There are several things that God said that we have to do being that apostolic prophetic church. Understanding the kinds of revelation God gives us causes us to begin to embrace that we come into understanding how important we are to the local church. Being that church, we acknowledge that there are several things God desires that we do. God said that He had given apostles, prophets, evangelist, pastors and teachers. As one of these, why do you exist? Why did He give you to the church? Notice part of the answer in verse 12: "*For the perfecting of the saints, for the work of the ministry, for the edifying of the body of Christ:*" This is one of the reasons that I say as a prophet that you have to commit this scripture to memory. Anything you commit to memory will become revelation to you. If you commit it to memory, it will come into your spirit and you will have a revelation of this particular thing that God said regarding your office and your reason for being on the planet.

Now the rest of the answer is in verse 13. "*Till we all come in the unity of the faith, and of the knowledge of the Son of God, unto a perfect man, unto the measure of the stature of the fulness of Christ:*" (KJV)

It is imperative that we understand that you and I are designed to come into the fullness of God as a prophet of God. As an apostle of God it is your duty, your privilege to come into fullness. You are favored to the place where you will come into God's fullness. Now you have to ask yourself, What does the fullness of God look like? The fullness is the ability to operate with all of the virtues and excellencies of God the Father, the Son and the Holy Spirit. The operation of each can be found in one of seven dispensations. A dispensation is a period of time in history when, according to The New Unger's Bible Dictionary, man is tested in respect to obedience to some definite revelation of God's will. The dispensations are listed later in this chapter.

Most of us do not realize that we can come into God's fullness. As a matter of fact, most churches are not established for you to come into fullness. They are only established for you to experience a partial measure of God's fullness. We must operate in the fullness of the Godhead. Most of us in the body of Christ, particularly prophets, have not operated in the fullness. Sometimes we are handicapped so that we cannot operate in the fullness that God has wanted us to do.

If God said that He has fullness for us, then our very heartbeat should be going after His fullness. I wonder what you would literally have to take off in order to come into His fullness. Most of us are not willing to take off anything to come into the fullness of God. Every time you take something off or put something on it is attracting something in the spirit world. You are activating something in the realm of the spirit. We are not talking about clothes. For instance, God says put on the whole armor of God. This literally attracts something in the realm of the spirit. You are body, soul and sprit so you don't put the armor on your flesh. As a spirit being, you have ability to go into the realm of the spirit and begin to tear down anything that God wants you to tear down, but it's all according to what you put on. Think about this, what about the fruit of the

Spirit? The fruit of the Spirit found in Galatians 5:22-23: *"But the fruit of the Spirit is love, joy, peace, longsuffering, gentleness, goodness, faith, Meekness, temperance: against such there is no law."* (KJV) is designed to be put on.

Love is designed to be put on. You wear that. You literally put on love, joy, peace, long-suffering, gentleness, goodness, faith, meekness, and temperance: against such there is no law. You put that on as a coat of many colors. Joseph wore the coat of many colors. I believe if we take a look at the significance of the coat of many colors, we would literally see a connection between the fruit of the Spirit and that coat. If we put that on, particularly prophets and apostles, we are literally attracting something in the realm of the spirit. When we put that on (the fruit of the Spirit), when we put on the will of God, we are empowered in a way that we have never been empowered before and that is because of what we put on. The Bible says that against such there is no law; in other words, there are things that will work against other people that will not work against us.

It is imperative that we really understand exactly where we are, what God has called to come to life inside of us. As a prophet, in every season God is expecting us to put something else on. We are going to need a different piece of armor in a particular season that we may not have needed in the last season. This does not mean that we do not put on the whole armor of God. I am only giving you that as an example. But there are times we are going to need to put on particular parts of the armor for the particular season that we are in. For example, there are seasons when we have to wear the spirit of gladness as a coat. How about the Spirit of joy? There are particular times when you have to wear the Spirit of joy like a coat. Why? Because the joy of the Lord is our strength; therefore, it is an inappropriate prayer to ask people to pray for your strength in the Lord. That is not biblical because you have to put that on; joy is your strength in the Lord. I can't pray that on you; it is there for the receiving. The working definition of joy is an inward stability (the ability to stay or stand) that God through Jesus Christ has already worked out on my behalf.

When we understand that God wants us to put something else on and embrace this, we have to walk in a different place. You can't walk as a defeated foe because that is not who you are. Your mentality cannot be as if you are defeated; your conversation cannot be as if you are defeated. There is a level of responsibility that God puts on me, regardless of what the situation is I cannot look like I am defeated. I cannot verbalize anything as if I am defeated. The very second you come into that place, it is almost like stepping from where you are into another room where defeat does not exist. So even if you get defeated in an area, you are literally saying that it's not over because I have not manifested a winning attitude yet. I must manifest a winning attitude. If there is a sickness in my body, I must manifest healing or it's not done yet. You are stepping into another room where you cannot talk doubt and unbelief. Once you step into that room, God will chastise you with many stripes when you talk that way when you have already stepped out of the room of doubt and unbelief. God will tolerate doubt and unbelief from some people. They still do not walk in His blessing, but He will at least tolerate that from them. But once you step into this room, God will not tolerate that from you. Therefore, you don't even feel right saying I am broke, I am sick, or any of those kinds of things because you have stepped out from where you were to another room, another place.

Understanding that you are in another place gives you also the understanding that you are now going to require another level of information and revelation. The old revelation that you once enjoyed is over now. Last year's word is over now; you need a new word for this year. When we move into this new place, we need a new level of revelation. Not everybody is able to understand this level of revelation, not everybody is even privileged to come into this revelation because one level of revelation will help some people but the same level of revelation will destroy other people. Why? Let us look at Mark 4:1-13 to find that out.

And he began again to teach by the sea side: and there was gathered unto him a great multitude, so that he entered into a ship, and sat in the sea; and the whole multitude was by the sea on the land. And he taught them many things by parables, and said unto them in his doctrine, Hearken; Behold, there went out a sower to sow: And it came to pass, as he sowed, some fell by the way side, and the fowls of the air came and devoured it up. And some fell on stony ground, where it had not much earth; and immediately it sprang up, because it had no depth of earth: But when the sun was up, it was scorched; and because it had no root, it withered away. And some fell among thorns, and the thorns grew up, and choked it, and it yielded no fruit. And other fell on good ground, and did yield fruit that sprang up and increased; and brought forth, some thirty, and some sixty, and some an hundred. And he said unto them, He that hath ears to hear, let him hear. And when he was alone, they that were about him with the twelve asked of him the parable. And he said unto them, Unto you it is given to know the mystery of the kingdom of God: but unto them that are without, all these things are done in parables: That seeing they may see, and not perceive; and hearing they may hear, and not understand; lest at any time they should be converted, and their sins should be forgiven them. And he said unto them, Know ye not this parable? and how then will ye know all parables? (KJV)

In Mark 4:1, Jesus begins to share some things in a parable with the multitude, and when he finished, the multitude left. They were not interested in knowing any more. They were not willing to get any more information or pay any price for understanding what they heard, but notice in verse 10 there were those with the twelve that were willing to pay a price, and they were saying I am not willing to leave just because service is over. I want to know more. There are some things that I did not understand and they wanted to understand. When He was alone, they asked Him about the parable. They wanted the fullness of what He was saying. That is what we have to do. We have to make a decision that we are willing to pay the price to know more because we want the fullness of what God is saying. Those of you who have declared what you heard in the past have heard some great things, but what I heard and experienced there did not describe the fullness, and that is not enough because I want the fullness. Fullness is going to cost you something. Therefore, those in the multitude who are not willing to pay the price for the fullness will go in a different direction from those who are willing to pay the price.

Notice in Mark 4:11 Jesus said unto them, "*Unto you it is given to know the mystery of the kingdom of God: but unto them that are without, all these things are done in parables.*" You have to understand that the call that God makes is not a call that everybody hears, and He is saying that you are not one of the multitude. Because you are interested in having this level of information and revelation, you are not part of the multitude. You have marked yourself as one with the twelve. Jesus said to them, "*Unto you it is given to know the mystery of the kingdom of God*". As a prophet of God, you are given the mysteries of the Kingdom of God to know. You must know the dispensations of God. You cannot operate without knowing the dispensations that have passed this dispensation of grace and the dispensation to come.

The first dispensation was the Dispensation of Innocence and everything that God is doing is to bring us back into the dispensation of innocence. Adam and Eve blew it for us. Think about this. How did Adam and Eve operate? What opportunities did they have? How were they to travel? They were not meant to stay in the garden because worlds (plural) were created. They were not stuck in the Garden of Eden. That was their place of residence. How were they to travel? We don't have the answers because these are the mysteries of the Kingdom of God. A mystery is something that is hidden. We do not have the answers, but we can get them. Remember, dispensation 1 was The Dispensation of Innocence. God is getting us back to this place in this particular dispensation. The following is the list of dispensations:

1. The Dispensation of Innocence, from the creation of Adam/Eve until they fell into sin.
2. The Dispensation of Conscience, from the fall into sin to Noah's flood.
3. The Dispensation of Human Government, from Noah to Abraham.
4. The Dispensation of Promise, from Abraham to Moses.
5. The Dispensation of Law, from Moses to Christ.
6. The Dispensation of Grace, from the death of Christ to the rapture of the Church.
7. The Dispensation of the Kingdom of Christ, His personal 1000-year reign, yet future.

We are currently in dispensation number 6 the Dispensation of Grace. All of the previous dispensations have passed, but God gave us the awesome ability to shift between dispensations. All we have to do is to read about it, and we can have some of those that are past. We have to get this because most of us who are called into this next room (place) are not exploring all of our benefits. We are in this dispensation of Grace, or God-unmerited favor, that we did not work for or deserve. As prophet, you have to know the dispensations, because you can experience all of the things in all of the past dispensations. We can shift between dispensations. For instance, we can have the promises in The fourth dispensation. Prophets have to know these things. The seventh dispensation is the Dispensation of the Kingdom, which means that you and I need to understand the mysteries of how that kingdom works. This is the reason that you cannot hold onto your will. Get rid of it because our current dispensation is the only dispensation where our will works. Therefore, we have to get rid of our will because in the seventh dispensation, the dispensation of The Kingdom, our will does not exist. We have no will in the King's kingdom. He reigns and rules.

RELINQUINCING OUR WILL

As prophets and prophetic people, we must know how to operate in the Dispensation of The Kingdom of Christ. Many of us do not know how a kingdom works because we live in a democracy, not a kingdom. We understand that when the president comes into a room, all stand and clap, but when a king comes into the room we bow and clap from that position. Can I give you some alarming news? Remember David? He was a king. Uriah and his wife Bathsheba were subjects of his kingdom. So, if Uriah's wife was a subject of the king and when look at it strictly from the standpoint of the kingdom, David did nothing wrong but had a man killed, because they were both subjects of the kingdom, and every person and every thing were subjects of the king. David was the king, and everything in the kingdom was his. We are all subjects of the kingdom of God, and I believe that God has many of us practicing. We are practicing how to submit to the authority of our King.

We know Jesus is King of Kings, and we know from Psalms 24:1: "*The earth is the LORD's, and the fulness thereof; the world, and they that dwell therein.*" (KJV) or 1 Corinthians 10:26: "*The earth is the Lord's, and everything in it.*" (NIV) and from this we understand that God owns everything and everything that we have belongs to Him. When he tells us to give Him ten percent of what belongs to him, this should help us appreciate the ninety percent that we keep because it all belongs to Him, and when you do not, the King says they are not submitted to my kingdom. For instance, if you purchased a house with your own money and the king commanded you to give up the house and said, "I want you to be out of the house this time tomorrow"; you have to go because you, your spouse and your children all have to go, because all of you are subjects of the king. You paid for the house, but you have to go. Most of us cannot go into the kingdom of heaven the way we are because we are accustomed to a system of democracy; but in a kingdom, when the king says bow, we must bow. We are still talking about relinquishing our will. How can God create you with a will and all of a sudden you do not exercise the rights of your will? It is because we are in a kingdom and it is not our will but the king's will. As a prophet we have to understand this so that we do not make excuses for people's flesh.

Jesus said in Mark 4:11: *It is given "to you" to know the mystery of the kingdom....* Why this group and not the other group? It was because the other group was not hungry enough to want the information or the revelation that comes from heaven. How do you explain to someone not wanting to relinquish their own will to do so knowing that God gave us our will in the first place and nothing on the earth is more powerful than our will, God will not violate the sovereignty that He has given us with our will. However, we must give it up freely in order to get more revelation and information.

God is teaching us that we must search for wisdom like hidden treasure. God spoke this to me when I was just a baby in Christ. I had no idea what God was talking about. All I knew is what I had seen on television about people who search for treasures and they never gave up until they found it. That was the only picture I had in my mind. You keep on looking and searching and never give up until you find it.

There are people who read the Bible, and it all seems as if it is some idle story, but we pick up the Bible and we understand it and we take it for granted. How do you know that we take it for granted? You know when we decide that what we know today is enough. Wanting to know more puts us in another category and another place. But the ones who do not want to know more will settle for hearing the parable and be content with not understanding. I cannot tell you how many people come to the School of the Prophets and do not understand what is being taught and never ask a question. I asked the group, How many of you understand? And people knew that they did not understand and would not say anything. That tells me that they are a part of the multitude and are not interested in knowing more. Jesus said that I have given to you to know the mystery of the kingdom of God, but to those that are without these are mere parables. Jesus taught the parable of the sower and part of what he said was that the sower sows seed; these are they by the wayside where the seed was sown. The multitude listen but most of them were not thinking about asking him "What are you talking about Jesus?"

For prophets that cannot be enough. As prophets, we have to literally understand all of these dispensations and who was operating in what dispensation. Jesus was born in the closing in The Dispensation of Law. In every dispensation there is always a prophet that has to close it out. Will you be that prophet? There has to be a prophetic voice on the planet that is talking about the coming dispensation. God never closes a dispensation if we are not ready. Some of you are wrestling with your will, and you do not have a clue. Why? Because there must be a breaking of your will. Because when the king comes, every knee must bow. When the King says I require more of you, everybody must say yes to this command. Everybody who does not say yes will be beheaded. There is another place that we must come to. Remember Pharaoh (the king) and Joseph (the second man). When they were coming through, Joseph's chariot was right behind Pharaoh's, and when Joseph passed by there were people with poles in their hand saying bow the knee, bow the knee. Joseph was not king, but he was the second man. Pharaoh honored him. Therefore, when Joseph came through, they had to bow the knee also because Pharaoh honored him.

God wants us to come to another place, and we have to go because we are closing The Dispensation of Grace and preparing for the Dispensation of Kingdom. We have to go to another place, and that place is further in God than where we are now. This does not happen until after you relinquish your will. Some people on this planet will never come into this because they will not relinquish their will. Glory be to God! Can you handle going to another place in God? Take a look at Hebrews 6:1-6: "*Therefore leaving the principles of the doctrine of Christ, let us go on unto perfection; not laying again the foundation of repentance from dead works, and of faith toward God, Of the doctrine of baptisms, and of laying on of hands, and of resurrection of the dead, and of eternal judgment. And this will we do, if God permit. For it is impossible for those who were once enlightened, and have tasted of the heavenly gift, and were made partakers of the Holy Ghost, And have tasted the good word of God, and the powers of the world to come, If they shall fall away, to renew them again unto repentance; seeing they crucify to themselves the Son of God afresh, and put him to an open shame.*" (KJV)

The place where we must go is the place of perfection mentioned in verse 1, and perfection is in the next room. It is in the room that we are in now that we declare things like "nobody is perfect." That is because you and I are in two different rooms. We may have never reached that stage of perfection, but in this room where we are in now, it exists. In the next room, perfection exists. Now this passage says not laying again the foundation of repentance from dead works, and of faith toward God, of the doctrine of baptisms, and the laying on of hands, and of resurrection of the dead, and of eternal judgment. And this will we do, if God permits. Some of us don't know what all of these things mean, but we must know and be able to walk in all of these things.

Now look at verses 4 – 6: "*For it is impossible for those who were once enlightened, and have tasted of the heavenly gift, and were made partakers of the Holy Ghost, And have tasted the good word of God, and the powers of the world to come, If they shall fall away, to renew them again unto repentance….*" Anytime God says impossible, we need to open our eyes and ears and listen. Now, notice that there is a comma after each one of these conditions, indicating that you have to master all of these. After we master all of these, if we fall away it is impossible to renew us to repentance. None of us have mastered all of these; therefore, we all still need repentance. Thank God for repentance! The reason we have not mastered all of these yet is because we are in the other room. But, when you come into the next room, you don't want to go back out because it is possible to reach perfection in this room. The time is coming when repentance is the last thing that you preach, if you preach it at all, because you will be so deeply in the next room that the message that you preach will not be the foundation of repentance. Once you get there, the crowd you will be preaching or teaching to will be smaller because many will not understand what you are saying.

Notice Hebrews 5:13-14: "*For every one that useth milk is unskilful in the word of righteousness: for he is a babe. But strong meat belongeth to them that are of full age, even those who by reason of use have their senses exercised to discern both good and evil.*" (KJV) In the Garden of Eden, Adam and Eve took of the forbidden fruit because they were after the knowledge to know good from evil. Now God is saying it is time for us to have our senses exercised to know good from evil. Sometimes a good thing could look like a God thing unless you know good from evil. Could a preaching engagement or an opportunity to be used in ministry be evil and not be of God? Yes, since the devil cannot kill you, he will try to get you out of the way so that you are not where God wants you to be at the time He wants you to be there so that you can make the connection. If we are off doing something else, we can miss our connection. We have to be able to say that I sense in my spirit that I cannot go, even though it would be an honor to preach there. We have to be like Nehemiah, who had an opportunity to meet with a government official who was high in office, but sensed in his spirit that he should not go to meet with him, saying, Why should I come down and leave this great work? When Nehemiah sensed (discerned) that the meeting was evil, not good, when he decided not to come down, that official started trying to weaken the hands of the workers. Anytime someone starts to speak into your ear telling you that they think that you are working too much and you are working for God, it is the wrong spirit.

We are working for God, but we are on a time clock. And when the time clock goes off, we are going to be in the Dispensation of the Kingdom. God is going to snatch us up out of here, and there will be seven years of great tribulation on earth. All that is left on earth will go through that period. I was listening to the news today, and they were talking about a national ID card. I was waiting to see if they were talking about inserting it, because they do have the technology to insert that, and that process of insertion is called the "beast". The Bible calls getting the ID inserted the mark of the beast. This is found in Revelation 13:16-17: *And he causeth all, both small and great, rich and poor, free and bond, to receive a mark in their right hand, or in their foreheads. And that no man might buy or sell, save he that had the mark , or the name of the beast, or the number of his name.* KJV One day we are going to wake up and we are going to realize that what we have in our hands is a mark for life, and it says that no man will be able to buy or sell unless they have that mark.

A dispensation is an era of time during which man is tested with respect to obedience to some definite revelation of God's will. The period of time that began with the death and resurrection of Christ is known as the Dispensation of Grace. This period of testing was no longer directed toward legal obedience to the law as a condition of salvation, but toward acceptance or rejection of Christ. As we look at the period of time covered in the New Testament, we understand this is when the Holy Spirit was sent to the earth. The Holy Spirit was and is responsible for preserving that which the Lord has redeemed and saved.

Key Point: We MUST understand that the Holy Spirit has the awesome responsibility of stabilizing mankind to bring us to a place where we will stop our continual falling.

Therefore, the Holy Spirit could be recognized as our "enabler." Through the Holy Spirit, the Lord also gave gifts to the body of Christ that would mature them in the things of God. This brings us to the purpose of the New Testament prophet.

The ministry of the New Testament prophet is submitted and responsible to the ministry of the apostle. The prophetic ministry is a valid ascension gift ministry given to the church by Jesus. The prophetic office is under (and/or accountable to) the apostolic office. This is because all functioning of the prophetic office must be based upon the historical facts and teachings of Jesus Christ, which were recorded by the apostles.

The prophet must understand his or her purpose in order to be an effective prophet. So, in order to be effective, one must understand the purpose of the prophet.

THE PURPOSE OF THE PROPHET

Like the apostle, the prophet is a special messenger from God. The prophet is the one divinely inspired to communicate God's will to His people and to disclose the future to them. The primary reason or purpose for the prophet is to declare, announce or utter a communication from God to man.

The prophet has a practical office to discharge. His essential purpose is to be an "interpreter" for God. Within the prophet's commission is to show the people of God their transgressions and sins. It is their duty to admonish and reprove, to denounce prevailing sins, to warn the people with the terrors of divine judgment, and to call them to repentance. Also, the prophet brings the message of consolation and pardon.

Prophets may also maintain the role of pastors and/or ministerial monitors of the people. Prophets could have the responsibility of one or more ascension gift. But the apostle, pastor, evangelist or teacher may or may not be prophetic. One may be in one office, yet flow in an anointing from another office.

In the Old Testament, the prophet's function differed from that of the New Testament church leader or priest. The priest approached God on behalf of men by means of sacrifice. The prophet comes to men as an ambassador from God, appealing to them to turn from their evil ways and life. The person maintaining the office of the prophet has the authority to rebuke the leadership offices of the church, providing that they are released as prophets. Those functioning within the boundaries of prophetic ministry have the responsibility to encourage and not to rebuke.

The prophetic and priestly classes were not antagonistic or in opposition to one another. The prophet was to understand all aspects of the church and God's plans and expectations of the full church body. This is extremely necessary if or when church leadership (the priesthood) moves out of the will of God. The one in the office of the prophet is raised to give severe rebuke.

In the Old Testament, the prophet's role in relationship to government was in exerting godly influence upon rulers and state affairs. The prophet was not an officer of the state, but a special messenger from God.

BECOMING A VOICE FOR THE 21ST CENTURY

In Matthew 3:1-3, the word said that John was a voice crying in the wilderness to " . . . *prepare ye the way of the Lord, make His paths strait . . .*" John was a powerful vehicle (or prophet) that God had chosen to use. Through John, God caused the word of His Son to continue to go forth as the final proclamation of the coming of Jesus Christ. God uses the prophet to bring about change to educate in order to reproduce. This is the way that God speaks audibly. He speaks in your inner ear, by dreams and by visions, yet all should be a confirmation of what God has already said.

TO RECEIVE PROPHETIC RESPONSIBILITY

Old Testament prophets were categorized as "seers." They had a great responsibility to the kings and leaders who depended upon them to both see and hear accurately. God placed the responsibility of the nations on the prophets. For that reason, the sons of Issachar had understanding of times and knew what Israel ought to do (I Chronicles 12:32).

And he said unto him, behold now, there is in this city a man of God, and he is an honorable man; all that he saith cometh surely to pass: now let us go thither: perad-

venture he can shew us our way that we should go. (I Samuel 9:6) KJV

The Old Testament kings and rulers placed their hearts and the direction for the nations into the hands of the prophets. God depended on Gad, the seer, to deliver to David the message of his impending state of sin for numbering the army of Israel. God did not speak directly to David at that time. He spoke to Gad, the seer (II Samuel 24:12,13).

BEING A PORTRAIT OF PROPHETIC ACCOUNTABILITY

Many times, in the midst of being lost, God will speak to the prophet. The prophet must maintain accountability. Who are you accountable to? It is mandatory that the prophet maintain a line of open communication with the Lord, his covering, and a good relationship with the recipient of the word. The lack of accountability destroys the charge one may have for a greater anointing.

USHER IN CHANGE

Whenever God decides upon change, He always calls for a prophet. God ushered in change during the period of time when the Jews had begun to relax in their spirit. They became very religious. God sent the prophet, John the Baptist, as a voice to prepare the way. This was because it was the appointed time for Jesus to enter the earth. The purpose of the prophet that must be remembered is that he promotes the vision of another and introduces the visionary. Therefore, the prophet has a word regarding what God is doing.

Often, when this voice sounds, there is no "thus saith the Lord" to signal you that it is God.

Surely the Lord God will do nothing, but He revealeth His secret unto His servants the prophets. (Amos 3:7)

THE PROPHET PREPARES THE WAY FOR A NEW MOVE OR ANOTHER MOVE OF GOD.

There is a great need to develop the voice of the prophetic utterance in today's church. A person may be receiving and speaking a one-word prophecy and have to graduate to paragraphs of utterance. This brings us to the making of the prophet and prophetic people. If you will be a prophetic voice, you will go through the making.

Prophetic utterance should bring forth prophetic truth. As a prophetic voice, deliverance should come forth from the prophet.

Prophetic Accountability Moves you to Maturity

If we are going to operate effectively, we must understand that we must leave from where we are now and desire to move toward the fullness of God. God wants us to operate in the fullness. If we want to do that, we must eliminate all carnality around us. We must leave where we are. We may have to leave some people, things, or churches and go from this room where we live now.

In Hebrews 5:13-6:2: read, *"For every one that useth milk is unskilful in the word of righteousness: for he is a babe. But strong meat belongeth to them that are of full age, even those who by reason of use have their senses exercised to discern both good and evil. Therefore leaving the principles of the doctrine of Christ, let us go on unto perfection; not laying again the foundation of repentance from dead works, and of faith toward God, Of the doctrine of baptisms, and of laying on of hands, and of resurrection of the dead, and of eternal judgment."* (KJV)

Whenever we see the word "therefore," we must ask what it is there for. What are we leaving? We are leaving the principles of the doctrine of Christ and going on unto perfection.

Do you realize that if God brings about the rapture in our lifetime and you as an individual refuse to give up, your will cannot last that long. The relinquishing of our will brings us to a place of death where we no longer exist.

Most of us in the prophetic are still wrestling with our will. Someone could be standing in front of you and you will not be able to help them because God cannot open their files to you and give you their information because you still have a will and God cannot trust you with their information. If we mishandle the information that God reveals to us about people, God will have to judge us. Remember, what God reveals He intends to heal, and He wants to use you to heal them. God may want to give you all of their pertinent information so that they can be launched into their destiny. That is where God wants you to be as a prophet. Too many prophets want to just prophesy to someone, and they think that when they give the word their job is over. But that is not over until you launch the person. There are many prophets around, but they do not all have what is known as a real prophetic presence, voice, and anointing, because if you have all three of these things, you can get results. If there is submission on your part, you will have authentic prophetic presence, voice and anointing.

Remember, the woman that Elijah was dealing with in 1 King 17 did not need a word; she needed results, and she needed a man of God that was going to launch her. The woman that stated that the creditors are coming for my sons did not need a word; she needed to be launched. You have to abandon where you are, abandon your flesh, relinquish your will and move into the next room where the prophetic presence, voice and anointing exist. Can God speak to you and ask you to give up something, and you are able to give it up without a second thought? That requires us to have the understanding that God is King and we can trust Him to provide provision, prophetic presence, voice and anointing. No matter what God asks us, we must trust Him and be willing to give Him anything He asks. Remember King David and Uriah. Uriah completely trusted King David. David had a bad heart. That is why he was so convicted, because he knew that Uriah trusted him. King David is highly trusted, but King David is subject to the prophet, so the trust that is on the prophet has to far surpass the trust of the king. Many prophets are not ready to be released into the office of the prophet. We think we are because we can prophesy, but most are not ready because our will is too big and because we cannot figure out this next move. We won't move at all, and we are not ready to be released.

The Old Testament prophet moved just this way, and the New Testament prophet has to be greater. When the Old Testament prophet came into the presence of the king, this prophet did not bow because he was not a subject of the kingdom on one hand, but on the other hand, he was subject to the kingdom, whatever kingdom he was from, and there was a perfect marriage between the king and the prophet. The prophet and the king were submitted to each other. Remember in 2 Kings 3:14,"***Elisha said, "As surely as the LORD Almighty lives, whom I serve, if I did not have respect for the presence of Jehoshaphat king of Judah, I would not look at you or even notice you."*** (NIV) Elisha honored Jehoshaphat because they were submitted to each other. It was for that reason Elisha gave them a word, helped them, and gave them direction. Elisha did not consider the other kings because they were submitted to his authority.

Jehoshaphat submitted to the prophet Elisha, and the prophet Elisha submitted to King Jehoshaphat. Because Jehoshaphat asked for help, the prophet was ready to help.

We have to really evaluate whether or not we want to be that prophetic presence on the earth, if we really want to be the prophetic voice, or if we really want to be the prophetic anointing in the earth. Because whenever that is the case, we must understand that when God wants to speak, it is imperative that we come to the forefront and say what God wants to say. It is frustrating to me when prophets come to me and say that "I had a word." How is it that you had a word that we did not hear? Once the time is gone, that word is old, and you are correct if you say that you had a word because it is gone now.

Chapter 4
EMBRACING THE PROPHET IN YOU

$\mathcal{R}$emember, one of the things that God wants to do is to bring us into this next place in Him. Now according to the office of the prophet, prophets and prophetic people are designed to be the prophetic presence, prophetic voice and the prophetic anointing in the earth. If you know that you are going to be the next voice that God is going to use, do you think that you might have a particular silent time as Jesus did? He went off the scene and is not heard from again until he is baptized, having a wealth of information to the point where the high priests are wondering, Where did this guy come from? Jesus understood that he was going to be the next voice of God that would literally speak some things that earth needed to hear. If that is going to be you, there are particular things that we have to eliminate.

Remember that you are designed to be a prophetic presence, a prophetic voice and a prophetic anointing where you operate in the earth. Remember that God did not make any mistakes by choosing you. He properly categorized you according to divine order. Look at Numbers 12:1: *"And Miriam and Aaron spake against Moses because of the Ethiopian woman whom he had married: for he had married an Ethiopian woman."* (KJV) The characters in this passage are Moses, Miriam and Aaron. This is a three-person team. Now look at Exodus 7:1. *"And the LORD said unto Moses, See, I have made thee a god to Pharaoh: and Aaron thy brother shall be thy prophet."* (KJV) Miriam and Aaron disconnected from Moses, the man of God, because they did not like something that he did. Miriam and Aaron spoke against Moses, and you never speak against the one who has your oil. Miriam and Aaron stepped out of line; should not Moses be able to choose his own wife? Numbers 12: 2 reads: *"And they said, Hath the LORD indeed spoken only by Moses? hath he not spoken also by us? And the LORD heard it."* (KJV) Now they are mentioning that God uses them, too. That is not an issue, because God said that they were both prophets. Now is a progression with these two because their attitude is leaking down to whom God is talking to. Now we have a problem because up to this point God had not spoken directly to Miriam and

Aaron concerning the church. Notice Numbers 12:3-4. "*(Now the man Moses was very meek, above all the men which were upon the face of the earth.)*" Moses did not hear what they said, and even if he did, he was meek and kingdom minded. He was not going to be angry with them. But God heard it and He took issue with what they did. We see that in verse 4: "*And the LORD spake suddenly unto Moses, and unto Aaron, and unto Miriam, Come out ye three unto the tabernacle of the congregation. And they three came out.*" (KJV)

Notice that God was still speaking to Moses concerning what they did. Why would God give them directions for the church when he told Moses to pastor it? Up to this point, God had not spoken directly to them; He would tell Moses to bring them up. When God starts to give you direction for the church when He told Moses to pastor it, and when God starts to give you directions concerning the church, you are in trouble, not Moses. Why would God give you directions for the church when he told Moses to pastor it? This means that somewhere in this church there was the usurping of authority. God treats them as if they are in authority and starts talking to them. Now that God has started to talk to them, He has to judge them. Notice what God said to them in Numbers 12:5-9: "*And the LORD came down in the pillar of the cloud, and stood in the door of the tabernacle, and called Aaron and Miriam: and they both came forth. And he said, Hear now my words: If there be a prophet among you, I the LORD will make myself known unto him in a vision, and will speak unto him in a dream. My servant Moses is not so, who is faithful in all mine house. With him will I speak mouth to mouth, even apparently, and not in dark speeches; and the similitude of the LORD shall he behold: wherefore then were ye not afraid to speak against my servant Moses? And the anger of the LORD was kindled against them; and he departed.*" (KJV)

Notice what God said to the prophets Miriam and Aaron in this passage: I speak to prophets and make Myself known in a vision and a dream. I do not speak to Moses this way, I speak to him mouth to mouth. We find in Genesis 2:7 what it means to speak to Moses mouth to mouth: "*And the LORD God formed man of the dust of the ground, and breathed into his nostrils the breath of life; and man became a living soul.*" (KJV) We use this to bring people back to life when a person is near death and we call that mouth-to-mouth resuscitation. We are sharing our breath with them, and they come back. They resuscitate. The reason Moses had life to give was because God had breathed the breath into him what was in His mind. Remember, the woman that did not have a child. Read 2 Kings 4:16: "*And he said, About this season, according to the time of life, thou shalt embrace a son. And she said, Nay, my lord, thou man of God, do not lie unto thine handmaid.*" (KJV) The prophet, having already been breathed on by God, now breathed life into that woman and said you shall have a son. And in nine months she gave birth to a child. That is calling it short. Her husband was very old so something had to happen for him because she could not do this by herself. Later the child died and the woman went to get the same prophet because what he breathed on her in the first place in order to conceive and give birth was the thing that she needed to get the child back. It was going to take the same breath to bring him back. The prophet laid on the dead boy, put his mouth to his mouth, and breathed life into the boy. We see this in 2 Kings 4:34-35: "*And he went up, and lay upon the child, and put his mouth upon his mouth, and his eyes upon his eyes, and his hands upon his hands: and he stretched himself upon the child; and the flesh of the child waxed warm. Then he returned, and walked in the house to and fro; and went up, and stretched himself upon him: and the child sneezed seven times, and the child opened his eyes.*" (KJV) We are looking to get this a different way. When you look to get this the kingdom way, it is possible for you to be revived.

Moses was in the next room. He had a kingdom mindset, but Miriam and Aaron did not. We know this because Moses had completely relinquished his will, but Miriam and Aaron had not because they were saying that we do not will that Moses marry an Ethiopian woman. God let them know that He was judging Moses on his faithfulness, not who he married. In the room where Miriam and Aaron operated, God could only speak to them in dreams and visions. When you are in that other room, having left the doctrine of Christ, you realize that whatever God says, you will obey God. Whether you are asleep or awake, you will obey. Everything that you hear is not God and everything that you hear from God is not for now. If you refuse to relinquish your will, God has to speak to you in dreams and visions, but when you are in the next room as Moses was, God speaks to you mouth to mouth.

It is our desire to reveal, through the word of God, an understanding of some of the many things that are going on within you that have caused you to believe that you have a prophetic calling on your life. There is a tremendous amount of information to be understood about the prophets of God. It is not complicated to understand if this calling is for you.

The Word of God tells us in Prov 4:7: 7 "*Wisdom is the principal thing; therefore get wisdom: and with all thy getting get understanding*".(KJV) *We desire to impart understanding to you regarding the "call of the prophet."*

And the Lord said unto Moses, See, I have made thee a god to Pharaoh: and Aaron thy brother shall be thy prophet. (Exodus 7:1)

What Aaron was to Moses, we are to Christ in this world. God has chosen or called each of us for a particular role and responsibility in Him. He did this before the foundation of the world. In the case of Moses and Aaron, God instructed Moses and called Aaron to speak to the people and Pharaoh on His behalf.

Throughout the Old Testament, God chose men or women to speak to an individual, the church, and the nation on His behalf.

And he said, Hear now my words: If there be a prophet among you, I the Lord will make myself known unto him in a vision and will speak unto him in a dream. (Numbers 12:6)

God established and utilized the role of the prophet in the Old Testament. The order and structure of leadership in the New Testament church was put in place at Jesus' ascension.

Ephesians 4:11 identifies the role of church leadership that Jesus Christ ordained for the plan and operation of the New Testament Church.

And he gave some apostles; and some prophets; and some evangelists; and some pastors and teachers. (Ephesians 4:11)

Our focus is on the purpose for which God gave these prophets and how they correlate with the four other offices within the church.

Understand: Your ministry gifts are never for you. It is never for your gain, but it is for the perfecting of the saints, the work of the ministry, and the edifying of the Body of Christ.

As we come to understand the ministry and role of the prophet, we come to realize that his gift is not for himself. Now, we must understand the process that it takes to "answer the call."

Those who are called must understand that before they ever came into being, God knew and called them. An example of this is found when God told Jeremiah,

Before I formed thee in the belly I knew thee; and before thou camest forth out of the womb I sanctified thee, and I ordained thee a prophet unto the nations. (Jeremiah 1:5)

There is nothing that you can do that will catch God by surprise. He knew you before you were anything. God also came into a knowing of what you would do, what you would not do, and every mistake that you would make, yet He still called you and sanctified you.

Understand: God set you apart for His purpose and for His glory before you came into the world.

The reason the prophet must and will undergo challenges is so that he or she will experience and understand what it means to be "set apart." For some prophets, the prophetic gifts have been in operation within them since they were children. Don't get the operation of a gift confused with the release of a call or office. Some problems and challenges come because no one was available to fine-tune the prophet in his gift. The proper awareness and training for his call would cause him to develop and to answer the call of God. It is necessary for each prophet to go through the period or season when he will come to accept Jesus, to go through the fire, the desert, and testing, and to seek the face of God for himself.

After seeking the face of God and discovering your prophetic calling, there is yet another step—"prophetic maturity."

PROPHETIC MATURITY

The prophet must come into prophetic maturity. Those things that were allowed or acceptable when they were babes are no longer acceptable. God does not permit excuses. The Lord will no longer allow those in the prophetic to make excuses for why they cannot go or cannot obey Him.

As you mature in the prophetic gifts, God does less and less in order to bring you to the place of having a face-to-face relationship with Him. God will let you go through the maximum challenges or desert experiences in order that you might come to know His heart. It is time to come to know the heart of God and to move on from just knowing His voice. If you learn the heart of God, you will come to understand what Moses understood. Moses wanted to know of God's way, "...*show me now thy way...*" Exodus 33:13.

We want to help you to take the proper steps into maturity that will lead to your ultimate destiny. Therefore, from point to point in your walk, you are setting stones in place in order to fulfill your destiny. We also understand why, at this particular point of our destiny, there have been challenges that have come to prevent us from entering the next phase of our destiny.

All prophetically gifted people deal with some form of complex within themselves. The majority of the time the obstacle that would prevent us would have much to do with our self worth. The thought of being unworthy to function in basic prophetic, prophetic gifting, prophetic ministry, and/or the office of the prophet would cause us to make the excuse that we would not or cannot wear the prophetic mantle.

One of the greatest battles that you will ever fight and have to endure will be the battle of your mind. If the devil is to ever defeat you and disqualify you in the prophetic, he must win the battle of your mind. Therefore, let us guard our minds with everything that we have (Ephesians 6:11-18).

Let's look at some Old Testament examples of great prophets who dealt with forms of personal complexes illustrating the mind's battle of unworthiness...

1. The Samuel Complex

Samuel had a problem accepting the call because of his age. He was approximately 10 years old when God spoke to him concerning the priest, Eli. God would not accept his age as an excuse or as a reason why he shouldn't give Eli the message from God.

2. The Jeremiah Complex

Jeremiah had a problem accepting his calling because of his age and because of the value he placed on being accepted by people. God would not accept Jeremiah's youth as an excuse for not answering the call. But, God encouraged him.

He told Jeremiah in Jeremiah 1:7: *"Say not that I am a child"* . . . and in Jeremiah 1:8, *"Be not afraid of their faces . . ."* In all of this, God is showing that there will be a time of preparation. There will, no doubt, come testing and situations in the life of the budding prophet.

Note : God wants us to clearly understand that He is always with us to deliver us in any and all circumstances. This confidence helps us to carry out His command to anyone within the ascension gift ministry of the prophetic.

Understanding: When Jeremiah said that he could not speak for he was a child, God told him what not to say, and then touched his mouth (Jeremiah 1:4-10).

In the life of a prophet, God will always touch that which is incorrect. It's up to the prophet to accept or to reject the touching of God. This is why our study is so very important. If we accept the touching of God, God will perfect us in the areas where we are mentally, spiritually or physically handicapped.

3. The Isaiah Complex

Isaiah lived among unclean people, and he had an unclean mouth just as the people. We have to be very mindful that we don't become what the people are whom we are helping. Our assignment is to bring change. Amazingly, God did the same for both Isaiah and Jeremiah. He touched their mouths.

Then said I, Woe is me! for I am undone; because I am a man of unclean lips, and I dwell in the midst of a people of unclean lips; for mine eyes have seen the King, the Lord of Hosts. (Isaiah 6:5)

Isaiah declared that, saying he could not speak for he had unclean lips and he dwelt in the midst of people with unclean lips. Therefore, God touched his mouth, because of his uncleanness, with hot coals. Regardless of how God has to touch one who is to be His mouthpiece, He will touch them – with a hot coal or with a warm hand. Everyone must have a touch from God (Isaiah 6:5-8).

Yet, there was a prophet whose mouth God would not touch. That prophet was Jonah. It is important that we understand how we are being used of God. Is God just using us, or is God pleased to use us? The choice is yours! Let's look at how He used Jonah.

4. The Jonah Complex

Jonah was a man who was concerned about how people would view him. He carried bitterness and resentment against the people of Nineveh, and he was self-exalting. In other words, Jonah had a heart condition that was toward himself and not toward the people. It is important that everyone who has a call to the prophetic office, prophetic ministry, prophetic gifting, or basic prophetic has a heart toward the people and God. We must examine Jonah's life, lest any of us come to the same destiny that Jonah came to. Not only did the book of Jonah seem not to have a complete end, Jonah was never mentioned any more in terms of a prophetic assignment. Therefore, God used him but was not pleased to use him.

Understand: Do not get caught up in desiring that what you speak prophetically to come to pass, especially when it involves condemnation, damnation and the degradation of the very people that God wants to bless. Our assignment is to say what God is saying and not to force our manifestation. There were things that Isaiah prophesied that he never did see in his time.

Key Point: God wants to bless and save all people. He loves the people, but he hates the sin. We must learn to separate the sin from the person whom we may correctly judge. When the men brought the woman that was taken in adultery, Jesus refused to judge the woman, not being an eye witness. But He did judge the men that were the carriers of the complaint or sin. They carried the thing that should have been judged. Jesus gave them the opportunity to make a judgment on the woman if they were without sin (John 8:7). Remember to judge the thing or (sin) and not the person. Let's make the separation. I Corinthians 2:15, "But he that is spiritual (mature) man judges the thing and restore the person. Our frame of thought here must be new covenant minded. Jesus said "I came to save that which was lost (Luke 19:10)".

Therefore, prophetic people need to perform a heart examination on themselves in order to bring forth, from within, the very heart of God – that we love the people like He loves the people.

The lesson learned from Jonah was that God's grace went beyond the boundaries of Israel to embrace all nations.

5. The Habakkuk Complex

Habakkuk was a complainer. His letter seemed to be filled with complaints about God not hearing. Habakkuk complained that God would show him situations that He was not willing to change. After his first complaint, God said, "***Behold ye among the heathen, and regard, and wonder marvelously; for I will work a work in your days, which ye will not believe, though it be told you.***" (Habakkuk 1:5)

I MUST EMPHASIZE: Within the above statement God is making a clear statement to prophets! God is not talking to the people; He is talking to the prophet. He is saying to the prophet what He is going to do. A prophet or prophetic people who have the Habakkuk Complex will not believe the word God told to them. This was because of the break in the pattern to which the prophet was accustomed. Therefore, it is imperative that we do not get so locked into custom that when God would move in an unorthodox way, we would not be able to follow Him.

Key Point: If you have this kind of problem, you will be limited in what God can say to you.

It is important that your will line up with God's will, and God's will be in line with His word. Carnality can interfere with clearly knowing God's will for your life. You do not want to operate in a position to which you were not called. Therefore, you need to know whether your calling as a prophet is direct or indirect.

Was Your Call Direct or Indirect?

In many cases, not all, we walk in areas of ministry for which we have never been called. This is because of the misconception of what we think we have heard. When Samuel heard God call his name, he was not sure who called him. It is not abnormal to hear and not understand what you heard.

Remember: Most of your prophetic gifting has to do with hearing and speaking.

Therefore, your first challenge is to hear God regarding your call. You will wrestle with hearing until you hear accurately. The question remains: Was your call direct or indirect?

A biblical example of an indirect call was Isaiah, although it did not take away from the authenticity of his call as a prophet.

Example: I call a secretary whom I know to do a job, and then someone in my company volunteers for the job. They both are equally secretaries.

God will grant us the privilege of working for Him in whatever area we desire if He sees that we can pay the price for that area of work. There is a price to pay for every level of the prophetic. I am not sure that God had predetermined that James and John would be a part of the inner cabinet of Jesus. But since they volunteered for the job and were willing to pay the price, Jesus invited them to drink of His cup and to be baptized with His baptism.

Warning: Do not ask for anything you can not pay the price for.

There are people whom God has specifically called into the office of the prophet. He expects them to develop, grow and blossom where they have been planted. When God plants you in a specific place and/or office, know that you can blossom there because God planted you there. As difficult as it may seem, you are able to blossom where you have been planted. As one within the prophetic ministry, there is a specific climate that is necessary for your development. God has planted you in a specific climate for a specific reason.

A climate is a region, or area with certain prevailing weather conditions that affect life, activity, growth, etc. Your climate always has to do with your spiritual season. If you adjust your spiritual thermostat, you are able to control your physical temperature. Yet, adjusting your physical temperature will never change your spiritual thermostat. You can change from church to church, and your season will not change, providing that the difficulties that you are experiencing are actually caused by your season.

1. Indirect Calls

Isaiah 6:8, "*Also I heard the voice of the Lord saying, Whom shall I send, and who will go for us? Then said I, send me.*"

Hosea 1:1, "*The word of the Lord that came unto Hosea, the son of Beeri, in the days of Uzziah, Jotham, Ahaz and Hezekiah, kings of Judah.*"

Malachi 1:1, *"The burden of the word of the Lord to Israel by Malachi."* It is uncertain whether Malachi was called directly or indirectly. If Malachi was in fact his name, we are led to believe that he was directly called. The name Malachi means: My Messenger or Jehovah's Messenger.

2. Direct Calls

Exodus 3:4, *"And when the Lord saw that he turned aside to see, God called unto him out of the midst of the bush, and said Moses, Moses. And he said, Here am I."*

1 Samuel 3:10, "And the Lord came, and stood, and called as at other times, Samuel, Samuel. Then Samuel answered, speak, for thy servant heareth."

Jeremiah 1:5, *"Before I formed thee in the belly I knew thee; and before thou camest forth out of the womb I sanctified thee, and I ordained thee a prophet unto the nations."*

Stay tuned to the voice of God. Many distractions will come. It is important that you stay focused and walk in your calling. Why is that important? It is important because you have a preordained destiny. You're going for the goal of the high calling. In order to reach that destiny or goal, you must be able to recognize "the touching of God."

Chapter 5
SOMETHING HAS TO HAPPEN TO YOU

THE COST OF THE ANOINTING

*D*o know where you are in your growth process? There comes a time when you have to actually know where you are in your development process. When you have grown to the point of receiving your own anointing something has to happen to you in order to facilitate that happening. God has to touch you. We will talk more about the touching of God later in this chapter.

For prophets and prophetic people, it is important that you understand your season of preparing to receive your own anointing. This process will cost you something. One way to recognize this season is your wanting to get out of your preparation process. This usually takes the form of wanting to quit their jobs, jump ship, leave town to start over or quit their marriages. These are the kind of things to look for in this particular season.

Because, now remember, as prophets or prophetic people you are to guide other people into peaceful and stable life situations and lifestyle. In order to make this happen for someone else your life must be stable, if not, there is no way that you can lead anybody else into a place of stability in their lives. With that in mind, I think that one of the things that we really do need to understand is where we are within this particular season. Where are you in terms of your thought process in this season. Where are you? Are you ready to quit, ready to jump ship, ready to just stop and do something else. I mean are we really totally determined that we are going to be prophets or prophetic people, being able to grab hold of a lot of other people that are being shaken right now and lead them right in to the Kingdom.

You have to actually figure out where you are in this particular season. Are we willing to sell out for a lesser piece of bread? Are we really willing to sell out and leave town? Are we really willing to quit? Are we really willing to just side step off course for a morsel of bread? Where exactly are we? What season is this? As the people of God, we need to know and understand where we are. The book of Philippians really deals with this season and teaches us how to stand; how to really take a stand in the midst of our costly anointing process.

I think there are some things that we really need to deal with because if you are going through a challenge, then you need to know how to handle the challenge that you go through. You and I should not be moved by our challenge. Our challenge should be moved by us.

If we are prophets or prophetic people, we are going to have to go through a particular period where we must be tried. We have to have a testimony and the way we obtain our testimony is to be tried. We really don't know whether or not you are capable of guiding others without your testimony of overcoming challenges. God does not know that you are capable of leading others if you don't learn how to deal with a particular challenge.

One of the things about prophets and prophetic people have to consider is that we have to lead people in a lot of different areas. One of the areas that we have to lead them is in their ability to take a stand. So, where are you? Have you gotten to the place yet where you know how to stand and not be moved? In the event that you have gotten to that place somebody is going to come along behind you and want to follow you; want to understand how do you really do that. How do you stand when all of the odds seem to be stacked against you? How did you stand every time no matter what is going on? How do you keep your joy in the midst of chaos? How do you do that?

I was thinking back on when I was a minister at my home church. I was thinking about some of those time periods that I had to come through. One in particular was going through a time period when you are not the key leader. The key leader is compensated for the work that they do, but I was not the key leader and I was not compensated for the work that I did at church. I have 5 children that I was raising by myself. I was a single parent with girls and boys. There were church responsibilities (Sunday service, bible study, Bible College and volunteer work) that were actually on me. There were home responsibilities for me and my children that were on me. I did not know if I was going to be able to provide the best for my family. I seemed to just exist during this time period. How do you handle being in that particular place? How do you handle that particular period?

LEARNING TO FOCUS

One of the things that I think that I learned in that period is gain a focus. That was lesson number one. I had to really gain a focus. In other words, Rodney, where are you going? What are you hoping to accomplish? Because there are lots of people that are actually operating within the structure of leading people and sometime we don't really see where this thing is going to end up. In other words, we don't really know how we are going to get through this season, how we are going to make ends meet, how we are going to accomplish all that we need to do, how we are going to take care of our responsibilities naturally or spiritually. We don't really know how this state of affairs is going to end up. And so when we really think about our dilemma, we wonder how I am going to get out of this. How am I going to take care of my children? How am I going to do this? How am I going to do that?

Well, all of these questions are actually on our mind and now we have to develop a plan of making it through this dilemma or getting out of this situation. In that particular period of my life I came up with a plan to go to Tulsa, OK. I had a plan to get out, and I was going to pack my belongings and my family and move to Tulsa, OK. I believed that was what I needed to do. But God had set me at that church under the teaching that I was receiving for that particular season of my life and I could not leave until God released me to do so. Many of you reading this book may be thinking that you are capable of selecting the place where God wants you to grow but you are not. When God created Adam He did not ask him where he wanted to be. He created the environment and the place that He wanted Adam to be and put him there. We find the account of that in Genesis 2:8 *And the LORD God planted a garden eastward in Eden; and there he put the man whom he had formed.* (KJV) God knows what He has put in every pastor or teacher or set gift and he also know who has what you need, you cannot possible know who has what you need only God knows that and He makes sure that you are at the right place at the right time.

My reason for going to Tulsa was not so that I could make it better financially, my purpose and my focus was to get deeper into the word of God. I wanted to gain something more spiritually than what I was actually gaining at the church where I was. But now understand this, the church where I was, is where I was actually called to be. I wasn't conscience of this kind of thought process. I was where I was actually called to be; and so what I was getting was what I needed spiritually at that particular time.

But now, my thought process was to go to Tulsa, OK. Now here is the thing that God corrected me on. He said this to me: "You have no need that man should teach you. For of the same anointing that teaches them will teach you also." And, I really did not know what that meant and I didn't even pursue to understand what that meant at that particular time because that was way beyond my thinking; God just spoke something to me and I didn't even know that this was in the bible. God spoke something to me that really helped me because I was getting ready to jump ship or ship wreck. You have got to jump ship first before you ship wreck. You don't know that ship wreck is coming until you jump ship.

As a prophet or prophetic person, I needed to make sure that I was not going to ship wreck. I needed to make that decision before I knew that ship wreck was coming. I didn't know that ship wreck was actually coming, but it was definitely on the way. Ship wreck is inevitable when we are not in our set place. Ship wreck is inevitable and it is going to happen, it is just a matter of time.

God began to deal with me about that. He said this to me: "You have no need that man should teach you." Well, He wasn't talking about I didn't need to set under the Pastor teaching the word or other church leaders teaching the word; that is not what He was talking about. Because He set up teachers to make sure that I was going to be taught, perfected, rebuked, corrected, and all of that, encouraged. He wanted to make sure that I knew that I had reached a level where my dependency had to change. In other words, my dependency had to be shifted now on the anointing and less on man.

If there is no shift in my dependency as a prophet the first thing that is going to happen is that I was always going to fall prey to whatever my environment was doing at the time. The second thing is that I was going to fall prey to being addicted to people. And the third thing is that I was going to fall prey to an inability to tap into the source of revelation for myself.

Understanding that, then the next place that I have to come to is just understanding that I am about to enter the season where the anointing is going to teach me. And so now understand this, as a Prophet, I had to understand that this is the season that I was getting ready to go into. And understanding that I knew that I had to cling to the word because, the enemy always comes after the word.

The enemy wants to make sure that we, you or I are handicapped to the point where we will not be able to receive this next level of God's word. He attacks us for the word sake. He does not attack us just because we are anointed. That is not why he attacks us. He attacks us for the word sake. He does not want you to come into the next level of receiving God's word.

If I am having any challenges in my life, all I need is a word from God. Prophets and prophetic people do not always get their word from God in church. They get their word at their place of revelation. Their place of revelation is not necessary a geographical location; you may be at home; you may be riding in the car; you might be at church; you may be listening to the word but it is because you have tapped into another source. And so, my objective for including this in this book is to push you to the place where God will be able to speak to you.

You have a problem if you are still dependent upon a man or a woman for revelation. If that is true of you then I can never push you to the place where you are going to be of some great help to your pastor or your set gift because you need your place of revelation activated. But this cannot happen if you have an unwillingness to go through a challenge.

When I started to go into this next place of revelation, my trials and my tribulation was turned up. This happened because the enemy comes after the word. If I can show you this and if you can understand this, the way it needs to be understood, then what is going to happen is that you are going to come to this next place of just standing where you are, regardless of what you are going through, regardless of what the lack is, regardless of what the challenge is; you learn how to take a stand and put God in remembrance of His word to bring the resources or bring peace to wherever it is that you are going through right now.

If you are merely just trying to get out of this situation because you are tired of it that will not work because it is going to follow you wherever you go. You are not going to out run it, because that has been assigned to you. One of the worst things that we can ever do is to be out of our set place with that trial. Because then, at that particular point, you are out of your set place (the church that God has assigned you to); in other words, you are not getting the specific word from God that you are needing in order to stand. Yet the trial won't leave you alone. The trial is assigned to you and God knows the address of the place where He set you or told you to be and that is the place He must send the word to help you stand.

If you are not there you will miss getting the word from God that you need. In Mark 4:10: "*And when he was alone, they that were about him with the twelve asked of him the parable.*" verse 14, 15: "*The sower soweth the word. And these are they by the way side, where the word is sown; but when they have heard, Satan cometh immediately, and taketh away the word that was sown in their hearts.*" (KJV) Satan comes immediately; he comes immediately for the word. When he identifies that you have word that is getting ready to take root in your heart, he comes after that word. And the reason he comes after that word is because if that word ever takes root, then he is not going to know what to do with you,

When I got to the place where I understood this, then I realized that it was going to have be something that I was going to do with the word. Let me ask you this question now? When the word comes to you, what do you do with the word? Because now understand this, if you are not using that word then you are no more than this person over in the book of Mark. Mark 4:14, 15: *"The sower soweth the word. And these are they by the way side, where the word is sown; but when they have heard, Satan cometh immediately, and taketh away the word that was sown in their hearts."* (KJV) The word was sown in their hearts. Understand this now, regardless of anything, when you hear the word, that word is sown in your heart. That is where it is sown. What I am saying to you right now is the word of God is sown in your heart. Your heart is the ground, so just like a seed is sown in the ground (the earth) you should not leave that seed alone. You have to take care of the seed sown in the earth, you cannot just put it there and leave it alone. If it is to grow to its fullness you must cultivate the soil around it, make sure that no weeds choke it out from where you planted it, make sure that it gets proper fertilizer, water and sunlight etc. whether it is sown in the grown, likewise you can not leave that word of God alone that was sown in your heart. Because this is what is going to determine whether or not you are going to stand.

When God starts to grow you up you will have no standing power without His word. But you say, I thought the Holy Ghost was my standing power. No, not by Himself; you must listen to the Holy Ghost and obey the word of God.

When you first come to Christ you have an enemy (Satan) at that particular time that you are more acquainted with than the Holy Ghost. Unless you have been saved all of your life, you have an enemy that you are more acquainted with than you are acquainted with the Holy Ghost and because of this you are more likely to believe the enemy than you are to believe the Holy Ghost. Why would you listen to the enemy rather than the Holy Ghost? Because you have been walking with him from birth until you got saved and during that time he is all you heard.

Up to the time of your salvation, you had not heard anything from God. You did not even listen to God. You did not even like God. The enemy is who you fellowshipped with all of that time and now all of a sudden you need to fellowship with Jesus (the word) and the Holy Ghost. Now Jesus is trying to get His word in you but you reject His word.

Jesus had to deal with this same issue when he was talking to His twelve disciples. He was trying to get them in on this new move of God. He had to literality say to them; look fellows this is how this whole process works. I realized that I had to understand what Jesus was teaching his disciples and once I understood the importance of having the understanding that they had one the things I literally had to do was to put me in with them, I had to act as if Jesus had thirteen disciples. Not twelve, but thirteen and I was number thirteen. I had to get in within the pages of what He was saying to them, now remember these guys were not saved. Peter was a killer; you have got to understand that Peter was a killer; Peter was a sinner. He was not saved but he was busy. Jesus says, look I think I can use him. Jesus didn't go to get religious people. He didn't go to the synagogue or what we would call the church to find people to follow Him. He went out into the streets. He found some of His peers; He found Peter who was a business man and a killer if you crossed him. He found Matthew, a tax collector, a sinner, a publican, he was not one of the religious order, he was who he was. Those are the kind of people that he selected and once he selected them He taught them the process.

The fact that you were not brought up in church is not an excuse for not understanding this process. Peter didn't understand it; Peter didn't know anything about what Jesus was teaching. Peter didn't understand what Jesus was talking about, and knowing this Jesus says, look, here is how this whole process works. It will work for you if you are not one of the religious people. None of His twelve disciples were religious people therefore, it will work for them but they have to get to the point where they understand how the system works.

Let's go to Mark 4:15 *And these are they by the way side, where the word is sown; but when they have heard, Satan cometh immediately, and taketh away the word that was sown in their hearts.* (KJV) So now, these are they by the way side where the word is sown, right? But when they have heard, Satan cometh immediately. When you finally get God's word is when Satan shows up. He does not care that you go to church. He does not care that you study the word of God. He don't care that you go to a church that teaches the word of God. He does not care about any of that. When you finally get the word of God that is when he shows up.

You may be one of those that wonder why Satan does not bother some of those folks that feel that they do not need God; the reason is that he already has them wrapped up, he doesn't need to bother them, he needs to bother you because you are at the point where you just have received the word of God. Now he is coming after that word. Whatever portion of that word that you understood, he is coming after that. Why? Because, if that word that you have just received ever takes root then he can count you out of reach. One of the reasons that he has not counted some of you out is because there is still a word from God that needs to take root. The foundation of the word needs to take root in you as prophet or prophetic person. Any time you can think that there is an alternative, other than what God has said then, the word has not taken root yet.

If you and I actually come to the understanding that we do not have any more options, we'll understand that the word of God has taken root now. We finally understand that God is our only way out of this mess.

With this in mind we need to get involve with how Jesus' system works. This is how His system work the sower sows the word. The sower sows the word. Anytime any of you are trying to get something by going through another door, it is not going to work; unless you are going through the door of the word of the living God. That is the only way out.

This is one of the things and we need to deal with and realize that nothing is going to work but the word of God. Even when we deal with other areas of our lives we must be focused the same way. For instance, our reason for getting married should not be because we can now enjoy two incomes or because there will be an additional income in the house, it should not be just to get extra money. If that is the reason it is not going to work. It is not going to work because more money is not really what we need. Proper management of whatever it is that we have, is what is actually going to cause a snowball effect for more to come in.

We must understand how to get things to work for us. Many of you are wondering how you are going to make it in the situation that you now encounter. You may be saying "how am I going to make it; I know that I have a gift on the inside of me, but what am I going to do with it?".

Do you realize that some of you may be struggling with many different things that the enemy is actually doing in order to trip you up. Knowing that you have that gift and making a decision about what to do with it is a position of vulnerability for us. Now the enemy wants to trip us up because we know that we have a real gift but we have not decided to use it for the glory of God.

Whatever your gift is, whether it is a gift to sing, a gift to act, etc. many of us have stopped pursuing God as our number one assignment which is ministry. We started to pursue an acting career, a singing career, whatever kind of career you actually go after, whether it is something that you have learned, a learned trade; you pursue that and you are really saying, the heck with God right now because I need to make something to make something happen; because God is not working; I need to do something; God is not doing His job; I need to do something. And so for you as a prophet or prophetic person it is a trick to try to trip you up and have you thinking that the world will pay you better than God and you go after that.

Here is one of the things that we actually have to understand, God has to set along the side and watch this happen. During this process you are being tried and God has to just watch to see what you will do, because if He doesn't set along the side and let this happen you will not be effectively tried. God has to watch and see what you are going to do. Are you going to pursue your acting career? Are you going to pursue your skill? Are you going to pursue this or that? If we let the enemy trip us we and pursue in this manner is to say, God you don't work; I am god, now. I am god of my own life.

Let me tell you something, this was one of the greatest trials, I think, that I have ever had to encounter. My uncle presented me with business opportunities a long time ago; but I knew that I had to be in the face of God. I knew that God had to be number one for me. I had to study the word of God; I had to get the necessary training in the word of God. I was not making a lot of money but God had to be God to me. I had to trust Him for the extra money that I needed, because I was raising five children as a single parent and I was not making enough money, that meant that God had to show up because I had five children and I had to be the provider in my house. There was nobody else to make sure that this thing happens for me, it had to be God and me. Otherwise, this thing is not going to go over and I can't make it without God's help. I knew that I could not pursue a business option to make the extra supply that I needed where God was not supplying, because I can not be god for myself.

In other words, I have no more options; God you are my only option. And so as a prophet or prophetic person, you must stop wrestling trying to find other options. You must come to the conclusion that God is your only option. If you don't come to that place you are going to be wrestling all of your life. This is true for all of us, we have to literally become like the three Hebrews boys found in Daniel 3:16-18: "*16 Shadrach, Meshach, and Abed-nego, answered and said to the king, O Nebuchadnezzar, we are not careful to answer thee in this matter. 17 If it be so, our God whom we serve is able to deliver us from the burning fiery furnace, and he will deliver us out of thine hand, O king. 18 But if not, be it known unto thee, O king, that we will not serve thy gods, nor worship the golden image which thou hast set up*".(KJV) We have to say if God doesn't, I still won't bow. If God doesn't provide for me, I still won't bow. I still won't bow because God is God.

If God called me then it is His job to provide for me; but I have to make it through that season. So, I can't fizz out, faint, quit, turn coward in that season; I can't do it.

Okay, here is what I had to do, the sower sows the word. I had to come to a place where I understood, okay, God gave me a word. Now that word is in my heart; now Satan is after that word and he is looking to tear that word down; but I can't let him. Because I am the only guard that protects that word that I have received.

The word that God spoke to you; you guard that word with your life. I mean literally guard that word with your life because you are a steward of words. We find that in 1 Corinthians 4:1: *Let a man so account of us, as of the ministers of Christ, and stewards of the mysteries of God.* (KJV) declares you as the steward of mysteries of God, as ministers (prophets and prophetic people), you are the steward of that word.

God hands you a word and say, here make this word work, this is the one right here that you need. You make this word work. There are many times that we as prophets or prophetic people try to go another route and get something other than God's word to work, but we have to run out of options.

When I was coming up in ministry I ran out of options. Some of the options some of you are trying, I have already tried it. I have already tried that; I am telling you, it doesn't work. It really just doesn't work. I tried to go to another city, it didn't work, and the reason that it did not work was because everything that I was trying to run away from followed me. I found out that quitting was not an option. I could not just throw my hands up and quit because I had five children to take care of and no one was going to love them more that I loved them. I could not quit, run, turn coward or faint. I simply ran out of options. As I mention before everything that I tried to run away from followed me. You may think that leaving the city, county, country or nation is the answer, but let me tell you the problem will follow you.

When you leave your set place, the place where God told you to be you now have a big problem, since your situation followed you and you are not in your set place you are headed for shipwreck. This is true because you have now positioned yourself not to receive the level of the word of God that you were accustomed to getting and you have that same trial that was trying to kill you in your set place. You are not getting the word from God that you need to stand. Remember, your situation or problem followed you. You cannot run from it. God will give you what you need to stand if you are at the address where He sends your mail. If you are not at that place you are destined for a bigger problem then the one you are running from.

What did I do when I left my set place? Once I understood that I must be where God had set me I went back and now that I am back in my set place, what do I need to do next? Well, Rodney, now you need to pick up where you left off. You have lost time but you still need to pick up where you left off because you did not escape the touching of God. I did not escape those things that I had to go through because I thought of something better to do.

To Further The Word of God

Take a look at Philippians 1:12: *"But I would ye should understand, brethren, that the things which happened unto me have fallen out rather unto the furtherance of the gospel;"* (KJV) What is the gospel? It is the word of God. Can we settle on that, the gospel is the word of God? The things that happen to me happened to me to further the word that I received from God. Everything that happened to me happened to further the word that I received. This is something that we absolutely have to understand that what happened to me was to further what was spoken to me. What happens to you? What did God say to you, what did God say He was going to do? What did God impress upon you that He was going to do? Well what happened to you, happened to further that word. Well, let me give it to you this way, God spoke a word to me and said, I want you to preach faith to My people. I want you to instill faith in their hearts. Well, I was a minister; I had not even preached my first message when He said that to me. Well, now I get busy going in that direction and I become disabled in my body. When I become disabled in my body I had a wife and five children. Then my wife decides that she wants to leave the family and she walks out. I became immediately a single parent of five children, I now have to be a father and a mother to my children; the oldest one was about six and a half years old. I still have to work; I still have to do everything that I am supposed to do; what am I going to do now? Being disabled did not change any of my responsibilities. What do I do now? I have to do what the word of God said.

Remember, those things did not change the fact that God said to me, preach faith to My people. It did not change that at all. So, now I am positioned to still fulfill that word that God spoke to me and do all of my other responsibilities too. What did that scripture say, in Philippians 1:12: *"But I would ye should understand, brethren, that the things which happened unto me…"* I would you to understand, brethren, that whatever happened to me, happened to further that word: "Preach faith to My people." That is why those things happened. Because, how am I going to further the word: "Preach faith to My people," I need a demonstration and a testimony of faith. If I didn't have faith to believe financially; if I didn't have to believe God to keep a place that we were living at that particular time; if I didn't have to believe for healing; if I didn't have to believe for those things I would not have opportunity to move to another level of faith. I have to believe for all of those things at the same time. Why?

Because of what happened to me. Well, how did something like that happen to a man whose is obeying God? How does it really happen? Well, because where I was right then at that time was not where God eventually wanted me to be. I was not at the destiny that God was calling me to; that was just a place of starting. But God says, look I am calling you further; I am commanding you to go further in Me. Well, now, I need something to happen to make sure that this place where I am right now is not my destiny. So I need something to push me out of this place. Why? I was comfortable at the place where I was and that place was working for me right then. I would not have been motivated to go up to a higher level of faith if those things had not happened to me, therefore something had to happen to me to cause me to go further in God than I had ever done before.

I was comfortable, but God says, look Rodney, this is not your destiny, you have just started; don't get comfortable here. You are in a church that teaches and preaches the word of God; you are listening to the word every single day; you are feeding off of the revelation of your pastor, somebody that was hit with cancer and bounced out of it. You are feeding of her revelation. You are feeding off of her testimony. You are feeding off of what she went through. What she went through was to further the gospel. All that she went through was to further what God spoke to her. But Rodney, what God spoke to her, now you need to be released from that. Now something needs to happen to you. Why? To further what I have spoken to you. Something needs to happen to you because I want you to preach faith to My people.

I was setting there as a minister feeding on her word; feeding on what God was speaking to her; feeding on her level of revelation. I was comfortable because I was receiving from her and understanding the revelation that she taught; Now, God says, something needs to happen to you and I began the process of coming into my destiny.

The same must happen to you because of the word of God that has been spoken over your life. I am talking to prophets and prophetic people right now and I am telling you right now in the Name that is above every name, in that Name of Jesus Christ, you are feeding on the revelation of what happened to your pastor or your set gift, but there comes a time that something must happen to you in order to further the word that God has given you.

I encourage you to go through the process, just as I have those that are members of the church that I pastor, those that I am spiritual father to and those that are submitted to my teaching, and are feeding on what happened to me. And I am telling you like I understood then, something must happen to you. Something needs to happen to you to push you out from where you are. Something needs to happen to you that pushes you out of that comfortable place where you are.

Something has to happen to cause you get uncomfortable at where you are. When you reach the point where God wants to further His word to you, you may want leave town and relocate, leave a relationship, leave your current situations or whatever you come up with to get relief from what is happening to you. But, remember something has to happen to you to further the word that God has given to you and when that process begins you will begin to be very uncomfortable where you are naturally and spiritually.

Your comfort zone will be snatched from under you and glory to God; you will be pushed to another level in God. Let's take a look at what happened to Jesus to further the gospel. It happened to Jesus the same way. Something had to happen to Jesus to further the gospel. The Bible mentions many things that happened to Jesus that were not so pleasant including His crucifixion, death, burial and being raised from the dead, all of these and more were used to further the gospel.

Now, Jesus says to His disciples, the twelve that had been feeding on His revelation, Peter, James, John, Matthew, all of the rest, something needs to happen to you, because the gospel needs to be furthered. Then Paul comes on the scene. And Jesus says to Paul, something needs to happen to you. And then something happens to Paul to further the gospel. Paul raises up Timothy, Silas, and John Mark and all of them. And then Paul says all of them, look something needs to happen to you. This process is passed down through generations through the years all the way down to our time; to my pastors and then to their spiritual sons (male and female) of whom I am one – something needs to happen to you. And the gospel goes further. Now all of us that are their sons have to say to our spiritual sons, something needs to happen to you. Every one of you that are reading this book and you are a prophet or a prophetic person, something needs to happen to you. Why? For the furtherance of the gospel; and then you are going to rise up some years down the road and you are going to tell somebody, something needs to happen to you. And it is going to be the furtherance of the gospel. Because if something does not happen to that particular generation, they stay where they are, and they need for something to happen in order to further the gospel.

Things that happen to us happen for the furtherance of the gospel. We don't understand why we are where we are. Why is all this happening to me? You know that you are trying to obey God and you start to think about your situation and you say "I am trying", glory to God. I can't begin to explain what I felt when I was obeying God; and then all of a sudden my body breaks down and the doctors don't know what is wrong and I have five children, in addition, their mother walked out, and now I have five children to raise by myself. What happened? To a man that is obeying you, God. How does this happen to me? This was not supposed to happen to me, I was obeying God and I wanted God to go after some of those folks that were not obeying Him.

But Rodney, they can't handle this if it happens to them. Why? Because they have nothing to further in God, if they are not walking upright before God, they are not doing anything for the glory of God, they have nothing to further. What are they going to further? But you are obeying God and you have a word, the devil is coming after that word. I will never ever forget this in all of my life, when I had to leave the church that did not believe in the manifestation of the Holy Ghost, and we went back to the church where God had set me, something happened to me. Everybody that attended our church could not stay but I could not leave because I had no other options. I said to God, this place is giving me options. This place is feeding the one option that I have, in other words. This place is feeding the one option that I have, there is not another church in the city that is feeding me like this. There is no other place that I can go that is feeding me like this. It is feeding the one option that I have. You are my only option, God. You are my only option; this place is feeding that option.

At that time I started writing book that I never finished but God was teaching me how to go through the process and stand. This is where I started in Philippians 3:1: *Finally, my brethren, rejoice in the Lord. To write the same things to you, to me indeed is not grievous, but for you it is safe.* (KJV) Wait a minute, How do you tell somebody rejoice that is going through what I was going through? I finally realized that rejoicing was a choice. You have got to understand that rejoicing was a choice; we didn't have any place to go to; we were not living in a place where you wanted to invite people to visit. My family was struggling at that time. We were struggling; but we loved the Lord.

You Must Have A Place of Dying

Now remember, I was going through some things, not just one, my body was broken down, I had become a single parent, I had financial responsibilities, had church responsibilities and I was studying the word of God. I was doing all of those things trying to live the best that I knew how for the glory of God. How do you tell me to rejoice? This is how I understood I was to rejoice, in Philippians 3:1-3: *Finally, my brethren, rejoice in the Lord. To write the same things to you, to me indeed is not grievous, but for you it is safe. 2 Beware of dogs, beware of evil workers, beware of the concision. 3 For we are the circumcision, which worship God in the spirit, and rejoice in Christ Jesus, and have no confidence in the flesh.* (KJV) Okay, wait a minute now. And have what? No confidence in the flesh. You know what that means, that means abandon all of your ideas that you think will work over what God has said. Abandon them all because it will not work. Please understand that you have to abandon them all because they do not work, those are your ideas. Now you know that you have to get rid of your ideas, those ideas you have about quitting, leaving the city, leaving the state, leaving your marriage or whatever you have come up with to get out of your situation. Abandon those ideas because they are not going to work because the reason you are going through those things is to further the gospel, the word that God has spoken to you. All that you come up with is based on your own understanding and your understanding is based on everything that you have learned from birth until now from parents, relatives, friends, education, school systems or society.

It gets better as we continue to understand what the Apostle Paul is saying about his situation to the church at Philippi in Philippians 3:4-7 *4: Though I might also have confidence in the flesh. If any other man thinketh that he hath whereof he might trust in the flesh, I more: 5 Circumcised the eighth day, of the stock of Israel, of the tribe of Benjamin, an Hebrew of the Hebrews; as touching the law, a Pharisee; 6 Concerning zeal, persecuting the church; touching the righteousness which is in the law, blameless. 7 But what things were gain to me, those I counted loss for Christ.* (KJV) *Can you see what Paul is saying here: "But what things were gain to me, those I counted loss for Christ."* Everything that I gained I had to count it as a loss. Do you understand what that means? Let me tell you exactly what that means: wherever you are right now, whatever you have accomplished in life up to now, you count that as loss. Count it as dung; count it as nothing. Why? The answer is here in Philippians 3:8 *8 Yea doubtless, and I count all things but loss for the excellency of the knowledge of Christ Jesus my Lord: for whom I have suffered the loss of all things, and do count them but dung, that I may win Christ,* (KJV). That I may win Christ; that I may win the anointing. The anointing must be won. It is not going to be handed over easily. There are things that you have got to go through, it is not handed over easily. What I am talking about is stepping into your own anointing.

One of the things that many of us don't understand is the difference between operating off of somebody else's anointing and operating off of the anointing that we have won. When it comes to your maturity you have got to operate off of what you have won. In other words, you are not going to win it as in a match with someone else, you are going to win it because you gave up something. You gave up some things that you loved. There was a place that was a comfort zone for you and you loved to stay right there, but you gave it up, glory to God. Now God says, I'll give you the anointing. Why? It is because you gave up those things that you loved. Can I be absolutely honest with you? On every new level that you come to, there is a safe place that you come to know on that level; there is a place of comfort that you will find that you absolutely love. I want to ask you this question—what is it that you as an individual find as your comfort zone? Whenever you get stressed, what is it that becomes your comfort zone? And then, is it God? What is it that becomes your comfort zone? I had choice comfort zones.

When I was smoking, one of the reasons that I didn't want to give it up is because when I got stressed a cigarette helped me, now if that cigarette helped me when I was stressed that cigarette became god. Because that was a place that God wanted in my life. Rodney, when you are going through, let Me comfort you. So now, if I want God to comfort me when I am stressed, this means that I have to evict that cigarette; and the only way to evict that is to give up the habit. What is it that you have to give up? What is it that you cling to at the place when you are going through? Is it seclusion? You have got to give it up; because seclusion can become your god. Why? Because that is what you like to do. You start to going through and then all of a sudden, you just go somewhere by yourself. Why? Not to get in the face of God, that would be a good reason, but that is not the reason, it is not to get in the face of God, you just don't want to be around people. If you have anything that comforts you other than God, now God says, you have got to give that up; that is a place that you have to give up lest I snatch that from under you. Now wait a minute, how would God snatch that away from you. Watch this, Where is the place that you normally go for that seclusion? He will snatch it away. Why? Because God wants a relationship with you and He wants the thing that He spoke to you to be furthered; and in order, to do that He now has to limit your options. We see that in Philippians 3:9: *And be found in him, not having mine own righteousness, which is of the law, but that which is through the faith of Christ, the righteousness which is of God by faith:* (KJV) Not have what? Mine own righteousness; you can't have your own stuff. You can not have your own righteousness. So that is a place that you have to abandon. Most of us hold onto something that makes us feel godly and therefore when we sin, we cling to it. Release it that is your own righteousness. That is your own stuff; you have got to let that go. We say to ourselves "well at least I am not as bad as this person or that person"; no, you have got to let that go that is your righteousness because what you really need has to be the righteousness of Jesus Christ, Himself. When we operate by our own righteousness, we want to justify where we are and what we do, but as prophets and prophetic people we have got to let that go.

Take a look at Philippians 3:10: *That I may know him, and the power of his resurrection, and the fellowship of his sufferings, being made conformable unto his death.* (KJV) What? Know him and the power of his resurrection, and the fellowship of his sufferings, being made conformable unto his death. Now you and I have to ask ourselves this question, have we conformed to anything that looks like His death, as a prophet or prophetic person? Have you conformed to anything that looks like His death? What was your dying? What did your dying look like? I can talk to you about mine. I can tell you what my dying looked like. I can talk to you about that. You have to be able to explain and express what your death looked like. What did your death look like? Where did you die or are you still very much alive. Can you explain to anyone your death? You need to be able to do that because it is at the place of your death that you end up with your one option and that option is God.

Do not feel bad if you can not name the place of your death. And please, whatever you do, don't try to cover it up and say, I died, when you didn't die. Some of you may not have a place where you died, because if you still have your comfort zone, you did not die. Death is to come. Here is what happens when you die; the only thing that you have to look back at is an old rugged cross. That is where I died. What does your cross look like? Where were you crucified? Some of you have not died yet; you are still holding on to your comfort zone. Because when you die you let go all of your places of security and you end up with one option: God, you are my only option.

Once you die to all other options where are you going to go back to -- the cross? For some of you the cross may be before you. Some of you, you might be on your cross right now. Some of you, the cross might be behind you. But you need to know where you are. Now, if you are on your cross right now, do what Jesus did—don't come off. Because the burial has to take place; but you are looking forward to and rejoicing in the resurrection. You are at a point where you can remember the words of an old song: "go on and drive the nails in my hands; go on and scandalize my name; go on do whatever you have to do; not even the grave is going to be able to hold me". You have got to understand that, not even the grave is going to be able to hold you; not if you go on leave your comfort zone and die. You can prolong your time of going to your cross but the cross is inevitable, one way or the other. It is going to happen. I am telling you we as prophets and prophetic people what we go through furthers the gospel. What we go through, it furthers the gospel that is the word that God has spoken to us.

Your Will is Required of You

Giving up your will is what is really required of you. Giving up my will is one of the things that I am qualified to talk about. I am qualified to talk about this particular subject, because I relinquished my will. That is what makes me qualified to really talk about this subject. It was not an easy task but I am telling you it was something as a prophet of God I had to do. I had to give up my will.

God won't come in and take your will from you because He gave you a free will. Since He gave you a free will, now it becomes your responsibility to really sell out to God on that, whatever it is that God wants you to do, to just sell out on that and just surrender your will.

Remember that place where you died, there is more to it than that. Go with me to Isaiah 9:6 6 *For unto us a child is born, unto us a son is given: and the government shall be upon his shoulder: and his name shall be called Wonderful, Counsellor, The mighty God, The everlasting Father, The Prince of Peace.* (KJV) *He starts it out with a birth, "For unto us a child is born,"* (KJV) but when it deals with a son being given, "… unto us a son is given:" it is marking the place where He died. Keep this in mind: until there is a place where you have actually died you have not even started living yet. This is not just for prophets, this applies to all 5 ascension gifts, I am talking about apostles, prophets, evangelists, pastors or teachers you have not even started ministry until you have actually come to the place of your death.

My question to any of you, when will you start ministry? When will you start it? You see, it doesn't start because you are about to sing your song, because you are about to preach your initial sermon or when you are about to teach your first lesson. It doesn't start until you can name the place of your death, name where you died. You will never forget the place where you died. Why? Because it was there that you surrendered every facet of your will. You surrendered every facet of your will right at that particular place. It is almost like you come to the end of your road; now nothing else really even matters. You know at that point that nothing else matters. That is where you set God up as number 1 in your life and nothing else matters. Jesus' place where that happened was called what? Jesus' place where that happened was in the wilderness. You may think it was Gethsemane. You may think it was Calvary. But it was actually the wilderness when He started ministry. Let us take a look at that in Matthew 4:1-2 *4: Then was Jesus led up of the Spirit into the wilderness to be tempted of the devil. 2 And when he had fasted forty days and forty nights, he was afterward an hungred.*

(KJV) It was at that place that He knew His assignment and He also knew that He was getting ready to embark upon that assignment, He knew that He was going to have to die in that wilderness. He knew that the wilderness was going to have to be the place of His death. He knew that He had no other options at this point. Now He has a place of reference to return to if He needed comfort.

I trust you know your bible well enough to be able to understand that when Jesus needed an overhaul (comfort), the wilderness is the place where He actually went back to. He went right back to the wilderness into a solitary place to pray. If you really never died, what place are you going to go back to when you are suffering or when you are in trouble or when you feel like you need an overhaul? You are going to go back to that place, and most of the time it is not back to the place of prayer and it is not back to that place of God being your only option because you have never really died. And so, where do you go back to? Maybe, you will go back to a man so that he can make you feel more comfortable. Maybe, you will go back to momma or daddy so that she or he can make you feel a little more comfortable. Maybe, you will go back to a woman or a man because she or he is going to make you feel more comfortable. It may be solitude or eating. Wherever that place is for you, that is where you are going to go back to. That is the reason you need a death. That is the reason you need a place where you are literally going to die; otherwise you never start living. Jesus started living when He came down out of the wilderness under the power of the Spirit. He realized something happened to me in that wilderness.

So probably most of us can not really say, something happened to me at this particular time in my life; it was at this place that I died and something happened to me. And I am telling you, we actually need that. We need that kind of a place. When we really understand this then we know where to go in times of suffering and trouble. Our place of death is the place that we need to go back to whenever we need reinforcement of the reality of God being our only option. What is the reality here? The reality here is that I now am really in a place where I am burned out again and being at that place you are drawn right back to the place of your death because you know that is where something happened for you. That is where your life was changed again. This is not where you came to know Jesus. After you came to know Jesus, this is where you actually came face to face with your death. And you started living.

It is very important that we understand that not making a decision for the will of God how it shortens our life. A lot of us don't really understand that. Understand it from this perspective: Jesus said it this way; He said the reason that I am here is to carry out the will of My Father or to carry out the will of Him that sent me. He said that is My reason for being on this planet, that is My reason for being on the earth to carry out the will of Him that sent me. If that is the number 1 objective of our being on the earth that should also be your objective to carry out the will of Him that sent you.

That is the number 1 reason for our being here, but I wonder how many of us really see that as number 1. Some of us can't even do a simple assignment because it is not our will to do so this week. If God ask us to do something this week, that is His will for us this week, but if we refuse that is not our number 1 objective this week and we start to make excuses to God. In order to carry out God's will and make that our number 1 objective we must surrender our will. I had to do just that, I had to surrender my will. Now, I am here to tell you that it is not really an easy task but it is a possible task.

When we study our bible we find out that something had to happen to those that God wanted to use in His plan for us. Something happened to every one of them and they had to carry that thing that happened to them to the next generation. We can go all the way back to Abraham. The account of what some of them carried to the next generation can be found in Hebrews 11:17-12:1: *By faith Abraham, when he was tried, offered up Isaac: and he that had received the promises offered up his only begotten son, 18 Of whom it was said, That in Isaac shall thy seed be called: 19 Accounting that God was able to raise him up, even from the dead; from whence also he received him in a figure. 20 By faith Isaac blessed Jacob and Esau concerning things to come. 21 By faith Jacob, when he was a dying, blessed both the sons of Joseph; and worshipped, leaning upon the top of his staff. 22 By faith Joseph, when he died, made mention of the departing of the children of Israel; and gave commandment concerning his bones. 23 By faith Moses, when he was born, was hid three months of his parents, because they saw he was a proper child; and they were not afraid of the king's commandment. 24 By faith Moses, when he was come to years, refused to be called the son of Pharaoh's daughter; 25 Choosing rather to suffer affliction with the people of God, than to enjoy the pleasures of sin for a season; 26 Esteeming the reproach of Christ greater riches than the treasures in Egypt: for he had respect unto the recompence of the reward. 27 By faith he forsook Egypt, not fearing the wrath of the king: for he endured, as seeing him who is invisible. 28 Through faith he kept the passover, and the sprinkling of blood, lest he that destroyed the firstborn should touch them. 29 By faith they passed through the Red sea as by dry land: which the Egyptians assaying to do were drowned. 30 By faith the walls of Jericho fell down, after they were compassed about seven days. 31 By faith the harlot Rahab perished not with them that believed not, when she had received the spies with peace. 32 And what shall I more say? for the time would fail me to tell of Gedeon, and of Barak, and of Samson, and of Jephthae; of David also, and Samuel, and of the prophets: 33 Who through faith subdued kingdoms, wrought righteousness, obtained promises, stopped the mouths of lions, 34 Quenched the violence of fire, escaped the edge of the sword, out of weakness were made strong, waxed valiant in fight, turned to flight the armies of the aliens. 35 Women received their dead raised to life again: and others were tortured, not accepting deliverance; that they might obtain a better resurrection: 36 And others had trial of cruel mockings and scourgings, yea, moreover of bonds and imprisonment: 37 They were stoned, they were sawn asunder, were tempted, were slain with the sword: they wandered about in sheepskins and goatskins; being destitute, afflicted, tormented; 38(Of whom the world was not worthy:) they wandered in deserts, and in mountains, and in dens and caves of the earth. 39 And these all, having obtained a good report through faith, received not the promise: 40 God having provided some better thing for us, that they without us should not be made perfect. Hebrews 12:1 Wherefore seeing we also are compassed about with so great a cloud of witnesses, let us lay aside every weight, and the sin which doth so easily beset us, and let us run with patience the race that is set before us,* (KJV)

Something happened to Moses; something had to happen to Abraham; something had to happen to Jesus; something had to happen to Peter; something had to happen to all of the twelve; something had to happen to them in order for us to come into the place where we are now. Something had to happen to my man of God, my woman of God, where I first started ministry. Something had to happen to them; something had to happen to me but it is always a place of dying where you ended up with a testimony. Your place of dying is where you end up with something that you could not walk away from; it is something that removes all of your options.

What was the thing that took place in our lives that has removed all of the options? You need to know the answer, because it is really at that place where God steps forth because you allow Him. No other point in your life was He able to come forth like that. Why? You didn't let Him. Do you realize that God always gives us an option to just relinquish our will without tragedy? He always gives every last one of us that option.

So this becomes tremendously important for us to really understand. Now when we get to the point where we really understand that then we actually are now in this position where God is saying, here is what I want to be able to do for you. I want to be able to let you on purpose make it up in your own mind that you are going to walk my will out. On purpose you decide that you are going to walk according to the will of God. Remember the strongest force in the earth is not the will of God, it is your will. Your will is the strongest force in the earth—it is not the will of God, it is your will. God is actually looking for you and me to make a decision if we are going to do this. Anything that you or I decide on we actually carry out regardless of whether it is the will of God or not, we carry it out. There are people that decide to get married and God is no where in that marriage and it happened because they decided on it. All of the signs, all of the warnings were there, they ignored every bit of that because it was what they wanted not God. Well of course later on they end up blaming God. Well you know, God was not anywhere in it. He says well you know there is nothing I can do about it. You wouldn't listen to me.

God deals with us in the area of our will. He is saying to us "go ahead and surrender your will to me. If you surrender your will to me then I can work with you. But if you never surrender your will God says, look there is nothing I can do. I can't even use you because every time I have something I want to bring across you don't even want to listen to Me". This is key, because we get to a point where we are flowing in the Holy Ghost, the Holy Ghost is speaking, the Holy Ghost is saying something, we are doing exactly what he says, we have results in what he said but then there comes that point when the Holy Spirit stops talking to you. Why? Because you stopped listening to Him, you are no longer yielded to Him and so therefore he stops talking. We have to start a relationship with the Holy Spirit and listen to Him if we want Him to continue talking to us.

Jesus really deals with some things here in Mark 10:13-15 *13 And they brought young children to him, that he should touch them: and his disciples rebuked those that brought them. 14 But when Jesus saw it, he was much displeased, and said unto them, Suffer the little children to come unto me, and forbid them not: for of such is the kingdom of God. 15 Verily I say unto you, Whosoever shall not receive the kingdom of God as a little child, he shall not enter therein.* (KJV) Let's take a closer look, "Suffer the little children to come unto me, and forbid them not: for" what? of such, "for of such is the kingdom of God. Verily I say unto you, Whosoever shall not receive the kingdom of God as a little child, he shall not enter therein." The kingdom of God is actually a place where God's will is carried out. Remember when the disciples asked Jesus to teach them to pray and He says in Matt 6:9-10: *After this manner therefore pray ye: Our Father which art in heaven, Hallowed be thy name. 10 Thy kingdom come. Thy will be done in earth, as it is in heaven.* (KJV), and so the same way the will is carried out in heaven God says, this is the way I want you to pray because this is the thing that is not happening. My will or the will of God is not being carried out in earth like the will of God is carried out in heaven. So to reject the will of God from happening in the earth is to reject His kingdom.

Okay, let me help you out with that a little bit. Take a look at what He says here again. "Suffer the little children to come unto me, and (what) forbid them not: for of such is the kingdom of God. Verily I say unto you, Whosoever (listen to this closely) shall not receive the kingdom of God as a little child, he shall not enter therein." Now what does that mean? Let me tell you what it doesn't mean first. It doesn't mean that if you don't receive the kingdom of God as a little child receives the kingdom of God. Well let's go right back to verse 13, what does verse 13 say again, now I need you to see this because we have to keep this in context. Verse 13: *"And they brought young children to him,"* (okay they what?) brought (notice the word brought) *"that he should touch them: and his disciples rebuked those that brought them. But when Jesus saw it, he was much displeased, and said unto them, Suffer the little children to come"* (notice the word come) *"unto me, and forbid them not:"* (notice the word forbid) *"for of such is the kingdom of God. Verily I say unto you,"* notice what the next phrase is saying (truly I say to you, I am not lying to you folks is what He is really saying) *"Whosoever shall not receive the kingdom of God as a little child,"* in regard to the words "not receive" what did Jesus do? He received a little child and was displeased because His leaders would not receive a child. Jesus did what? He received the child and was displeased with His leaders because they did not receive a child or the children in this case. And now He is saying, for of such is the kingdom of God (the kingdom of God is as the children) and He is further saying that whosoever shall not receive kingdom of God as a little child, (as a little child; in other words, the same way you receive the child you receive the kingdom the same way. And if you don't you can't even enter it.

You must understand that! Let me say it another way, if a child runs to you to be picked up you will usually pick that child up quickly without thinking about it even if that is not your biological child, it may be a friends child, it may be a niece or a nephew but just as you received that child so must you receive the kingdom of God. You just received the kingdom of God without a second thought and everybody receives a child just that same way. And so the bible says, if you do not receive the kingdom of God like that you are not worthy of the kingdom. Most people receive a child just like that. When a child is running (abounding) toward you; immediately you pick the child up and receive that child without thinking about it and during the time that child is in your arms you protect it with all that is in you. You take ownership and will not allow any harm to come to the child while you have it in your arms. We are to receive the kingdom of God just like that, the reason that we do not is because we know that if we receive the kingdom like that it is going to cost us something. And therefore, when we see the kingdom abounding toward us just like children abounding toward us we won't receive it, because we know this is going to cost us something.

This gets better, look what Jesus did in verse 16: *"And he took them up in his arms,"* *(what did He do?) "He took them up in his arms…"* because this child is as the kingdom. What do you do with the kingdom? You take it up in your arms as to say, I will protect this, I will carry this out, whatever your will is right here God it is mine just as much as it is yours. You have the mindset that you did not bring that child into this earth but in as much as the child is abounding toward me and I received the child into my arms I might as well be my biological child because I took responsibility of the child in my arms at that particular moment and I say that, when this child is in my arms I am going to protect the child as my own. I don't know what is the child's social security number or date of birth, I don't know any of that but I will protect this child. Why? Because the child abounded toward me and so therefore I received the child and as the child ran to me that is how fast I received the child.

When you decide to refuse the will of God it can shorten your days on the earth, because you are not here for you. Remember this, when you received the kingdom of

God it is going to cost you something.

Let's go a little further to verse 16 - 18: *"...put his hands upon them, and blessed them. 17 And when he was gone forth into the way, there came one running, and kneeled to him, and asked him, Good Master, what shall I do that I may inherit eternal life? 18 And Jesus said unto him, Why callest thou me good? there is none good but one, that is, God." Let's understand that. If you are seeing me, Jesus, as a mere man and calling me good then you are off; but if you are seeing me, Jesus, as the Holy One of Israel as God Himself then you are correct in what you are saying. So if that is who I am to you then do what I say. That is what He is really saying. Verse 19-21: "Thou knowest the commandments, Do not commit adultery, Do not kill, Do not steal, Do not bear false witness, Defraud not, Honour thy father and mother. 20 And he answered and said unto him, Master, all these have I observed from my youth. 21 Then Jesus beholding him loved him, and said unto him, One thing thou lackest: go thy way, sell whatsoever thou hast, and give to the poor,"* Now watch what Jesus says next *"one thing thou lackest"*; what He is getting ready to say is not what the guy is lacking but what He is actually saying is going to reveal what he is lacking. That is exactly what happened; it revealed what he was lacking. *"go thy way, sell whatsoever thou hast, and give to the poor, and thou shalt have treasure in heaven: and come, take up the cross, and follow me."* What you have go sell it. And so what does it reveal? It reveals that the thing that he has is dearer to him than the kingdom he is trying to enter into. Do you realize how many of us in the body of Christ that wear titles, believers that are leaders would not go through one ounce of suffering for the kingdom of God, most of us won't. We wouldn't go through anything for the kingdom of God, not anything. You know why? Because your mindset is really not kingdom, what was Jesus asking him, *"Go sell what you have"?* Let's see you detach yourself from that which is important to you. Now think about this now. What are we involved with that deters us from our destiny.

Sometimes distance is what deters a person from their destiny. Sometimes it is just too much trouble for me to be going through, I want that but that is just too much trouble. Look, it is not really a matter of this or that, it is a matter of kingdom. It is a matter of the kingdom of God in as much as the kingdom of God is advancing toward you, therefore you have to advance toward it. This becomes extremely important, Jesus is saying, now look if you really want the kingdom of God it means that you have got to sell what you have. We have to sell out to God at the expense of what ever it is that we actually enjoy, which is what most of us won't do. Jesus was talking to leaders, Prophets and prophetic people. And when we really think about things that we accommodate over what God wants. What is it really going to take? What would you give in exchange for an anointing? See, because remember the anointing flows from the kingdom. You must understand that? What would you give in exchange for it? God says that if you are going to come into it you need to give all, give it all up. I really do question how bad we really want what it is that we say we want. For many of us it is just a matter of having a title. I am telling you it is much more than that because once you get that title God says, I require your will from you.

Let us take a look at what Paul has to say about surrendering his will in 1 Corinthians 9:16-18: *For though I preach the gospel, I have nothing to glory of: for necessity is laid upon me; yea, woe is unto me, if I preach not the gospel! 17 For if I do this thing willingly, I have a reward: but if against my will, a dispensation of the gospel is committed unto me. 18 What is my reward then? Verily that, when I preach the gospel, I may make the gospel of Christ without charge, that I abuse not my power in the gospel.* (KJV) God requires our will. He will not make us give it up, we must do it willingly. I remember a situation with one of my spiritual daughters. Her will was blocking God's will in her life. I went through a trying time trying to minister to her of the importance of God's will for her life. As I reflect on the last conversation we had prior to her death, I begin to recall the wrestle that she had with her will and how I reasoned with her for about an hour and a half about surrendering to the will of God; that whole thing was of great concern to me. I am telling you I was really battling hard with that; so much so that I called my mentor, Dr. Mike Freeman and spoke with him sharing my concern about the situation and he said this to me, "do you realize that if she could have only surrendered her will it could of changed the whole state of her existence.

Just surrendering to the will of God could have changed it all." And you know what, and my whole thought process went back to how many of us do the same thing. God says look it is not just a matter of doing what I want, you know that you should do that, but you must obey the leaders that I placed over you to guard your soul. This becomes one of the biggest tests we encounter, because if we don't obey our spiritual leaders (pastors and set gifts) who you see every Sunday and every bible study night, we are not about to obey God.

I Corinthians 9, verse 16, is the scripture that God used when He called me to ministry. Because God knew that I was a tough case. He knew that He was going to have to hit me right at the gut, He already knew that He was going to have to hit me straight forward with this. Verse 16: "*For though I preach the gospel, I have nothing to glory of: for necessity is laid upon me…;*" (KJV) Wait; though I preach the gospel I have nothing to glory of, a necessity is laid upon me. Rodney I need you to do something. And I am not asking you, I am laying it on you. I am laying this responsibility on you as a leader. How many of you have ever really experienced something that you felt that God wanted you to do and it almost felt like it was just laid on you? You know, almost no questions asked, it is just laid on you. But even though it was laid on you, you still understand I can do this or I can reject this. I did know that God had a plan for my life and that is the but if I can do this, or if I can reject this but I also know that God is the reason that I am still here on the earth because I tried to commit suicide but God did not let that happen. Keeping that in mind, how can I reject God's will for my life, He is the only reason I am still here.

You know I was just thinking not long ago when I was about 18 years old I was driving somebody else's car, I will never forget that, that thing was about a 1968 Fleetwood. I was driving with my girlfriend and I pulled up to the McDonalds drive-thru window and I was placing my order, all of a sudden a car rolls up slowly and I saw him through the mirror because my background caused me to watch everything you and the car pulled up slowly and I am still watching it through my mirror, now I knew that I had done nothing to anyone because I didn't bother folks. Then all of sudden he pulled up on the side of me, and I saw the window roll down and he put a shot gun right up out of his window just like that. And I looked over at him and he pulled it back, I wasn't the owner of the car. And it was a good thing that he at least waited to see if I was the one that he was really looking for. God protected me from that. He could have not waited to see if I was the owner; how can I reject a God that protected me when I was unsaved? How can I reject what He wants? Then there was another time when I decided to get smart with another guy, was calling him some names that were definitely going to make him angry.

I got this old cougar that needed a lot of maintenance and it was out of shape and I was busy aggravating this guy. Now, everybody in my neighborhood understood that people who expected trouble kept guns under the car seat. I did not have a gun in my car because I knew better, but I pretended as if I had one under my seat. I was doing all of the name calling that I could do and at the same time going up under my seat pretending to get a gun I did not have and he said OK, it's like that and began go under his seat to get his gun and I knew I didn't have a gun, understanding that I put my foot on the gas pedal as hard as I could and that car did not want to move at all and I was really pushing it because I knew that he was going to use his gun. He was driving a Volvo that was running good and fast. I thought, what am I going to do? The best thing that I could do was to use my driving skills in that worn out car I was driving, and I used every bit of the skill I had. I had the gas pedal to the floor but that Volvo was just cruising up on me and so when I got to my exit even though I was in the left lane I took the exit, I waited until I was just a few yards from the exit and quickly took that exit. The Volvo was coming upon me fast in the left lane and he was going so fast that he had to miss the exit, he couldn't follow me. I certainly was not going to out run him on a straight shot. He had almost caught up with me and would have if I had not taken that exit so quickly. In the nest moments he could have shot me with that gun and could have taken me out of the earth. God protected me at that time also, how can I now say no to God.

These are just two of the many times that God protected me. Now that I am years down the road why would I not do His will. He protected you all this time, why would you years, months, weeks or days down the road say no to His will? What reason could possibly be good enough for you to say not to God. And you know, I'm sure you have some stories too. I mean God protected you all that time, why wouldn't you say yes to His will? He laid a necessity on you. For though I preach the gospel, I have nothing to glory of: (a) necessity is laid upon me; woe is unto me, if I preach not the gospel. For if I do this thing willingly, I have a reward; but if against my will, a dispensation, (a God-given order) is laid on me. A what? a God-given order. A dispensation of the gospel is committed unto me if I don't do it willingly. (1 Corinthians 9:16, 17 KJV) You can do it with reward or you can do it by force where God can just go ahead and remove you from earth.

The only thing that God has to do in order to remove you from the earth is just to remove the hedge He has around you, Satan is already after you. He already does not like you, come on saints don't fool yourself; he already does not like you and I at this particular time because we have already caused him enough trouble. And if he already doesn't like you please understand what that means is that he is already trying to wipe you out and get you out of the earth. Let me repeat that, he already wants to wipe you out. What that means is that you and I are just going to have to go ahead and submit to whatever His will is. But now remember the strongest force in the earth is the will of man not God. I said the strongest force in the earth is the will of man not the will of God. Now, if the strongest force in the earth was the will of God that means that God could make us do whatever He wanted us to do; but His will is not the strongest force in the earth. Why is that true? Because God has turned over the authority of the earth to you and I and since that is the case, we have to relinquish our will in order to do His.

This is one of the scriptures that God dealt with me about when He called me to ministry Verse 18: *"What is my reward then? Verily that, when I preach the gospel, I may make the gospel of Christ without charge…"* In other words, I am going to preach whether you give me an offering or not is what Paul is really saying. Why? Because I do not preach in order to get an offering. But can I help you with this; you are going to be tested to see if you will preach without expecting an offering. I am going to say that one more time, you will be tested. Your test may end up like mine. I live in Maryland and I went to South Carolina one time to do a revival and they took up offerings but I didn't get any of it. We went out to breakfast and I guess the people forgot their money so I paid for breakfast. Then the question was asked: "would you go back?" I said: "Absolutely!" I didn't get an offering, brought my own food and theirs and "would you go back?" Absolutely! I went to a church in North Carolina to do a three day prophetic conference and they gave me a $100 offering for all 3 days and we paid for our own hotel, food and travel and all that was needed for the trip. And the question was asked again, "would you go back?" Absolutely! Absolutely! I would go back in the drop of a hat if it is God's will. So, at this particular point I don't conjure up what I think the will of God is. God called me to preach; so now if I have a release to go then I go and we would pay the bill on that. Why? Because it is the will of Him who sent me; and so if you as a leader, prophet or prophetic person are not at that level in your will you are in trouble.

I would like to ask the question, "Why do we preach?" We went to Delaware one time to do a prophetic conference; I think in that conference we only had a couple of people that really showed up for that conference. We were just going there to test the ground to see if they were receptive to the prophetic. We do that occasionally. We also did that in Elizabeth, North Carolina one time to see whether or not if they were receptive to the prophetic because the prophetic is not excepted everywhere. Not everybody is receptive to that. So we did that and the question was asked, "Would you do it again?" Yea, if it is the will of God. If it is the will of God, we would do it again. Why? Because we are not moved by how many people show up, we are not moved by any of that. We are not moved by what people think. We obey God, wherever God wants us to go that is where we go, that's where we take the word.

As a leader, prophet or prophet person you have to set your will to obey God. I am telling you, I had to set my will to obey God because some of the people that you will have to minister to are people that have talked about you, people that have scandalized your name, people that just simply don't like you at all and now this amazing God that you serve say, I want you to give them a prophetic word. For what! I mean that is probably what you are thinking in your head, for what? They don't like me God. Then God says, I don't care, tell them what I said. This is where I had to get, God and I don't go through those kinds of exchanges anymore. Because I developed the same love for you that God has for you and now it doesn't matter what you do to me or what you did to me I am still going to give you the same word. I am not going to polish it over.

Likewise if you give the biggest offering in the church, and you put it in my hand, please understand you are still going to get God's will and God's word for your life. So it doesn't matter how big the offering is, doesn't matter how small it is, doesn't matter if you have been wonderful to me, doesn't matter if you have not been wonderful to me, you are still going to get the will of God. Why? Because I can't give you anything else; does that make sense? That is just where I am, I can't give you anything else, I am going to give you God's word, I am going to give you what God said to give you. This is where your feelings have to bow out because somebody just blessed you real good but they need a real rebuke, now we are about to find out whether or not you are more tied to the riches or to God. You know just some weeks ago, I kind of lightened up on some of my spiritual sons because I guess most of them felt like I was being a little too hard on them so I lightened up a little bit but let me tell you something when you have a leader that dies it just brings me back into focus: I am called to bring you into purpose. And if I have to rebuke you in the hardest way possible because I am telling you, my wife asked me and one other person asked me regarding the death of one of my spiritual sons, "was it anything else that we could have done?" And you know what my answer was "No." Do you realize, can I say this honestly because I did everything that I could to help bring her into her purpose.

The same is true of my wife, if my wife was called home to God today, and I thank God that God has given my wife long life and the length of days, do you realize that if she went home to be with the Lord today I wouldn't have any apologies that I need to make. I wouldn't have any more love that I wish that I could have poured on her; I wouldn't have any more. You know why? Because I treat my wife every single day of her life as if this is her last day. And if she went home to be with the Lord, I would miss her dearly but I would have no regrets. I wouldn't try to climb in the casket crying because I needed to make something right that was wrong and now its too late.

Oh I would miss her dearly but let me tell you right now, I wouldn't be able to think of anything that I wish I could have done. Why? Because I am doing everything I know to do right now while she can yet enjoy it. If I am going to walk according to the will of God it involves her. What do I mean by that? I can not say that I am walking the will of God out for my life and I mistreat my wife. If you do that you are not in the will of God. The same goes for you that are reading this book and anybody else. I can't be nasty and mean to you and say I am walking the will of God out for my life. I can not do that and still say I am in the will of God. If you do that you're not walking the will of God out for your life; even if you try to say that you are, please understand that you're not walking it out.

These are God's people we are talking about and that includes you and knowing that we must understand what we need to do. We need to love the people of God. Since I understand that I need to treat you just like this is your last day on earth. I can't think of any person within our congregation, the church where I am senior pastor or within our leadership (I thank God that because God has given each and every one of them long life), that I have not given my all for. If anyone of them were to go home to be with the Lord I have already given them my all. I have given everything that I have to give and I have held nothing back from any of them. Remember what Paul said in Acts 20:20: *"And how I kept back nothing that was profitable unto you, but have showed you, and have taught you publicly, and from house to house,"* (KJV) He says, I kept back nothing from you. That is where I live. I can honestly say that I kept back nothing.

THE TOUCHING OF GOD

The touching of God is essential and important to the destiny of the prophet at any level. Abraham received the touching of God and brought forth life out of that which was dead. Jacob received the touching of God and got his name changed, which produced a nature change. Joseph received the touching of God that literally thrust him from the pit to the mansion. This was the beginning process that thrust him, eventually, to his destiny. Moses received the touching of God that brought him from the backside of the desert to being a deliverer in the forefront. Isaiah received the touching of God and had the foulness of his mouth and language changed. Jeremiah received the touching of God and received destiny in his youth, to the point of having authority over kingdoms and over nations. Joshua received the touching of God and fulfilled a portion of destiny by becoming the successor of Moses.

If we reject the touching of God, then God will reject us from being His mouthpiece, even as He said in the book of Hosea: Hosea 4:6 *My people are destroyed for lack of knowledge: because thou hast rejected knowledge, I will also reject thee, that thou shalt be no priest to me: seeing thou hast forgotten the law of thy God, I will also forget thy children.* (KJV) My (God's) people are destroyed for two reasons: lack of knowledge and rejection of knowledge. Therefore, God said they would not be priests to Him.

Esau rejected the touching of God and lost his birthright, which encompassed his destiny. Korah rejected the touching of God, and the earth swallowed him up with his destiny. Miriam and Aaron rejected the further touching of God, through their leader, and lost their destiny.

Understand: If God will reject a priest that mishandles the sacrifice then, certainly, He will reject a prophet that mishandles the people.

It takes courage to go forth once you have received the touching of God. There will be trials and tribulations, obstacles to overcome, and stumbling blocks in the way. *Take hardness as a good soldier* (II Timothy 2:3) because now you're in the development of the "making of a prophet."

The touching of God moves us out of a place of comfort. When God touched Jacob, Jacob's thigh was now out of its socket. When He touched Abraham, Abraham had to leave his hometown, family and friends. When God touched Esther, she had to come to the point of being willing to perish if necessary. Being touched of God is a place of sacrifice.

What is it that causes you not to be able to advance to the next place? Could it possibly be your will? What is it that causes us not to obey God when God tells us to do something? There is a level of security that causes us not to be able to break free and advance into the next place. If God has already spoken and said some things regarding where you are designed to go in order to bring about a rich manifestation of what He said, then there may be some things that we must let go. When God gives us an assignment, the next thing that He must do is touch us, and we get to an uncomfortable place of unrest. There were times when I would be doing just about anything and there would seem a problem when there was nothing wrong. I had to shift to a place of prayer because I knew that there was nothing wrong in the natural. God just started to pull on me to prep me for His next move. When the shift happens, you have to be ready. You cannot be getting ready.

The prophet always lives ahead of the game. That is a blessing, but it is also a problem. God is talking to you about something, but He is not talking to the house (your local church) about those things and this causes unrest on the inside of us. Now you have no one to talk with because no one understands what God is saying to you, and it becomes lonely sometimes. You have to now begin to understand and think like a prophet. I did not have anyone to teach me these things and I did not know what to expect, so I had to learn these things.

There are times when you have to let people that you love run into walls because what God is saying they don't understand. And because they are not operating in a level of trust that they need to, they are not going to believe you, and sometimes you have to just release what God is saying and step back. It becomes difficult to watch someone that you love run into a wall, but if the person does not believe your report and you are hearing God on this next move, then something has to cause the person to hear, and often what causes people to hear is trouble.

Now what would make Moses want to leave Pharaoh's house? Moses was in the house of the king. What would make him want to leave that comfortable place? Purpose made him want to leave. Purpose caused him to get involved in killing the Egyptian on the behalf of the Hebrew slave, but it was not time for him to come forth. Moses was still in Pharaoh's house, so it was not time. God let Moses know that he had come into the season; the season alarm went off. It was the season, but not the time. When you come into your season, the alarm clock goes off. But since it was not the time, Moses could have pushed the snooze button on his alarm clock because it was not yet time for him to deliver God people. If you are a disciplined prophet, you do not need an alarm clock in the natural because God will get you up. He utters His voice and you get up. You cannot oversleep. You will be the only one that hears Him, even if other people are in the area where you are sleeping.

When you step into the time, there are no more moments left. We find this in Genesis 12:1-3: *"Now the LORD had said unto Abram, Get thee out of thy country, and from thy kindred, and from thy father's house, unto a land that I will shew thee: And I will make of thee a great nation, and I will bless thee, and make thy name great; and thou shalt be a blessing: And I will bless them that bless thee, and curse him that curseth thee: and in thee shall all families of the earth be blessed."* (KJV) In this passage, God told Abram to leave his father's house, family including Lot, and friends and to take no one with him except his wife. Anytime there is a greater place, there is always an abandonment of another place. This is not always a geographical shift. We have to understand what kind of shift it is, whether it is a changing of position, mentality or whatever it is, because all of them feel the same. God did not give him the exact address or location. All he knew was that God was going to show him where at some future time.

Abram departs, having only the information that God provided in verse 1. He does not know how he is going to provide for his family, he does not know where he is going, and he does not have transportation. All he knows is that he must go and take only his wife. Now Abram does not know who God is, so he cannot connect the dots. He must operate on faith alone. He does not know at this time in his life that God considers him His friend or even what it means to be a friend of God. Abram served the god of the sun and he did know who god was at that time. God is expecting Abram to do something without having all of the information. That is how God knows that He can trust you. Some of us are so stuck on the security of where we are that we will not leave that place. When you respond to what God is saying and doing without knowing all the details, God knows that you are worthy of His touching you; otherwise, He will not touch you. Not that you are not worthy as a person, because God sent Jesus. His only begotten son Christ has taken care of that part of making you worthy, but this is about the activation of purpose and He knows that He must get you to leave where you are before He is ready to touch you.

An example of what I am talking about can be found in the account of the people building the tower of Babel. When God saw what they were doing, He decided to go down Himself. He did not send an angel; He went Himself. We see this account in Genesis 11:4-7: "*And they said, Go to, let us build us a city and a tower, whose top may reach unto heaven; and let us make us a name, lest we be scattered abroad upon the face of the whole earth. And the LORD came down to see the city and the tower, which the children of men builded. And the LORD said, Behold, the people is one, and they have all one language; and this they begin to do: and now nothing will be restrained from them, which they have imagined to do. Go to, let us go down, and there confound their language, that they may not understand one another's speech.*" (KJV) They were a people of one language and one mind, and God said that there is nothing they cannot accomplish because they are operating in unity as one and they were about to accomplish something before the time.

Since that time God has restored us to one language and that is the language of tongues. He is expecting us to operate as one. God does not tolerate disunity. Remember the account of Moses, Miriam and Aaron. They were not unified because Miriam and Aaron ignored the authority of Moses. If God puts you over anything, you cannot tolerate disunity. When God created Lucifer, sun of the morning and the anointed cherub, he did not create another like him and gave him a very important position to lead worship. But when he broke the unity and caused disunity, his position was not so important that God would tolerate that, and God kicked him out. Jesus mentioned Satan's fall in Luke 10:18: *"He replied, 'I saw Satan fall like lightning from heaven.'"* (NIV)

Why would God be interested in coming where we are? It is because we worship Him. We worship Him more than we worship man. Abraham gives us an example of why God would want to come into our presence. Abraham honored God as God, and God met Abraham because he honored Him as God. Abraham is also a prophetic presence at this time. Therefore, being a prophetic presence will cause God to want to meet with you. Abraham was to be the father of nations, and God needed to touch him. Many of us with the title prophet are not a prophetic presence because if we were, we would be able to change some things. If the best thing that we can do is prophesy, we are not a prophetic presence, a prophetic voice or carrying a prophetic anointing. If a person with a deadly disease such as AIDS comes into our presence, we can turn it around when he or she is ready to submit to God, if we have all of these.

Remember, the widow in 1 Kings 17:9: *"Arise, get thee to Zarephath, which belongeth to Zidon, and dwell there: behold, I have commanded a widow woman there to sustain thee."* (KJV) God told the prophet to go to Zarephath and be a prophetic presence, and that is what he did. The prophet Elijah changed the widow's situation. She was expecting to eat her last meal, and she and her son were going to die. We find the account of this in 1 Kings 17:13-16: *"And Elijah said unto her, Fear not; go and do as thou hast said: but make me thereof a little cake first, and bring it unto me, and after make for thee and for thy son. For thus saith the LORD God of Israel, The barrel of meal shall not waste, neither shall the cruse of oil fail, until the day that the LORD sendeth rain upon the earth. And she went and did according to the saying of Elijah: and she, and he, and her house, did eat many days. And the barrel of meal wasted not, neither did the cruse of oil fail, according to the word of the LORD, which he spake by Elijah."* (KJV) Elijah was a prophetic presence that God needed him to be.

The Making of a Prophet

The prophet is one who is divinely inspired to communicate God's will to His people and to disclose the future to them. When the seeds of the prophetic are planted in God's select people, at His determined time, He will cause an awakening of their call within them. He will also put in place a means for their development.

The Wilderness Experience

God takes prophetic people into wilderness places for preparation. It would seem, from the natural perspective, that we should not have to always be in that kind of place. It is a great place for preparation. In the desert, the climate is right for prophetic people to grow. When the seeds of the prophetic are planted and are developing in God's select or hand-picked people, the climate that they are in determines whether their growth will be good or stagnated. The climate is important.

The definition of climate is:
1. the prevailing weather condition of a place, and/or
2. a region having definite climate conditions.

The training of the prophet Moses was done on the back side of the desert in the wilderness. His training and his testing in the prophetic were in the wilderness.

The training schools of the prophets were also in the wilderness. They were in parts of particular countries. We understand that the wilderness is an uncultivated, uninhabited region, or wild area. A wilderness area may be an area of public land, likened to a virgin forest, preserved in its natural state by prohibition, by law, or by the construction of roads, buildings, etc. An example of this kind of wilderness training can be seen in the life of the prophet Elisha. Just like the prophets of old, no one is excluded from the climatic conditions of the wilderness experience.

John the Baptist, the forerunner for Jesus, had to spend some time in the wilderness before he could speak for the Messiah. John the Baptist's clothing was camel's hair, and his food was wild honey and locusts. God seemed to have taken this prophet more into the rough for the kind of people he would reach.

And the same John had his raiment of camel's hair, and a leather girdle about his loins; and his meat was locust and wild honey. (Matthew 3:4)

Before Jesus would come into power, cast out demons and heal the sick, He would go through the wilderness and be tempted, tried, and tested of the devil, and then come out of the wilderness in the power of the Spirit.

There is a wealth of experience in the wilderness. A prophet will never reach his full potential, prophetically, without investing real time in the wilderness. In order to survive, time spent must be for development and growth and then – like Jesus -- come out of the wilderness in the power of the Spirit.

And when the devil had ended all the temptations, he departed from Him for a season. And Jesus returned in the power of the Spirit into Galilee: and there went out a fame of Him through all the region round about. (Luke 4:13-14)

Key Point: Do not go into the wilderness to stay. The wilderness is where God will teach you. Like Jesus, the prophet must come out of the wilderness in the power of the Spirit.

Every School of the Prophets, in the time of Elijah, was in the wilderness. All of the prophets were trained in secluded places. This is, sometimes, why when the prophets would run into trouble, they were accustomed to going back into a solitary place. That place would be where they were accustomed to hearing from God.

It is important to hear from God. Once a prophet hears from God, he usually acts in obedience and in accordance with what has been said. It is only in adherence to the word of God that you will develop effectively as a prophet.

THE DEVELOPMENT OF THE PROPHET

The scriptures teach that the prophet receives his communication by the Spirit of God. It is essential for the prophet to understand all the aspects of growing in the prophetic. What could be complications for a budding prophet can be handled through the insight and understanding of a senior and/or fathering prophet.

Senior Prophets (II Kings 2:6)

1. All senior prophets are fathering prophets, but not all fathering prophets are senior prophets. In this chapter, we find that there were prophets called "the sons of the prophets," yet they were not their biological sons but spiritual sons. Elijah was a senior prophet, and Elisha called him father. We do understand that Elisha was fathered (prophetically) by Elijah.

Fathering Prophets

2. It is imperative that we understand the responsibility God gives fathering prophets regarding those sent to you to father, care for, and develop.

One of the reasons for the greatness of the prophets was that they were specifically selected by God. They did not come into their roles or office by inheritance, nor were they sons of a former prophet automatically called to prophetic work.

One of the main points we must understand, as prophets, is that God selects or handpicks prophets. Some people receive positions in other areas of ministry based on inheritance such as the priests. But, the calling and choosing of a prophet is specifically based on being picked from among others by God. Therefore, great honor has been bestowed on one called as a prophet of God.

False Prophets

3. A false prophet is one who speaks a vision of his or her own imagination, not from the mouth of God. A false prophet declares something that is not of God, but may seem to be, or sound like, God. One biblical example is found in I Samuel 15:1-9. Saul was given the command to kill all of the Amalekites and to destroy all that they owned. But Saul was disobedient to the voice of the Lord through the prophet Samuel. He killed all except King Agag and kept what he considered the best of the herd and material goods. Whose voice was Saul obeying?

What makes a prophet true or false?

1. False prophets were simply false because God did not call them.

2. False prophets are habitual liars. They prophesy things that God did not say, nor the truth of what He is going to do.

3. False prophets are those who are following their own spirit and have seen nothing that God has spoken by His Spirit (Ezekiel 13:3).

God said to Jeremiah concerning false prophets:

The prophets prophesy lies in my name; I sent them not, neither have I commanded them. (Jeremiah 14:14)

Prophets prophesy by virtue of their office. The office of the prophet carries authority. Therefore, when the prophet speaks, supernatural power is activated.

Key Point: It is important to understand that the office of the prophet carries authority: (1) The authority on your office is activated by the words of your mouth. But prophetic authority only comes after you have been released by the one you are submitted to. If you become loose with your words, God cannot give you the power or authority He wants you to have. (2) The authority of your office is activated by the releasing of your man or woman of God.

Warning: 1) Saying what you want, when you want, will affect God's power in your mouth. 2) Lack of confidentiality will affect what God will say to you.

You must learn that it takes wisdom to speak what you hear and to know when you are to speak it. Using wisdom will increase what God will say to you while you are hearing from Him.

And to the false prophet Hananiah, Jeremiah declared:

The Lord has not sent thee but thou makest this people trust in a lie. (Jeremiah 28:15)

Remember also what God said to Jeremiah at the time that He called him:

Before I formed thee in the belly I knew thee; and before thou camest forth out of the womb I sanctified thee, and I ordained thee prophet unto the nations. (Jeremiah 1:5)

Key Point: You were known by God and patterned by Him before entering the earth.

The prophet Moses was called through a miraculous incident of the burning bush (Exodus 3:4). God caused Moses to operate out of a nature in which He formed him before he ever recognized his calling. While Moses was still in Egypt serving under Pharaoh, he killed a man because the man was trying to kill a Hebrew. Therein, we see Moses operating out of the prophetic nature of deliverance before God ever told him to go to Egypt and deliver His people.

The prophet must understand that he is one who is instructed by God not to operate as others in the nation in which he resides. Moses said to the people, in Deuteronomy 18:9, that upon entering Canaan they should not try to communicate with God by any form of divination, after the pattern of other nations. In other words, it is important that the prophet understand how not to cross over into divination, sorcery, or witchcraft.

God has given us dominion over all the earth, but not over people. The ministerial role of the prophet is not based on any method of control. The word says it is *"in Him we live, and in Him we move, and in Him we have our being"* (Acts 17:28).

Key Point: Learn to hear and listen closely to God.

Prophets are very unique people. Do not try to pattern after anyone but God. You are not unique to the point that you need, or should try, to invent some new thing.

Remember: GOD DOES NOT ALWAYS DO THINGS THE SAME WAY. The ministerial role of the prophet is based solely upon saying what God tells you to say, doing what God is doing, and moving in the manner that God says to move.

An inheritance relationship is not suitable for the prophet. Each prophet has to be a "special" kind of person, specifically selected by God—not just anyone would do. Many people function according to patterns, but the prophet does not function according to patterns.

The prophet is one of the most unpredictable offices among the five ascension gifts. The prophet often charts a new course that might be different from any before. Even when God gives the prophet instructions for his work and the course that he will take, that course often carries with it a great challenge such as with Hosea and Gomer (Hosea 1:2).

The beginning of the word of the Lord by Hosea. *And the Lord said to Hosea, Go, take unto thee a wife of whoredoms and children of whoredoms: for the land hath committed great whoredom, departing from the Lord.* (Hosea 1:2)

In the Scriptures, the prophet might anoint a king into office; later he might bring that king into severe reprimand. He might bring cheer, or he might impart sorrow.

A prophet's assignment might lead to great danger or high honor. The prophet must be prepared for suffering or injustice, as well as ease and plaudits. The prophet has to always be an individualist, encouraged in ingenuity. There is no room for mediocrity.

As God's newly called prophet, Samuel's first mission was to tell the high priest, Eli, that his house had been rejected by the Lord (I Samuel 3:4-18). This could have been a challenging task for Samuel, who was approximately 10 years old at the time. Later, Samuel anointed Israel's first king Saul (I Samuel 9:15-21; 10:1-8). Afterwards, Samuel had to inform Saul that he, too, had been rejected (I Samuel 13:11-14).

Later, Samuel was to anoint Israel's second king, who at the time was the shepherd boy who would become the great King David (I Samuel 16:1-13). Nathan was instructed, in due time, to rebuke David for his sin with Bathsheba (II Samuel 12:1-12).

All of these are periods of challenges. Challenging seasons must come to test the faithfulness of the nabi, seer, watchman, and man of God—all terms for the prophet.

TERMS OF DESIGNATION AND TASK

There are three terms that are specifically important for designating prophets. The most important is the Hebrew word "Nabi". Nabi means to declare or announce. The primary function of the prophet was "to declare or announce," or a prophet was "one who utters a communication". In the form of a noun, it is used nearly three hundred times in the Old Testament. The other two terms are used much less.

The Hebrew words ro'eh, and hozeh both mean "one who sees." They are both translated seer. "Hazon" is the word that is consistently used for the prophetic vision and is found in Samuel, Chronicles, Psalms, Proverbs and in most of the books of the prophets.

Sometimes the prophets are called watchmen (sopin in Hebrew) in Jeremiah 6:17, and Ezekiel 3:17; 33:2, 6-7, and shomer, a watchman, in Isaiah 21:11 and 62:6.

We should also mention a fourth term, although it is used less than any other. It is the phrase "Man of God" or "Ish-elohim." This term is significant and rare. It simply means or refers to the prophet as one who has been chosen and sent by God.

In the Greek, the word prophetes signifies "one who speaks for another," especially "one who speaks for a god" and so interprets His will to man. Hence, its essential meaning is "an interpreter."

The English language "prophecy" is the sense of prediction and in this sense has been retained as its popular meaning. The larger sense or use as interpretation has not been lost.

Therefore, distinction had to be made between the prophets of God and those who practiced demonic acts. The chosen nation, Israel, was warned against consulting and practicing in the mystical arts.

Chapter 6
PROPHETIC ORDER

*O*ne of the places in which I think that we are greatly challenged is the area of prophetic order, actually knowing what to do and when to do it.

This was a challenge for me. God started to use me in the prophetic before I started preaching, and there was no training. For some time I walked as an evangelist because God told me that He wanted me to do the work of an evangelist. But He did not tell me that I was an evangelist. I assumed that I was an evangelist with none of the traits of an evangelist. When you are heading a church, you cannot tolerate any level of disorder because any level of disorder breeds more disorder.

I came from a church with a tremendous level of order. One example that I remember is that of a blind person who stood up to give a prophetic word during the same time that the preached word was going forth. She stood up in the middle of the sermon speaking in the gift of tongues and the gift of the interpreting tongues, giving her prophetic word. She was sat down because she was completely out of order. You cannot tolerate any disorder, not even from a blind person. She stood up in the middle of the preached word, and this is clearly out of order. This happened because there was no training in the prophetic at that time. The best information available was limited. There was very little information available at that time.

God explained to me that I was not an evangelist but a prophet--I have called you to be a prophet to the nations. At that time I was not ordained or even a minister. I did not have a license or anything like that. God went on to say to me that your assignment will be to set order. You will have to rebuke leadership. I started to do that at that time. I was out of order because at that time I did not have my personal life in order. God expected me to ask Him when, because He was not talking about then. I am doing that now. I am rebuking leadership and strengthening them, but God spoke that to me twenty-two years ago, and I was not ready at that time.

The prophet is a divine gift and is used of God as His mouthpiece. Prophets have their ears to God's mouth. The Holy Spirit is speaking to prophets, telling them what to do and when, because prophets and prophetic people are sensitive to seasons and times. The Holy Spirit will tell you what is going to happen in the next season. You never have to worry about whether God will tell you or not, because He is always speaking. You may or may not hear Him, but He is always speaking. Nothing will happen in your house that you will not know, because the Holy Spirit will tell you prior to its happening. Now, if we speak what God is saying and according to His word, the Devil does not know if it is you or God talking because we are mysteriously hidden in God; so as long as you say what God is saying, the Devil does not know whether we are talking or God is talking. But when we deviate from the word of God, then the Devil can see us.

Being mysteriously hidden in God positions us to have knowledge of visions and revelations of the lord. This is found in 2 Corinthians 12:1-4: "*It is not expedient for me doubtless to glory. I will come to visions and revelations of the Lord. I knew a man in Christ above fourteen years ago, (whether in the body, I cannot tell; or whether out of the body, I cannot tell: God knoweth;) such an one caught up to the third heaven. And I knew such a man, (whether in the body, or out of the body, I cannot tell: God knoweth;) How that he was caught up into paradise, and heard unspeakable words, which it is not lawful for a man to utter.*" (KJV)

Now according to this passage, Paul cannot tell if he is in his body or out of his body. This is because he is hidden in God. When you are hidden in God, you come into visions and revelations of the Lord. Sometimes when people see you operate like this, they may ask you if you are like a palm reader, psychic or diviner. Having this knowledge, vision, and revelations of the Lord is nothing like a palm readers or psychics; they are of a different spirit. They cannot know anything until someone in the body of Christ speaks what the Holy Spirit has already given them.

Confidentiality is also a very important part of prophetic order. Gossip is one of things that prophets are challenged with, and gossip is unauthorized information. If you operate in unauthorized information, your anointing is at stake. We are managers of words and we must be good stewards of our words. When you are confidential, God will give you information about people in order to help them. When He knows that you are not going to put their information out in the street, He knows that He can trust you with people's hearts and with people's feelings, and, therefore, He will also give you unspeakable things. He will tell you some unspeakable things about people. God wants to fellowship with you. Married men can identify best with this because women have about 6000 words that they need to get out each day, but men do not want to hear it. But you married men should make yourself listen to all 6000 because your wife needs to get those words out but not to just anyone. She needs her husband to hear. I said that to say that God has some words that He needs to get out and He is looking for someone who will be able to hear Him because He is in heaven and He cannot do anything past your authority because He has given man authority over the earth. He needs you to hear it because you are your brothers' keeper. God takes you to a level where you have understanding that passes knowledge.

THE OLD TESTAMENT ORDER

The prophetic institution was not a temporary position established for superiority of position, provision was made for it in the law. The reason provision was made for it in the law was so that the Israelites might not consult with false prophets such as diviners, observers of times, and enchanters.

Diviners, observers of times, and enchanters were recognized as the pagan counterpart to the prophets of God. Diviners differed from prophets. A "diviner" is a human being used for unwarranted prying into the future by magical arts. The prophet is a divine gift.

The "observer" comes from the Greek word "skopos." From skopos, we get the English word "scope," to look or observe. "Times" is derived from the word "harra" or "horror." From this etymology derived the word "horoscope." The "enchanter" is one who practices exorcism. Incantations or magic ritual procedures enlist the aid of evil spirits or set free the demonized from their torments.

Moses gave them the promise of a prophet. Although this passage is considered as a reference to the Messiah, it does not exclude its reference to a succession of prophets between Moses and Christ, running parallel with the kingdom of Israel. The scriptures do not represent an unbroken series of prophets, each inducted into office by his predecessor, except in the cases of Joshua and Elisha, who were respectively inducted into office by Moses and Elijah. The prophets are described as deriving their prophetical office immediately from God.

In the time of the Old Testament, specifically during the days from Joshua to Eli, the visions of prophecy became less frequent. During the time of the judges the priesthood, which was the original instrument through which Israel was governed and taught in spiritual things, degenerated. Similar to today's religious era, the people became less sensitive and were no longer affected by the plans and order put in place by God.

Within the Levitical priesthood, God called out and raised up Samuel, of the family of Kohath (I Chronicles 6:28), as the instrument for effecting a reform in the priestly order and giving to the prophets a position of importance that they had never before held. Samuel did not create the prophetic order as a new thing. He orchestrated the qualities of both the prophetic and regal order given in the law to the Israelites by Moses (Deuteronomy 13:1, 18:18 and 20-22). Again, here we see the order, or role of the prophet, was not yet developed because there was not yet a demand for them.

New Testament Order

As we move to the New Testament order of the prophetic, we see some things that will help us in the way we move throughout the local assembly. For example, we have seen people that would prophesy in testimonial services. There would be incidents where a person would prophesy in the midst of a sermon, and they would not even be the guests. We, as prophets, MUST remember that God is a gentleman and will not break through to interrupt you or anyone else, not even to get His word through. God is a God of order.

It is always proper order to:

1. wait for the opening, and
2. wait for the leading to get the word through that God has given.

Remember: The delivery of your message will determine the reception to it.

You can have a genuine word from the Lord that could be rejected because of your lack of wisdom in delivering it. Don't assume that just because God said it, your message will be automatically received.

Key Point: Say what God has said and not what He seems to have said.

Someone who wants change rarely rejects accuracy. In the mind of the prophet, any accuracy is not easily rejected because of the pressure that God puts on him when He is giving it.

Understand: The office of the prophet carries the authority to rebuke, correct, root out, pull down, destroy, throw down, build, and to plant.

The Office of the Prophet: The office of the prophet also carries with it the authority to judge prophecy. The situations and circumstances that bring the prophet to judge can and should be done by the one who occupies the office. Those who fall in the other categories could possibly know some of the situations and circumstances that would come under judgment. However, they are not allowed to do anything about it. If they find themselves judging, they could be found fighting God or against the upline.

God has privileged some to know and understand certain things. He could very well be bringing those persons into the office of the prophet. These individuals must first test their level of discipline to prove whether God can trust them.

The Prophetic Ministry: Those with the calling into the prophetic ministry may flow in the gifts that are mentioned in the first part of this chapter, yet they do not move into judging the prophecies of prophets. They may be permitted to judge prophecy, but will not be allowed to judge prophets or the prophecy that comes out of the mouth of the prophet. These are definitely people who could mistake their call to the prophetic ministry for the call to the office of the prophet. The distinction will be found in the assignments that God releases them to do. You must be sure that it was God that released you to do it and not you releasing yourself.

Example: Phillip had four daughters that flowed in prophetic ministry. But it is very interesting that when it was time for the apostle Paul to be given an all-important word from God, God sent Agabus, a proven prophet, to deliver His word (Acts 21: 8-11). This does not speak to gender, but this does speak to quality, qualification, and responsibility.

Prophetic Gifting: These are people who are limited to operating within the prophetic gifting.

But he that prophesieth speaketh unto men to edification, and exhortation, and comfort. (I Corinthians 14:3)

1. Gift of tongues
2. Gift of interpretation of tongues
3. Prophecy

To move from the place of edification, exhortation and comfort is to move outside of prophetic order. Whenever we move from prophetic order, we move from the place where our anointing resides. The anointing is what makes our place easy. Those flowing in prophetic gifting will operate in prophecy well, provided they stay within these three parameters:

1. Edification
2. Exhortation
3. Comfort

It is imperative that the prophets understand this in order for the anointing to increase in their lives. People with the prophetic gifting may also flow in dreams, visions and other areas such as the inspiration gifts and revelation gifts. In many occasions, they are unable to understand what they see if it is a visual prophetic happening. When

it is a visual prophetic happening, they would need the assistance of a senior prophet. When we speak about the visual, we are mainly talking about dreams and visions
because they have much to do with symbolism. This is an area in which God started
dealing with me early on in my prophetic ministry. At that time, I was walking at that
level of prophetic gifting. For example, God dealt with me concerning snakes and what
they would represent.

*Example: When a snake is draped around someone, it would mean that the person was
a deceiver. If the snake was wrapped round the person's neck in a strangling hold, that
would mean that the person is being deceived and stands in need of deliverance.*

Reminder: I must always remind you that this is the way God deals with me!

Basic Prophetic: The prophet that operates in the basic prophetic is one that will flow
as Jahaziel, the son of Zechariah, in II Chronicles 20:14-21. We cannot assume that
Jahaziel was automatically a prophet because his father was one.

*I lifted up mine eyes again, and looked, and behold a man with a measuring line in his
hand.* (Zechariah 2:1)

The person who functions in this manner operates in basic prophetic. Prophetic
experiences may flow today and tomorrow. At other times, it may flow for months.
Whether they flow or not, the person functioning in this manner still needs to be just
as ready as the prophets themselves.

All of the above positions have full authority in their individual areas. Each of them
must follow proper order. Even those in the office of the prophet must prophesy by
two or three (prophets), and the other must judge.

Let the prophets speak two or three, and let the other judge. (I Corinthians 14:29)

The word also says that if the first has received a word, let him hold his peace, being
the first to receive it. This is where one of the misunderstood, misused scriptures
comes in. That scripture says:

And the spirits of the prophets are subject to the prophets. (I Corinthians 14:32)

This scripture means exactly what it says: The spirit of the prophets comes under
subjection to the other prophets. In other words, "I am not so important that I have to
be the first to say what God said." The important thing is that it gets said. Order can
only be possible when there is submission of one to the other. When we have a church
that God has authorized, peace resides. In any church where peace is absent, there is

no doubt that order is also absent. Teaching must be instituted in order for prophetic order to be established. In the Bible, you will discover that schools were established for the prophets in various regions.

THE SCHOOLS OF THE PROPHETS

Samuel took measures to ensure his work of restoration was permanent, as well as effective, for that time. In order to perfect the role of the prophet, he instituted companies or colleges of prophets. There were gathered promising students who were trained for the office that they would be destined to fulfill. These institutions were very successful from the time of Samuel until the closing of the canon of the Old Testament. Their chief study was the law and its interpretation. Oral, as distinct from symbolical, teaching was tactfully transferred from the priestly to the prophetical order. Subsidiary subjects of instruction were music and sacred poetry, both of which had been connected with prophecy from the time of Moses (Exodus 15:20), (Judges 5:4,5).

HISTORY OF THE SCHOOLS

These schools of the prophets were established in the following locations:

A. Ramah – or (Ramatha'im-zophim – the double height, Watchtowers). This was the birthplace of the prophet Samuel, his official residence and place of his burial. It is said among the ancient cities in Mount Ephraim that Samuel established a training facility for prophets. It bears tremendous history of a place of sanctuary and protection for great leaders and prophets of that time.

B. Bethel – (Beth'el – the house of God). Bethel was about ten miles north of Jerusalem and was originally called Luz (Genesis 28:19). It was one of the areas where Abraham encamped and received his name. It was in proximity to the place where Jacob had his dream. Bethel was assigned to the Benjamites, but they either were unable to possess it or were too careless about doing so. It was taken, later, by the children of Joseph (Judges 1:22-26). It is believed to have been one of the places where the ark was brought (Judges 20:26-28). Bethel was one of the three places selected by Samuel to hold court (I Samuel 7:16). Jeroboam chose Bethel as one of the two places where he set up the worship of golden calves or idols (I Kings 12:28-33). It was at Bethel where Josiah removed all traces of this idolatry and restored the true worship of God (II Kings 23:15-20). People returning from Babylonian captivity occupied Bethel.

Bethel was also a mountain fortress city located in the mountain range of Palestine. As a fortress city, Bethel was surrounded by an 11-foot thick stone wall. It was structured by what could be considered the best-laid masonry of the time.

C. Gilgal (gil'gal – rolling) was a place in the Jordan Valley not far from Jericho. This is where the Israelites first encamped after they crossed the Jordan and where the twelve stones were set up as a memorial. Samuel judged in Gilgal (I Samuel 7:16). Agag was slain in Gilgal (I Samuel 15:33). The prophets Elijah and Elisha frequented Gilgal, which was approximately four miles from Bethel and Shiloh. (II Kings 2:1, 4:38).

D. Jabbok (yab boke--pouring forth) Jabbok is believed to come from the word baqaq (baw kak'), which means to pour out, or to empty, or depopulate, or to spread out as fruitful vines, to make empty. Jabbok is a stream east of the Jordan that empties into that river between the Dead Sea and the Sea of Galilee. It was once the border of the Ammonites (Numbers 21:24; Deuteronomy 2:37; 3:16). It later became the boundary between Sihon and Og. Its earliest recognition precedes the struggle of Jacob and Jehovah and the interview between Jacob and Esau. Both events took place on Jabbok's southern banks.

E. Jericho ("yer ee kho"). Jericho is derived from the root word "ruwach"-- to blow; to breathe; to smell; accept; perceive; anticipate; make of quick understanding. Jericho ("jer' i ko'") "place of fragrances" or "moon city" is an ancient city in the wide plain where the Jordan valley broadens between the Moab Mountains and the western precipices. It is situated on the route of Israel after they crossed the Jordan under Joshua (Joshua 3:16). The first mention of Jericho in scripture is in connection with the advance of Israel to Canaan (Numbers 22:1). It seemed to have been a very important city of the Jordan Valley. The spies, sent by Joshua, were entertained in Jericho by Rahab. The promise of her protection was ensured when the city would be destroyed (Joshua 2:1-21). The miraculous capture of Jericho, the sin and punishment of Achan, and the curse pronounced upon everyone that should attempt to rebuild it again are recorded in Joshua 6:1-7:26. Jericho was given to the tribe of Benjamin (Joshua 18:21). There was a long interval of silence before Jericho is mentioned again. It is, incidentally, mentioned in the life of David in connection with his embassy to the Ammonite king (II Samuel 10:5).

Jericho was rebuilt and was identified with the sons of the prophets. Prophetic students sought retirement and recluse from the world.

(II Kings 2:2). Elisha "healed the spring of waters" and, beyond the Jordan, Elijah "went up by a whirlwind into heaven" (II Kings 2:1-22). The men of Jericho assisted Nehemiah in rebuilding that part of Jerusalem that was next to the sheep gate. The New Testament Jericho is mentioned in connection with Jesus restoring the sight to the blind in Matthew 20:29,30 and his being entertained by Zaccheus. Jericho was mentioned in the parable of the Good Samaritan (Luke 10:30).

F. Jordan ("yardane" from a descender, to descend, to go downward). Yardane is derived from the root word "yaw-rad."

As shown in this chapter, there were several regions that had established schools for the prophets. As students in the school of the prophets, just measurements must be taken within ourselves to see if we qualify for the prophetic.

Chapter 7

WALKING WORTHY OF YOUR PROPHETIC VOCATION

$\mathcal{N}$ot everyone qualifies for the prophetic office, prophetic ministry, prophetic gifting or basic prophetic. There has to become "a making" before one is actually qualified to be used in these areas of ministry. Those who are senior prophets must understand the importance of the qualifying for this office or area of the prophetic. In studying biblical prophets, we come to understand that there was a period of "making" before "using."

THE BEGINNING STAGES

The "making" is necessary in order to ensure accuracy. Let's look at the beginning stages of some of the Old Testament prophets. The prophet Isaiah:

In the year that King Uzziah died, I saw also the Lord sitting upon a throne, high and lifted up, and his train filled the temple. (Isaiah 6:1)

The fact that Isaiah said, "In the year that King Uzziah died, I saw the Lord" puts a question in my heart. The question I have is, "What relationship did Isaiah have to King Uzziah, causing him not to see the Lord before?" Isaiah kept close watch on King Uzziah. Isaiah watched him closely enough that it was only after King Uzziah died that he was able to see the Lord. Many times we will find that we will have to separate from the people and things that have so captivated our attention. This is the sure way that the Lord can speak to us accurately and we hear him without interference (2 Chronicles 26:22).

In the sixth chapter of this book, Isaiah was able to say, "When King Uzziah died, I saw also the Lord high and lifted up." So let's conclude with Isaiah, that one of the qualifi-

123

cations to ensure accuracy is to deal with your distractions.

Fine-Tuning the Prophet

When the call of the prophet is on your life, there will be little sparks of prophetic happenings—just enough prophetic sparks to make you interested. In this season come challenges to prove whether you are hearing the voice of God or other voices.

One voice calls you closer to leadership, and one voice calls you away from leadership. Still another calls you toward opportunity. Now, the big question is "Which is correct?"

Did God Call You?

The calling may be one of opportunity, but because of immaturity at this point in the prophetic, it is not yet time to go forth. The voice that is calling you away from present leadership may cause you to leave incorrectly by not being properly released into the prophetic.

When this happens, you are unsure of the voice you hear. "Which voice is correct?" At the same time, you are unsure of what to do.

You are being developed! Where do you go when you are hearing all of these voices and have no direction? This is where a senior prophet or sometimes a prophetic pastor comes into play. They may have gone through prophetic seasons and have an understanding of the prophetic. The word says that God places us under governors and tutors until we have been matured (Galatians. 4:1-3).

Many times we refuse to be governed or tutored because we believe we hear God well enough. Yet, there is a new level of hearing in accuracy that God desires to bring us to.

Key Point: I have noticed that many people who have a call in the area of the prophetic have a tough time receiving correction.

There is a need to be able to receive the correction to a word given, or given in your spirit. The senior prophet will judge your prophecy. You must be able to receive it without thinking that someone is coming up against your ability to hear God. Proper interpretation to a word given by God, or to a vessel receiving it, is often missed by the recipient.

Key Point: This is the testing period that will prove how well you have matured in the area of being submissive and receptive to the man or woman of God who is over you.

The proving season is a very important period in the life and ministry of the prophet. Some may think that surely it should not take that long. God gave me a word. He called me to the office of the prophet. It took me ten years to get there. There had to be some additional things burned out of my life so that my hearing would not be affected or infected. This process was necessary for my family, the body of Christ and for me. My hearing had to be correct.

CAN YOU HANDLE BEING DISLIKED?

This is a very popular test of prophetic people. Everyone wants to be liked. Yet, you will find prophetic people who will go overboard to try to get someone to like and appreciate them. Anyone who will stand in the prophetic role must come to know that they will be one of the most disliked people among the unsaved and Christian world.

CAN YOU TAKE LONELINESS?

Seeing that you will be one of the most disliked people, loneliness is almost inevitable. If you cannot take loneliness, which is one of the tests, you certainly are not ready to be a prophet, nor a prophetic person. The prophet is one who often stands alone. Once you have gone through what I call the "prophetic process," you will have many periods in your life when you actually want to be alone. Being alone in many cases is the only way that you can hear God accurately.

I trained myself to hear God under any circumstance by studying in crowds. Take the challenge to hear God while there is noise around you. Your Word level gets tested in this season of your life. You can never be fine-tuned without the Word of God and a prophetically trained individual in your life.

Many people may prophesy, but that is not an indication that they are prophets or prophetically trained.

THE TEST OF BEING OFFENDED

Offense hinders your ability to hear accurately. Jesus said that offense must come. Offenses will hinder your ability to hear. Until we can get past offense, we are not ready to occupy the office of the prophet. The real test of whether we have been freed from offense is the public rebuke from leadership rightfully or wrongfully. The test is whether we can take that rebuke and still serve well -- not be offended.

Handling Intimidation

One of the greatest tests in my life that I had to deal with, in its season, was the test of handling intimidation and not slipping off into a spirit called "jealousy" or "competition." When God started the process of molding me as a prophet, I fought with the spirit of intimidation. If you will be the prophet that God has called you to be, you have to be able to handle intimidation without welcoming any of its companion spirits, lest you be hindered from entering your season in the prophetic. There will be periods when you will feel intimidated and feel the need to compete with someone who seems to intimidate you. It could be the one you are submitted to. It could be someone you admire. Regardless of who intimidates you, you must understand that if you can be intimidated then you are not ready to be released as a prophet. The prophetic is not an area of competition.

When someone intimidates you, it means that the influence that comes from, or seemingly comes from, someone prevents you from walking in the door of who God says that you are. Oftentimes there will be spirits of intimidation that will rise up when you begin to prophesy. If you can be intimidated, that very spirit of intimidation will show up at the time that God wants to use you prophetically.

So before you can be used of God in the area of the prophetic, allow every ounce of insecurity to burn out because that is where intimidation stems from. Intimidation about or regarding an individual is never because of someone else. It is because of your uncertainty and insecurity.

Can You Take Rejection?

Can you take rejection from your leader or those close to you without feeling physically, mentally, emotionally or spiritually crushed? If you cannot take being rejected, then you are not ready for prophetic ministry. Can you really give a prophetic word and not be or feel rejected if it is not being received? Many times the budding prophet gives a word that he believes he heard from the Lord, and it is not received. How will the budding prophet (you) handle the rejection of God's word? God wants to see that you can handle rejection and not run, faint or fizz out.

Remember: Moses' word was rejected several times, yet God kept sending him back to the same person. (Exodus 5,6,7)

Jonah was tired of preaching to people who would keep falling back into the same sin. He knew God would continue forgiving them (Jonah 1:1-3). Jonah is frequently referred to as a prophet who ran away from God. The analogy of the prodigal son leaving home is referred to in the same respect. Yet, it was not the fact that Jonah ran, but it was the reason for his running that is important. He ran from God because he did not want to see another time that he would preach and prophesy to a people who would repent and change the mind of God. Jonah knew that God was going to forgive Nineveh although he prophesied judgment.

Warning: Maturity in the prophetic will not desire to see chaos, havoc or damnation to come upon people for any reason. It does not matter what they have done to us or anyone else.

As a prophet, you do not want to run from God, but commune with Him as friend-to-friend. Your actions will assist you in examining yourself to determine the type of prophet you are becoming.

What Type of a Prophet Am I?

The Office of the Prophet vs. the Gift

How do I know if I have the office or the gift?

As we come to understand whether we are called or whether it is a gift, we also want to determine if it is a ministry or an office. Below you will find a list of the characteristics that I use to locate the gifts and the calling of God that reside in the house where I am the set man. Out of this, I believe that you will find it helpful to distinguish between the various levels of the prophetic.

Key Point: It is very important to be sure that everyone functions in the area to which they have been called, ordained or gifted.

To allow someone to function outside of where he or she has been called, ordained or gifted will cause utter frustration.

Example: If one has been called to the office of the prophet and is only allowed to use his gifts when he has been released to the office, he will be totally frustrated. If one is only gifted and attempts to stand in the office, he will burn out quickly. The gift works as the Holy Spirit wills. One that stands in the office has his office always. He wears his anointing like a coat.

Prophetic Calling

1. Basic Prophetic: This is when any believer, through the gifts of the Spirit, speaks to someone or a group for the purpose of edification, exhortation and comfort (I Cor-

inthians 14:4). This does not include correction or new direction. It may include a predictive word of prophecy.

2. Prophetic Gifting: These are the people who have impressions, dreams, visions, or other types of revelations. They lack the understanding of what they saw or what was prophetically impressed upon them. This group receives more, prophetically, than the first group, but they are neither in the office of the prophet nor in prophetic ministry.

3. Prophetic Ministry: Believers whose gifting has been recognized, nurtured and commissioned in regular ministry and the local church are in prophetic ministry. There is still much symbolism that represents other things that God is saying. Through prophetic teamwork, it is possible to discern much of the interpretation and application of the prophetic revelation.

4. Prophetic Office: This one represents the group that is actually called to the office of the prophet. This is somewhat like the prophetic office of the Old Testament. They often minister in signs and wonders and are known to speak 100 percent accurate words of prophecy. This certainly does not mean that they do not miss. It means that what they speak happens most of the time. Their credibility has been established by a proven track record of accurate prophecies. Do the previous attacks stop? After coming into the office, those previous attacks continue. The prophet must master functioning accurately in the midst of being attacked.

Eventually you become immune to the people talking, not believing you and being rejected.

SERVING UNTIL YOUR DREAMS DIE

This is a part of the process. Matthew 10:39 says, "*He that findeth his life shall lose it: and he that loseth his life for my sake shall find it.*" Whatever I try to save will be lost. The word says: "*...except God builds the house they that build it labor in vain*" (Psalms 127:1). Joseph had to let his dream die in order for God to breathe life into it. Elisha had to go through the death process before his dream of receiving a double portion could live.

Whenever God gives you a vision of what He wants you to have, He always starts you out with seed. The seed must always go through a process before it goes through the development of the vision.

You begin with a seed only. When we neglect to be a seed, we neglect to have the harvest or the dream. There is always a waiting period to your calling.

Example: God spoke to me ten years before I was released as a prophet.

Key Point: There must be the sanctioning of your call by the one you are tied to.

THE ATTITUDE OF THE PROPHET

You must maintain an attitude of love, appreciation and worship.

Remember: You become the voice of God. Therefore, what you say MUST, WILL, and SHALL come to pass.

1. Love: Love is an essential ingredient in the prophetic. If your anger flares up and love is absent, you can speak someone's destruction.

Understand: God (Creator and Destroyer) sat down in order that Jesus (Redeemer and Salvation) might stand up. What did Jesus say to the disciples when they wanted to call down fire from heaven (Luke 9:54)? Jesus did not tell them that they were unable to accomplish that task, but He warned them of their spirit of operation, thus displaying and forbidding them in their decision. He gave them vision for the people, letting them know that He came to save, not to destroy.

But He turned, and rebuked them, and said, ye know not what manner of spirit ye are of. (Luke 9:55)

2. Appreciate: Raise the value of the recipient of the prophecy.

We must know the value of a thing, or a person, regardless of what it looks like. God carried Ezekiel through this test. God asked Ezekiel, "Can these bones live?" Ezekiel looked at the condition and became speechless. Then God said: ". . .these bones are the whole house of Israel." That is when it became Ezekiel's responsibility to raise the value of them and to speak the word.

Again he said unto me, prophesy upon these bones and say unto them, O ye dry bones hear the word of the Lord. (Ezekiel 37:4)

Next God told Ezekiel to prophesy unto the winds.

Then said He unto me, Prophesy unto the wind, prophesy, son of man and say to the wind, thus saith the Lord God; Come from the four winds, O breath, and breathe upon these slain, that they may live. (Ezekiel 37:9)

They would have never become what they were purposed to be until the prophet Ezekiel raised their value by speaking into them.

3. Worship: The prophet is one of those who become a drink offering that is poured out on the altar of service. God says through the apostle and prophet Paul—

Yea, and if I be offered upon the sacrifice and service of your faith, I joy, and rejoice with you all. (Philippians 2:17)

It is verbal worship that is often the vehicle that really keeps you sane. When the prophet loses his place of worship, he or she may become vulnerable to fall back into sin, depression, bitterness or unbelief.

Example: Elijah running from Jezebel (I Kings 19:1-4); Jonah under the tree (Jonah 4:6); David hung up his harp after saying, "I will bless the Lord at all times. His praise shall continually be in my mouth. (Psalms 137:1-4)"; When it seemed like God deceived him, Jeremiah said, "I will no more speak in Your Name" (Jeremiah 20:7-9).

What do prophets do when situations and circumstances happen to cause them to lose their place of worship?

The prophet is to stand with that last word of direction heard from God. There may not be another word until after the test.

Example: Sometimes when I think back on my prophetic maturity, all I had was the last word of direction from God. Through sickness, pain, and utter discouragement, all I had was a word. As a prophet stepping into the office, that was enough.

Chapter 8
MESSAGE OF A PROPHET

In many cases, prophetic people receive a word that is for an individual and may not be for the entire church. Therefore, it is important to understand whom the word is for. If the word is for an individual and you have been released as a prophet in that local assembly by the leadership of that house, then it would be appropriate to go and speak to that individual. In cases where the Lord gives you a word for an individual and you are not released by the leadership of that house, you should and must always give respect to that house and its leadership prior to speaking to an individual or the body.

Warning: Protect your anointing by avoiding giving anyone a private prophecy. It was a private prophecy, or word, that deceived Eve, but Adam became infected by the private word given because he did not take authority over the serpent.

IDENTIFYING THE RECIPIENT OF THE WORD

It is very important to be able to identify the individuals to whom God may give you a word. This takes great discipline because you may receive a word, and it may not be time to give that word to that individual.

Example: There are times when God may give me a word for someone at the beginning of a service; yet He does not allow me to release that word until the end of the service.

It takes discipline to hold a prophetic word through the entire service before releasing it. How does one identify the individual that God actually desires to minister to? At the point of your getting up in the morning, expect that there will be a vision or a word to you about who will be in the service that night. Never allow yourself to attempt to become familiar with an environment before you have arrived in the place where you are the guest. You should already have lain before the Lord regarding that place so that when you arrive; it is as though you have already been there. At that particular point in time, faces, images, and the surroundings will or should already be familiar to your spirit. This is because you have already lain before the Lord. Once you step into the building, people will stand out to you regardless of the size of the facility. The most important thing to remember is your main purpose for going there is to bring forth a word for the house. Along with bringing forth that word, there will be the added benefit of bringing forth a word to an individual.

Remember: Prophets are ministers to the body of Christ and not just individuals. There- fore, your purpose is to the whole body and not simply to an individual. Whenever the prophets try to minister on an individual level only, they limit themselves in many areas and cease from reaching their original purpose.

t is important that prophetic people understand that they are not above the rules of local assemblies, even if it is the location where they are members. Prophetic people HAVE NO AUTHORITY OR RELEASE to override the authority of the house.

Overriding authority is one of the ways to stop the flow of the prophetic in your life.

Understand: Sometimes when receiving a word, that word may be for the prophet only and not for others at that time.

LEARNING HOW TO FLOW PROPHETICALLY

It is important to understand prophetic order in the local church in order to govern the body accordingly. The word says that everything should be done decently and in order. The closer to order in the local church, the stronger that prophetic anointing will grow. Therefore, one must understand the methods of prophetic revelation.

METHODS OF PROPHETIC REVELATION

The word of God says that He is the same yesterday, today and forever. Throughout church history, we find that God never ceased to relate to His people. The Lord is re- storing the power of the Holy Spirit within the church in these last days. As the Lord is pouring forth His Spirit, He is bringing a great challenge to the body to not only pray and sing in the Spirit, but to walk and live in the Spirit. Within this tremendous out- pouring, the gifts of the Holy Spirit are becoming more profound within individuals. These experiences are identified as dreams, visions, and written and spoken prophecy.

As we enter this new millennium, the move of the Holy Spirit is bringing prophetic ministries, in various forms, to be increasingly common, in our time. It has become expedient that we, the church, accomplish our purpose in these times.

The ascension gifts are not only scriptural; they were operative throughout Old Testament history in Jesus' life and in the life of the early church.

Prophecies, in both the Old and New Testaments, were words inspired by the Spirit of God and spoken through the utterance of a man or woman for the edification, exhortation, and comfort of the body of Christ. There are two basic uses for the prophetic. The first is for revealing the present and future strategic will of God in certain matters. The second is given for the illumination of doctrine that is taught in scripture but is not clearly seen or clearly understood by the church. These prophetic experiences may be identified in several ways.

1. Prophetic Impressions

There are many levels of prophetic revelation. The beginning levels include prophetic impressions, which are genuine revelations. They can be extraordinarily specific and accurate when interpreted by those who are experienced and sensitive to them. However, we must be careful at this level because our own feelings, prejudices, and doctrines can affect our revelations.

Visions can come at the impression level as well. They are gentle and must be seen with the eyes of the heart. They, too, can be very specific and accurate, especially when interpreted by those who are experienced and sensitive to them.

2. Conscious Sense of the Presence of the Lord

There is a level of prophetic revelation that comes as a conscious sense of the presence of the Lord or the anointing of the Holy Spirit. This is when the Holy Spirit gives special illumination to our minds and will often come when one is writing or speaking. This conscious sense of the presence of the Lord will give greater confidence to the importance or accuracy of what is being spoken. Even at this level, the prophets must still be careful about being influenced by their own prejudices, doctrines, emotions, and so forth.

3. Open Visions

Open visions occur on a higher level than impressions. They give more clarity than when we feel the conscious sense of the presence of the Lord or the anointing. Open visions are external and are viewed with the clarity of a movie screen. We are not able to control them, and there is less change of mixture in revelation that comes through an open vision.

4. Trances

Trances are high levels of prophetic experiences and were common to the biblical prophets. Trances are dreaming when you are awake. Instead of just seeing in the manner of open visions, a trance is as though you are actually there in the experience. Trances are experiences on different levels. They can be mild. This type of mild stupor allows you to be conscious of your physical surroundings and interact within them.

The next level is where you experience actually being present in the vision. Biblical examples are recorded in the life of Ezekiel and in the life of the apostle John as his visions are recorded in the book of Revelation.

Example: Peter experienced this when the angel led him out of prison. No one ever touched the gates; they opened on their own accord. (Acts12:1-10)

Chapter 9
THE PROPHET AND DELIVERANCE

*W*ithin the general makeup of the prophet is the gift of discernment. This is, or should be, a gift that flows out of the prophetic person. The gift of discerning spirits, along with the other eight gifts of the Spirit, should be manifested in the life of the prophet, the prophetic minister, and occasionally those who function in prophetic gifting. It is the gift of discerning of spirits that will enable the prophet to see, supernaturally, the plans, purpose, and working of the enemy and its force. Also, the gift of discerning of spirits will give the prophet the ability to see in the realm of the spirit in order to clearly understand the maneuvering and the functioning of the spirit that is in operation and that is given physical manifestation at that time.

We need to look beyond what we see in order to recognize the plan, purpose and working of the enemy. We do this with the gift of discerning of spirits. The enemy has a plan to talk you out of obeying God and start doubting God. The enemy wants to stop the flow of what God is doing. The gift of discerning of spirits is not discerning what people are doing but discerning the operation of spirits. God will reveal particular spirits and not just tell people's business. Sometimes people are afraid of coming in the presence of a prophet because they have the misunderstanding that God is going to tell the prophet all of their business and he or she is going to tell everybody, especially if they know that they have some things in their lives that they need to change. God is not a gossiper and what he reveals He intends to heal. The prophets and some prophetic people are able to discern particular spirits, seeing in the spirit, and are able to know the plan, purpose and working of the enemy. And they can attack these plans, purposes and workings of the enemy and not people.

"To another the working of miracles; to another prophecy, to another discerning of spirits, to another divers kinds of tongues and to another the interpretation of tongues." (I Corinthians 12:10)

In Mark 9: 4-29 is the account of the physical manifestation of a deaf and dumb spirit that had possessed the young boy who was brought to the Lord Jesus by his father for deliverance. Let us take a look at some possible manifestations of a deaf and dumb spirit and how it would manifest itself at particular levels of oppression and possession. This example in Mark 9 is possession. But this spirit may not always be in the form of possession. It may come in the form of oppression. Possession is the total control by a demonic force over an individual's soul (mind, will, emotion and intellect). Oppression is a force that would come against or attack the mind and/or the flesh. Oppression works from the outside. It is more emotional than spiritual.

It is the role and responsibility of the prophet to recognize and/or identify the various levels of spiritual and demonic influence within the congregation.

It is important not to call what may be a work of the flesh demonic or what may be demonic a work of the flesh. We must identify what the works of the flesh are and must not attempt to cast out what is not demonic.

The person operating in the works of the flesh (Galatians 5:17-21) is not necessarily demonic. The individual must take authority and control over their own flesh, bringing it into subjection to their recreated or born-again spirit. This begins the developing of babes in Christ versus someone who continually walks in the flesh. The prophet would have to discern this area because of his authority to correct and/or chastise the body.

Those that are babes will find themselves wrestling with their flesh. Once again, this does not mean that it is a demonic influence.

RECOGNIZING DEMONIC INFLUENCE

We must be able to recognize the various stages of demonic influence. There are six stages:

1. Regression – Regression is to withdraw or to back away from. We should be able to discern this stage within the midst of our congregation. People who begin to become isolated from the body are in the stage of regression.

One of the ways to identify people who are headed out of the back door of the church is by their acts of regression toward the back of the church. This demonic activity causes them to be incapable of communicating. You have to go after them. You will notice that they will begin to change their seat from wherever they normally sit to a little farther back each time they come to church. The next time they come, they stop talking to people and will not say anything to anyone. They are literally backing their way out of the back door. This is the time when you go after them because you recognize the signs and they are not able to communicate with you. These are the beginning stages of demonic influence of regression.

WHEN IS THIS REGRESSION AND WHEN IS THIS PROPHETIC PREPARATION?

Regression does not allow you to interact with others. However, regressing prophetically will not prevent your interaction but will cause conflict in forcing interaction because of your season.

Regression also has a prophetic side. Regression is a prophetic act when you sense in your spirit that God is doing something with you prophetically that you cannot have interference with. At this time you begin to regress, and you really need to do that. You need to get away from people who will interfere with your process of receiving from God at this time. This does not mean that you are angry with anyone; you can talk to people and communicate with people. There are no demonic forces involved because you are not hindered from communicating; you are choosing to separate yourself so that you can receive from God.

2. Suppression – Suppression is manifested from lack of joy. A person begins to hide his or her feelings and is unable to express joy.

To suppress is to keep from being revealed, or to inhibit the expression of something. The prophet must be mindful of what he talks about or confesses. Men do this from time to time (suppressing things), especially married men. This is a dangerous thing to do because this act of suppression leads you to the next stage of depression. This demonic influence is leading you to a place of losing control and that is not what God wants to happen to us. Most of the healthy people just go off every time something happens; they do not suppress anything.

Prophetically, we use suppression to control the flow of information. This is prophetic preparation. Suppression is different. Suppression is denying what they feel.

3. Depression – Depression is a broken spirit. People are not able to overcome the things in their lives. God has been speaking to you through all of these previous stages. Now, He is saying, Come out of this. At this stage, you have started to follow the demon out of the presence of God, and God wants you to come out now because this leads you to the next phase of oppression. You cannot carry some things because you are not designed to do that. God wants to carry that care for you. The only thing that you are designed to carry is the word of God and the glory of God.

If depression is not arrested, caught or put in check at this point, depression will lead to oppression, which opens the door to possession. Depression is a period of drastic decline. There is that time when the prophet goes into a desert place, but never a drastic decline.

4. Oppression – Oppression describes one who is weighed down with the cares of this world. Oppressed people lack victory. At this stage, people cannot remember any of their victories in their lives. This shuts down the voice of God.

Oppression is to keep down by unjust use of authority, or to weigh heavily on the mind or spirit (I Corinthians 7:37; 2 Corinthians 9:7 NIV or NASB). The prophetic side of oppression is called discipline. Your flesh is being oppressed. Discipline is training expected to produce a specific character or pattern. School is the place of discipline and challenge.

5. Obsession – Obsession describes one who lacks reality. Obsessed individuals become focused on one particular sin in their life. At this stage, they are not functioning the way that God created them.

Obsession is defined as a compulsive, often unreasonable idea or emotion, or an irresistible impulse to act on an unreasonable idea, problem or thing. This quality should be on the prophet in a positive sense. It should happen in a time of preparation.

6. Possession – A person experiencing possession is someone who comes under total control of a demonic force.

In our prophetic preparatory period, we should come under the control of the Holy Spirit, which involves being totally submitted to Him (I Corinthians 16:14-16). They have addicted themselves to the ministry of the saints.

THE SPIRIT OF PERVERSION

Homosexuals are bound with the spirit of perversion. The word perversion means to deviate from the original form. There are men who are bound by that spirit that have never entered into a homosexual relationship. Likewise, people who are bound with that spirit make a choice to leave the natural use.

The first five of these stages are mental and emotional harassment by the enemy. The sixth is spiritual, a total yielding of the person's soul to a demonic force. All of these stages, through the gift of discerning of spirits, can be discerned, and the person can be delivered.

THE PROPHET'S ROLE IN DISCERNMENT

Through the prophet's spiritual insight, his or her ability to discern spiritual influence is great. Within the prophet's role and responsibilities in ministry, there will be times during impartation that it is necessary for him to be cognizant of various levels of demonic influence, oppression and/or possession. The prophet may, from time to time, discern, cast out and/or deliver an individual from whatever level of demonic influence present.

PARTICULAR SPIRITS AND HOW THEY MANIFEST

Mark 1:21-28 A Religious Spirit – The manifestation of this unclean spirit seemed to have a revelation of who Jesus was and a religious knowledge that would allow him to fit in with most religious people. The remedy: Jesus prophetically discerned the spirit and its function and commanded it to hold its peace and come out of the man.

Mark 5:1-19 A Spirit of Insanity – The manifestation of this unclean spirit was able to tap into a portion of this man's mind and cause him to have incredible strength. This is a man who manifested multiple personalities through the influence of a demonic spirit that brought much damage to his body. But, at a spare break from demonic activity, he, in the presence of Jesus, fell down and worshipped Him. This was a clear indication that showed an act on the man's part that he wanted to be delivered.

The scriptures can help us identify the difference between a demonic spirit and a sickness. When Jesus was in the presence of sickness, there was not a spiritual or physical reaction. But when He was in the presence of demonic influence, there was a manifestation or a reaction within the person. Both physical and spiritual are present. The demonic spirit responds with a physical manifestation.

The gift of discerning spirits is one of the many gifts within the body of Christ. *"Now ye are the body of Christ and members in particular."* Are you sure that you can recognize "the realms of prophecy"? (1 Corinthians 12:27)

Chapter 10
THE REALMS OF PROPHECY

$\mathcal{T}$here are four basic realms of prophecy. We are going to address each one:

1. Prophecy of Scripture

All biblical revelation prophesied through the Old and New Testament prophets is the prophecy of scripture. The prophecy of scripture speaks of the declaration and revelatory elements of the word of God as the highest revelation of God to mankind. All prophecy should be judged by the prophecy of scripture, which is the word. It should not contain any errors, mistakes or imperfection.

Knowing this first, that no prophecy of the scriptures is of any private interpretation. For the prophecy came not in old time by the will of man: but holy men of God spake as they were moved by the Holy Ghost. (II Peter 1:20-21)

The dictionary defines inspiration as "the supernatural influence of the Spirit of God on the human mind, by which the apostles and prophets and sacred writers were qualified to set forth divine truth without any mixture of error." The written word of God must be held as the highest and purest form of communication from God. The prophecy of scripture is the only kind of prophecy that can claim this level of inspiration.

2. The Spirit of Prophecy

The anointing of the Holy Spirit enables the Spirit of prophecy to operate in people who neither have the gift, the ministry, the office nor function in Basic Prophetic. The Spirit of prophecy enables one to speak under the inspiration of God and is often released during the powerful presence of God in church services. We can identify the Spirit of prophecy when there is a strong presence of the anointing in a service.

And I fell at his feet to worship Him. And he said unto me, See thou do it not: I am thy fellow servant, of thy brethren that have the testimony of Jesus: worship God: for the testimony of Jesus is the Spirit of Prophecy. (Revelation 19:10)

3. Gift of Prophecy

The Holy Spirit gives the gift of prophecy to certain believers to bring the word of the Lord to the congregation. The Holy Spirit brings the revelation of the Lord to teach, encourage, and comfort the body of Christ -- to exalt and crown the worship of Christ. Not all Christians have the gift of prophecy. The same goes for pastors and preachers. The gift of prophecy is not the same as the ministry of preaching. Each gifting has a different meaning and is for different purposes.

Now there are diversities of gifts, but the same Spirit. I Corinthians 12:4

To another the working of miracles; to another prophecy ... I Corinthians 12:10

4. The Office of the Prophet

The prophetic realm of foretelling and confirmation of ministries in the presbytery with the laying on of hands should only be done by those who have the mantle of the office of the prophet.

Prophets are vessels whom Christ chooses to function constantly and accurately in the realm of the word of knowledge, the word of wisdom, discernment of spirits, confirmation, revelation, illumination, prophetic utterance, prediction, visions, correction, and ministry confirmation.

In the New Testament Church at Antioch, men such as Agabus were considered to be prophets of God. Agabus moved in the realm of predictions. Other New Testament prophets moved in the realm of presbytery confirmation of ministry.

For one who holds the office of the prophet, his or her utterance must be according to the word of God. His or her revelation cannot be accepted if it were to contradict the words of Jesus Christ or the apostles.

If any man think himself to be a prophet, or spiritual, let him acknowledge that the thing that I write unto you are the commandments of the Lord. (I Corinthians 14:37)

Because the prophet is human and liable to error, his prophecy may contain an error. The Lord admonishes us to judge and evaluate his word by the scriptures and the witness of the Spirit in the hearts of the believers. At the same time, the Spirit quickens the word, or the hearts of other believers, to confirm the truth of the prophet's word. The deliverance of the prophet's word falls into three categories that consist of a total of nine gifts.

THE GIFTS OF THE SPIRIT

The gifts frequent the office or ministry of the prophet. The nine gifts of the spirit come in three categories:

<u>Revelation Gifts</u>: Word of Wisdom, word of Knowledge, Discerning of spirits

<u>Power Gifts</u>: Gift of Faith, Gifts of Healing, Working of Miracles

<u>Inspiration Gifts</u>: Gift of Tongues, Gift of interpretation of tongues -Gift of prophecy

All of these gifts work as the Holy Spirit wills.

REVELATION GIFTS

But the manifestation of the Spirit is given to every man to profit withal. For to one is given by the spirit the word of wisdom; to another the word of knowledge by the same Spirit; to another faith by the same spirit; to another the gifts of healing by the same spirit; to another the working of miracles; to another prophecy; to another discerning of spirits; to another diverse kinds of tongues; to another the interpretation of tongues; but all these worketh that one and the self same spirit, dividing to every man severally as he will. (I Corinthians 12:7-11)

<u>The Word of Wisdom</u>

The word of wisdom occurs when God gives a fragment of His mind to a Spirit-filled individual to know and understand that which he could not have known or understood on his own regarding future events. Jesus told Peter, "*Verily I say unto thee, that this night, before the cock crow, thou shalt deny me thrice.*" Jesus could not have known this on his own except God would reveal to him exactly what Peter would do in the future. This was a futuristic event unknown to man Matthew 26:34. It is always a fragment of God's mind.

There are many occasions when we must do a certain thing, yet we lack the understanding of how to do it. Therefore, God, in His supernatural ability and gift of the word of wisdom, goes into motion. This particular gift enables us to do and understand when our mental ability is disabling us in what we know that we must do. There was a time when King Solomon had to determine the owner of a child when he had no way of naturally knowing who the owner of that child was. Since Solomon had no way of knowing who the owner of this child was, it was imperative that he use the ability of God to supernaturally know what to do in this particular situation. Therefore, he told them to bring him a sword so that he could divide the baby and give each woman half. When the owner of this child yelled out to save the child's life, he had the answer that he was looking for in order to give the right mother the living child. Solomon could not have known to do this on his own. That was a word of wisdom that came to him supernaturally from God. It was a fragment of the mind of God that gave him understanding about what to do (I Kings 3:24-27).

The Word of Knowledge

The word of knowledge exists when God reveals a fragment of His mind to a Spirit-filled individual regarding past and present events. Jesus spoke to the woman at the well about her husband. Jesus asked the woman where her husband was. *The woman replied, "I have no husband". Jesus said, "You have answered right for you have had five husbands, and the one that you have right now is not yours"* (John 4:17-18). Jesus could not have known this on his own. The fragment of what was revealed to Jesus was the word of knowledge. Jesus told the woman what was going on at that time and in the past.

Discerning of Spirits

The gift of discerning of spirits exists when God reveals a portion of His mind to a Spirit-filled believer. The Spirit-filled believer will understand the operation of spirits. The Spirit-filled believer also sees into the spirit world concerning the operation of that which is going on in an individual at that time. It is important to understand that all of these gifts of the Spirit work only as the Holy Spirit wills. It is very important to understand not to make attempts to see in the realm of the spirit on your own. When people try to operate in the spirit realm on their own, they often lose sight of the original intent of God in their lives. When believers position themselves to see into the realm of the spirit without being led by the Holy Spirit, who actually possesses the gifts, they come to a place of being spooky and unbalanced. If you position yourself to see into the spirit on your own, Satan will position himself to show you things that God never intended for you to see. Let's concentrate on keeping balance with the gifts of the Spirit.

INSPIRATION GIFTS

The original purpose of the inspiration gifts is to inspire the body of Christ and to convict the sinner. The thing to remember is that the inspiration gifts are inspired by the Holy Spirit. Many people are trying to get the gifts to flow on their own. Maturity is the key through which the flow of the gifts comes. In times past, we have been instructed that the gifts only work as the Holy Spirit wills. What I found out after listening and searching out the scriptures for myself was that you can use your gift whenever you desire, providing you stay within God's will and purpose. In other words, you must have God's will in mind in order for the flow to be created and for you to be able to use the gifts. It should be understood that this is possible with those who are released in the office of the prophet. The word says that all of these worketh that one and the selfsame Spirit dividing to every man severally as the Holy Spirit wills. The Amplified Bible says all these (gifts, achievements, abilities) are inspired and brought to pass by one and the selfsame (holy) Spirit, who apportions each person individually exactly as He chooses. (1 Corinthians 12:11)

The Gifts of Tongues

The gift of tongues occurs when God allows a Spirit-filled believer to speak in a heavenly language or another language that the believer has not learned by natural means. The gift of tongues is a supernatural happening within the believer to reveal that which God desires to speak to a local assembly of people. As we noted earlier in a previous chapter, there is a vast difference between tongues and the gift of tongues.

Tongues would be classified as a heavenly prayer language with which an individual communicates with God. However, the gift of tongues occurs when God communicates to a group of people. In this process of the gift of tongues, God is always using a Spirit-filled believer. Some very good references to support the gift of tongues are found in 1 Corinthians 14:3: *"But he that prophesieth speaketh unto men to edification, and exhortation, and comfort."* Verse 4b says, *"But he that prophesieth edifieth the church."* Verse 5 says, *"I would that ye all spake with tongues, but rather that ye prophesied: for greater is he that prophesieth than he that speaketh with tongues except he interpret, that the church may receive edifying."* In the book of Acts, you will find many occasions when the people spoke with tongues and prophesied. That is, they spoke with the gift of tongues and prophesied. What we should get from that is that they spoke with tongues, interpretation came, and that together equals prophecy. How do we recognize when it is the gift of tongues? The tongues that are motivated specifically by the Holy Spirit come forth with power and authority. The Holy Spirit then calms the atmosphere and brings under subjection all other tongues as the gift of tongues seems to escalate. If it is only tongues in communicating with God, there is no regulating of the other tongues that surround the tongues that are coming forth at that time.

The Gift of the Interpretation of Tongues

The gift of the interpretation of tongues occurs when God reveals, supernaturally, to a

Spirit-filled believer the interpretation of that which someone has spoken in tongues. The interpretation process is a very important one. The interpretation oftentimes turns out to be a misinterpretation based on the zeal that one has that is not according to knowledge. There are many occasions when one desires to interpret tongues, yet the person's motivation is not the Holy Spirit. The motivation turns out to be the concern and care that the person has for this particular body of believers. As you seek to interpret someone's tongues, it is important to remember not to be moved by care, concern or the fact that you may like someone and want them to have a good word.

Our zeal has sometimes caused us to make mistakes in our interpretation of the gift of tongues. Please remember that everything that is spoken through this process is always according to the principles of edification, exhortation and comfort. The reason is that through this process you are dealing with a group of people who may not be able to handle the sharpness of a prophet. The sharpness of a prophet may cut some that need not to be cut because they are unable to handle the cutting at that time.

Remember the word that Jesus gave the disciples, "...*let the wheat and the tares grow together and the Lord at His coming will separate it.*" anytime God has to do a cutting or as it says in Jeremiah 1:10, "*See, I have set thee over nations and over kingdoms to root out and to pull down and to destroy and to throw down, to build, and to plant.*" This, according to New Testament times, is not normally done nor spoken in crowds of people. This is normally done on an individual basis. There are occasions when God would permit this to be done in a group setting, but normally, if it will be done in a group setting, it is because the whole group is judged. Therefore, never carry a condemning word that will rip up a whole house when the whole house is not guilty of an offense. This is when prophetic order and preciseness are absolutely important. Some have condemned whole houses because they were unskilled in the prophetic. They have done, basically, what the wife of Moses did as she got out of order because of her anger towards Moses, her husband. Moses' wife attempted to circumcise her son, the son of Moses, and instead could have castrated him because she was unskillful in circumcision.

<u>The Gift of Prophecy</u>

As we have already covered, the gift of tongues coupled with the gift of the interpretation of tongues equals prophecy. Yet, there are many levels of prophecy in scripture, and it is important for us to understand the different methods of prophecy. One never has to speak with tongues coupled with interpretation of tongues in order for it to be prophecy. That is not the only method of prophecy even though it is one of the methods. God may allow a Spirit-filled vessel to just know some things without the manifestation of tongues.

There are periods when God would supernaturally reveal to a Spirit-filled person a fragment of His mind in order to let the body of Christ in on a particular message that God desires to get to them. One method of prophecy is when God reveals a fragment of His mind to a Spirit-filled vessel. Another method of prophecy is when God reveals a fragment of His mind through prophecy of scripture. Thirdly, there is much scripture that has still not come to pass. Therefore, that type of prophetic utterance must be marked as prophecy.

It is important to remember that prophecy is God-breathed and not man-breathed, even if God does cause it to come directly from scripture. Lastly, written scripture is yet another method of prophecy. Some people may never prophesy verbally, but God has revealed a fragment of His mind to them through their writings and the very things that they write come to pass. It is imperative that we understand the different types of prophecy. One type of prophecy can never be belittled because all of it is inspired by God and God-breathed.

POWER GIFTS

The power gifts are a supernatural manifestation of the power of God on a Spirit-filled vessel. This vessel will flow in such power to bring forth what is in the mind of God. The prophet is one who will flow well with all nine gifts of the Spirit. If we ever get the prophet in his or her place, there will be a great move of God's power in the earth. These gifts of the Spirit are not just for the office of the prophet but extend to those who walk in the realm of the Spirit. Remember, these are the gifts of the Holy Spirit. The gifts of the Holy Spirit will work in whoever has the Holy Spirit inside of them and who made the decision to yield to Him.

The Gift of Faith

The gift of faith occurs when God uses a Spirit-filled believer to do what he could not do with his faith. This is when God supernaturally blows up the faith of a believer to do a supernatural thing. These are times that the faith that you have is just not enough to get the job done. There are times that you may find it to be a struggle to believe for something, but when the gift of faith kicks in, the struggle is over. The gift of faith is a supernatural happening in the life of the believer to manifest God's power in the earth. The word says, *"God has dealt to every man the measure of faith"* (Romans 12:3). When God desires to get the supernatural done, He causes your natural faith to explode to a supernatural level and gets great things done.

The Gifts of Healing

The gifts of healing occur when God uses a Spirit-filled vessel through the gift of healing. There are times when God will heal a certain type of sickness or disease at the same time. It may be that God is healing cancers at this time and a word of knowledge may come that God is healing cancers. If a word like that were to come, the gifts of healing would go into motion, and every cancer in the place would be healed. All of the gifts are a supernatural manifestation of God's power in this dark world. The gifts of healing could manifest the laying on of hands for the purpose of healing a sickness, disease, or sicknesses and diseases. It could be all of the above. What is very important to remember in this is that these gifts work through yielded, Spirit-filled vessels.

<u>The Gift of the Working of Miracles</u>

The gift of the working of miracles exists when God, through a supernatural happening, causes miracles to happen using the muscle of a man or a woman. Even this is a supernatural thing done by God through a Spirit-filled being to accomplish the will of God in the earth. This gift is like the time when God used Samson to kill one thousand people with the jawbone of an ass (Judges 15:16). That type of a miracle had to be through a supernatural manifestation of God's power. There's not a man in the earth that could have done that in his own strength. Therefore, it is called the working of miracles.

LEARNING TO FATHER LEADERS

Before any person can function as a father or a type of father (if the person is a woman), they must submit themselves under the hand of someone else on earth. There are times when the person to whom you would need to submit may seem to be less capable than you, yet God still would have you to submit under that person's hand.

There was a time when Jesus, becoming ready for ministry, had one more person to whom he had to submit outside of the one that posed as his natural father (Joseph). The person to whom he submitted after having left Joseph was John the Baptist at the baptism. John the Baptist felt very much incapable of baptizing him, and he bears this out by saying, *"I have need to be baptized of thee"* (Matthew 3:14). That was the point at which Jesus humbled himself and submitted under the hand of John. Now, He goes from there to the wilderness to be tempted and to go through His period of being tried.

Jesus returned from the wilderness and began the selection of His sons for ministry. Yes, He, Himself hand-picked His own sons that He would pour into. The interesting thing about hand-picking His own sons is that some had to leave their natural father and come under the authority of their spiritual father. Until we come under the authority of our spiritual father, we will never be able to function in the position as a son. There must be absolute submission under a father.

Let's look at some major details about their father-son relationship.

Now when Jesus had heard that John was cast into prison, he departed into Galilee; And leaving Nazareth, he came and dwelt in Capernaum, which is upon the sea coast, in the borders of Zabulon and Nephthalim: That it might be fulfilled which was spoken by Esaias the prophet, saying, The land of Zabulon, and the land of Nephthalim, by the way of the sea, beyond Jordan, Galilee of the Gentiles; The people which sat in darkness saw great light; and to them which sat in the region and shadow of death light is sprung up. From that time Jesus began to preach, and to say, repent: for the kingdom of heaven is at hand. And Jesus, walking by the sea of Galilee, saw two brethren, Simon called Peter, and Andrew his brother, casting a net into the sea: for they were fishers. And he saith unto them, follow me, and I will make you fishers of men. And they straightway left their nets, and followed him. And going on from thence, he saw other two brethren, James the son of Zebedee, and John his brother, in a ship with Zebedee their father, mending their nets; and he called them. And they immediately left the ship and their father, and followed him. And Jesus went about all Galilee, teaching in their synagogues, and preaching the gospel of the kingdom, and healing all manner of sickness and all manner of disease among the people. (Matthew 4:12-23)

1. Leaving Your Comfort Zone and Place of Support, vs 12

Jesus left the comfort of Nazareth where he was raised, along with his family support and all that he cared about and loved. He came to a place that, later on, he would have to weep over because they hadn't grasped their time of visitation. This is a place where every father and every son have to meet. It's what I call a place of surrender and a place of abandonment. This place is a strange place where there is no moral support or spiritual support, only a place of nothingness. This is that type of place that many will wonder why you left, and for what purpose could there possibly be for going to a place such as this Capernaum. Every father must learn to exist where there is nothing but surrender. Every son must come to a place with a father where there is nothing to do but surrender and sit at his feet. There is great power at the feet of a master teacher for the son if he only learns to wait.

2. Shining for/in Another Man's Dream, vs 16

Jesus, at this point, realizes that his only position was to shine for another man's purpose. As a son, it is imperative that we understand that unless we shine for another man's dream, we'll never see the fulfillment of our dreams. As we understand this very important position, we'll also understand the way to fatherhood. The ultimate is to become a father and not remain only a son. We find later that the disciples (sons) were called by Jesus (father) to shine in His dream, which was to reach the lost at all cost. My question to you is, "Are you trying to shine for yourself when you have been called into another man's dream?" If you are, your dream can never be realized because you are trying to shine in your dream when yours has never died.

3. Preaching Another Man's Word, vs 17

It is amazing to me that Jesus came preaching the same word that John the Baptist preached. Remember that Jesus submitted under the hand of John the Baptist and never showed himself until John the Baptist was going off the scene. A son can never show himself until the father is going off the scene. There is a problem in our society today. We, as sons, are trying to show ourselves before our father has gone off the scene. John the Baptist, being a type of a father in this case that we're using, was not dead, but just off the scene. It is not necessary for your father to be dead, but it is necessary for him to be off the scene. Note also that it is important to always stay in a submitted position under your father until he comes to a place of nonexistence. This marks the time for your arising. The real test of whether your time has come is how well you speak your father's word. There will always be an increase of knowledge and revelation that may supersede what your father has said, but it is only likely to happen after he ceases to exist. His death becomes your rising.

4. Locating Your Sons, vs 18-19

At this point, Jesus starts the process of locating his sons, who would function as his staff. God always causes a father to locate sons/staff. Not only does God cause a father to locate his sons, but He also causes him to place his spirit on his sons in order to reproduce what he has been made as a father. There is a word that comes to mind when I, as a father, think of a son or daughter. I have the awesome challenge to duplicate myself in them and to say what Jesus said, "Follow me and I will make you fishers of men." The condition of a son is to "follow me." Any son who has a problem following the father/leader forfeits the benefit of having a portion of that father on him or her. The word "follow" is extremely important to having a portion of your father's spirit. This means you must follow at all cost. Sometimes the cost is great and sometimes not so great. At any rate, there is a cost to capturing the spirit of your father.

The benefit of following is "I will make you." The making comes during the process of following. The word "following" is progressive, is continuous and illustrates a method of not topping the said action. The making happens as you continue following. Some have forfeited their making because they ceased in their following. Now, we return to the prerequisite "Follow me and I will make you fishers of men." I will make you that which I am. God told Moses to choose seventy elders faithful, of good report and full of wisdom. The elders/sons having all of these qualities still needed more in order to be effective. God said there is yet something lacking. They have great gifting and great qualities, yet the missing ingredient to activate all of that greatness was the spirit of their father. God said to Moses, "***You choose the men and I will take of the spirit upon thee and will put it upon them.***" Numbers 11:16-17. The spirit that God was referring to within the context of this scripture would be equivalent to the anointing that was smeared upon Moses.

5. Leaving the Natural Father and Cleaving to the Spiritual Father, vs 20

It was a custom for the natural father to teach natural hobbies and abilities. The spiritual father was the one who had the challenge to impart some spiritual gifts.

Chapter 11

UNDERSTANDING END TIME PROPHECY

A Snap Shot of Revelation

A snap shot is exactly what it says. A snap shot is specifically what it says; it is just a portrait of the Book of Revelation. There are a lot of things that people say regarding the Book of Revelation but we want to really see what the Book of Revelation is saying about the Book of Revelation. We want to make sure that we actually understand specifically what Revelation is actually dealing with; how do we really take a look at the book and not really go off course or become someone so deep that we are just way on the other side of things.

First of all, one of the things that I want take a look at is found in 1 Corinthians, Chapter 2:14: "*But the natural man receiveth not the things of the Spirit of God: for they are foolishness unto him: neither can he know them, because they are spiritually discerned. But he that is spiritual judgeth all things, yet he himself is judged of no man.*" (KJV) This is something that we should really understand. So let us make sure that we understand that the natural man does not know the things of the Spirit of God. So as we really look into the Book of Revelation, we can not look into this book with your natural mind because it is not really going to make sense to you and we have to make sure that we understand this according to the word of God; and I believe that the bible really does interpret the bible. So we do not have to look outside of the bible to see if we can get an understanding of the Book of Revelation.

So let us begin at Revelation 1:1: "*The Revelation of Jesus Christ, which God gave unto him, to shew unto his servants things which must shortly come to pass; and he sent and signified it by his angel unto his servant John: Who bare record of the word of God, and of the testimony of Jesus Christ, and of all things that he saw. Blessed is he that readeth, and they that hear the words of this prophecy, and keep those things which are written therein: for the time is at hand."* (KJV) Let us rest just a minute right there and see if we can go over this line upon line and precept upon precept. The Book of Revelation -- first of all let us correct some of our speech, it is not the Book of Revelations. This is one revelation that God actually intended for his servants, all of His servants, not just for John, his servant. So it must be understood that he intended that his servants understand this. Anytime you are going to do a study on anything, you first want to know who they are talking to because you can miss a whole plan basically not knowing who is being talked to.

This is the Revelation of Jesus Christ which God gave unto Him, Jesus, to show unto His servants. So, they are really servants of Jesus and if we are not really servants of Jesus, then we are really not going to have a revelation of this awesome book. We have to first of all qualify as servants of Jesus. And so now I really do question whether or not everybody in the body of Christ is really servants of Jesus. I really question that because now watch this, this is very, very important, what is a servant? One who serves, right? No, now if we are going to understand that, we are going to have to figure out what does Jesus really care about, and we need to know that to see or what is Jesus called to do.

We have to know if we are really servants of Jesus because if we are not doing the works of Jesus then we are not servants of Jesus. Remember who He wanted to get this revelation to. He wanted to get this revelation to His servants. Whether those servants were people in this day or people in our day, He wanted to get this message to servants. Why? Verse 3: *"Blessed is he that readeth, and they that hear the words of this prophecy, and keep those things which are written therein: for the time is at hand."* Why is it that He wants to get this message to His servants? Well, He wants to get this message to them so that they could actually walk in the fullness of the blessings of God. This will show you that we really should not stay away from the Book of Revelation; because of verse 3: *"Blessed is he that (what?) readeth, and they that hear the words of this prophecy, and keep those things which they (heard)."* So now watch this, one, two and three, blessed is he that (what?) number one: readeth; and they that hear the words of this prophecy; so it does not leave the blind man out or the blind woman out because if they hear these words, if they read these words, and they have to keep these words that they heard or read. And so, the bible calls them blessed. So you have to do three things, you have to read, hear and keep -- keep what, the words of this prophecy. Verse 2 says this: *"Who bare record of the word of God..."* he had a process by which this was suppose to be delivered. It came from Jesus Christ, it had several stops, remember this and if you can remember this, if you ever embrace this you will never walk in error and you will never walk away from God, if you understand this what I am about to say. It is the Revelation of Jesus Christ which God gave to Him, so the revelation really came from God, God handed it down to Jesus, Jesus handed it down to the angels, and the angels handed it down to John and John handed it down to the servants of these seven churches.

God is wanting to get this message to the seven churches, now that it has already gotten to the seven churches, now what happens is we have to make sure that we embrace this word so that we would know, number 1: how to walk; number 2: so that we would be conscious of what time we are in. We are going to have to really visit some places in order to really understand this because most of us, because we do not really understand signs of the times then we do not really know where we are right now. How many of you really understand that? I said, "Because we do not understand the seasons of the times we do not know where we are." We have no clue where we are. If we knew where we were, then we would not do some of the things we do. If you only knew how close you were to the end of the Grace Dispensation, you would not do what you do. You would not be idle and waste time like you do.

Now here is one of the things that says that most of us are not servants of Jesus Christ, because what He cares about is building the church and that is not really our concern. Let us look back real quick to Matthew, Chapter 16, I want to show you this; because you have to understand this is something that He passionate about. He is passionate about building the church. We find this to be true in Matthew 16:13-18 -13 *When Jesus came into the coasts of Caesarea Philippi, he asked his disciples, saying, Whom do men say that I the Son of man am? 14 And they said, Some say that thou art John the Baptist: some, Elias; and others, Jeremias, or one of the prophets. 15 He saith unto them, But whom say ye that I am? 16 And Simon Peter answered and said, Thou art the Christ, the Son of the living God. 17 And Jesus answered and said unto him, Blessed art thou, Simon Barjona: for flesh and blood hath not revealed it unto thee, but my Father which is in heaven. 18 And I say also unto thee, That thou art Peter, and upon this rock I will build my church; and the gates of hell shall not prevail against it. (KJV) Now lets focus on verse 13-16: "When Jesus came into the coasts of Caesarea Philippi, he asked his disciples, saying, Whom do men say that I the Son of man am? And they said, Some say that thou art John the Baptist: some, Elias; and others, Jeremias, or one of the prophets. He saith unto them, But whom say ye that I am? And Simon Peter answered…"* Who answered? Simon Peter. Now Simon Peter was in tune with God. He did not mind taking risks, somebody that is in tune with God does not mind taking risks. He took a risk and he jumped out there. And "He saith unto them, But whom say ye that I am?" Here is what He says, verse 16: *"And Simon Peter answered and said, Thou art the Christ, the Son of the living God. 17 And Jesus answered and said unto him, Blessed art thou, Simon Barjona: for flesh and blood hath not revealed it unto thee, but my Father which is in heaven."* So He is saying, my Father has revealed this unto thee, my Father who is in heaven revealed this to you. Now my Father who is in heaven revealed this to you which means that Peter was actually living with God beyond, he learned to live beyond where everybody else was living. This is going to make better sense later as you read and understand. He learned to live beyond. Why beyond, because he is a servant of Jesus Christ. And so now remember, the challenge that Jesus put before them is, it is upon this kind of revelation that I am going to build my Church. Revelation – do not separate that revelation from this revelation that we are talking about in the Book of Revelation, because it is the Revelation of Jesus Christ. Who gave it to Him? God! So God gave Him this revelation, now wait a minute, let us go back and take a look at Peter again; what did He say again to Peter, verse 17: *"And Jesus answered and said unto him, Blessed art thou, Simon Barjona: for flesh and blood hath not revealed it unto thee, but my Father which is in heaven."* Who revealed it? My Father!

So, it is the Revelation of Jesus Christ. Okay go back to the Book of Revelation, verse 1 says: *"The Revelation of Jesus Christ, which God…"* Who is God? God is Father. Go back over to Matthew, Chapter 16, again. Who gave this to Peter? Read verse 17, again: *"And Jesus answered and said unto him, Blessed art thou, Simon Barjona: for flesh and blood hath not revealed it unto thee, but my Father which is in heaven."* So where did the revelation come from? The revelation came from God but it was the Revelation of whom? Jesus Christ. How do you know? Because the question was: "who do men say that I am?" This is the key needed to understanding how to live beyond everybody else, all the other natural people. How do you live beyond? You have to live beyond in order to qualify for this level of revelation. The problem is that we fellowship with too many natural people that do not want more of God. If we are fellowshipping with the people that do not want any more than what they have right now then you are not going to want any more than what you have right now. So, this is something that we really have to understand, it is the Revelation of Jesus Christ which God gave unto Him, or God gave it to the servants.

He wanted the servants in on this. He wanted Peter in on this; why, because Peter was one of the servants. If you want to go beyond then you have to be one of His servants. Remember "He gave it to Peter. He wanted Peter in on this, why, because Peter was a servant." In Revelation 1: 4: *"John to the seven churches which are in Asia: Grace be unto you, and peace, from him which is, and which was, and which is to come; and from the seven Spirits which are before his throne;"* Let us take a look into that verse, it is so flooded and filled with information. Now first of all, John to the seven churches -- John to what, the seven churches. So it is John that is designed to speak to the seven churches. And so John is actually speaking at this particular point and he is saying, *"Grace be unto you, and peace, from him which is, and which was, and which is to come…"* He is, He was, and He is the same one that is coming.

We have to understand that what God is actually saying is that He is, He was, and He will be in the future. It is the same God; He is the same God of the Old Testament; He is the same God that was in that particular time; and, He is the God of today. He is the God of tomorrow. John continues to say "*…and which is to come; and from the seven Spirits which are before his throne;*" What are the seven Spirits which are before His throne? The seven Spirits which are before His throne and if you are really a child of God then we ought to be able to embrace according to Hebrews, Chapter 6, that which is to come. This describes a place where we are able to go far beyond what we are accustomed to in God. Take a look at what is possible in Hebrews 6:1-6: *Therefore leaving the principles of the doctrine of Christ, let us go on unto perfection; not laying again the foundation of repentance from dead works, and of faith toward God, 2 Of the doctrine of baptisms, and of laying on of hands, and of resurrection of the dead, and of eternal judgment. 3 And this will we do, if God permit. 4 For it is impossible for those who were once enlightened, and have tasted of the heavenly gift, and were made partakers of the Holy Ghost, 5 And have tasted the good word of God, and the powers of the world to come, 6 If they shall fall away, to renew them again unto repentance; seeing they crucify to themselves the Son of God afresh, and put him to an open shame.* (KJV) God wants us to leave the principles of the doctrine of Christ and go beyond that. God is trying to get us to live beyond, beyond where anybody else is willing to live. This is powerful, He is trying to get us to live beyond where we are accustomed and we can see that better once we bring some of this out that is found in the book of Revelation. We are also going to be able to see this throughout the word of God, because He is, He was and He is to come. He wants to get us to live beyond so that we would be able to understand all that is really going on here.

I do not want to leave you out on the seven Spirits; go with me over to Isaiah. Now, you are supposed to be able to access this, this is very important and I want you to really see this. Isaiah 11:1: "*And there shall come forth a rod out of the stem of Jesse, and a Branch shall grow out of his roots: And the spirit of the LORD (number 1) shall rest upon him, the spirit of wisdom (number 2) and understanding (number 3), the spirit of counsel (number 4) and might (number 5), the spirit of knowledge (number 6) and of the fear of the LORD (number 7);*" So you are really suppose to access the seven Spirits which are before the throne of God. This is powerful because the only Spirit that is before the throne that we have accessed is the Spirit of the Lord. It is the only one we have accessed but we have them all. Let us move a little further. Revelation 1:5 says this: "*And from Jesus Christ, who is the faithful witness, and the first begotten of the dead (which means that there will be other begotten of the dead), and the prince of the kings of the earth…*" He is the prince of the kings of the earth. That will be us. But do you realize how many of us are not really accessing that. This is the reason we can not sing that we are wretched because you can not be a king and a wretch at the same time. When you stand up as a king, wretch is gone. If you are a wretch, you are going to walk with your head hung down but when you stand up as a king and realize that you are a king then you are erected. I am telling you we are not thinking that way; why, because we are not living beyond. So, "*(He) is… the first begotten of the dead and the prince of the kings of the earth. Unto him that loved us, and washed us from our sins in his own blood, And hath made us kings and priests...*" And has made us what? kings and priest. Kings are not born, kings are made. Slaves are not born, slaves are made. You have to figure out what you want to be. Do you want to be somebody's servant all your life; somebody's slave all your life? Or, do you want to just go ahead and rise up and realize that He has made you kings and priests in this day. Revelation 1:6: "And hath made us kings and priests unto God and his Father; to him be glory and dominion for ever and ever. Amen. Behold, he cometh with clouds; and every eye shall see him..." Now watch this. One of the things that is easy to do in the Book of Revelation, is to forget that we are talking about the Revelation of Jesus Christ. It is easy to get off track and forget that is what we are talking about. Why? The reason is because John covers other information in this book. So it is easy to forget that we are really talking about the Revelation of Jesus Christ and that is why it keeps on going through who is, and was, and is to come.

It keeps on making reference back to Him (Jesus Christ) so that we don't forget that is who we are talking about. We are really talking about His revealing. He keeps on bringing that up because we have to understand the Book of Revelation is about Him. It is not about you going to hell. It is not about you going into Great Tribulation. It is really about Him and His unveiling. The word "revelation" means to reveal something or to unveil something. Then what is being unveiled? Jesus Christ, Himself; He is being unveiled. Verse 7: "Behold, he cometh with clouds; and every eye shall see him and they also which pierced him..." Well, that blows out the water what the Jehovah Witnesses believe. You know what the Jehovah Witnesses believe? They believe that the rapture happened in 1914 and the eyes that saw Him were the 144,000 in Kingdom Hall. Everybody over 144,000 are going to be lost because only 144,000 will be saved, as they think. Now we have a problem verse 7 says that every eye shell see Him and also they that pierced Him.

In addition, Revelation 7:9 says *After this I beheld, and, lo, a great multitude, which no man could number, of all nations, and kindreds, and people, and tongues, stood before the throne, and before the Lamb, clothed with white robes, and palms in their hands* (KJV) because now we do not know, according to what they believe who is that number that no man can number, that number clearly includes all nations, kindreds, people and tongues. We have some problems here with what they believe, so their belief is off. Let's revisit verse 7: "*Behold, he cometh with clouds; and every eye shall see him...*" How many eyes? Every eye, "*...they also which pierced him...*" they will see Him. So saved and unsaved alike will see Him. Now "*...all kindreds of the earth shall wail because of him. Even so, Amen. I am Alpha and Omega, the beginning and the ending, saith the Lord, which is (there it is again), and which was, and which is to come, the Almighty.*"

Revelation 1:9: "*I John, who also am your brother, and companion in tribulation, and in the kingdom and patience of Jesus Christ, was in the isle that is called Patmos, for the word of God, and for the testimony of Jesus Christ."* I John -- why does he start off this way? Because what he wants us to know is, the level of information that I am coming up with I want you to know that I have not arrived. I am your brother in tribulation. I go through tribulation just like you and I am in the kingdom just like you. Now we may have a little challenge, because most of us do not really operate like we are in the kingdom. Let me ask you this question: How is it that we could see our brother that sits beside us or our sister that sits beside us every single Sunday that have a business and we go outside because we can get it cheaper, outside, and we do not support their business? And then say we are in the kingdom. What kingdom? People in the kingdom support each other and that includes business. This is how it works in the kingdom. How can I talk about you, making negative statements and judging you knowing that you are in the kingdom and that I am in the kingdom and still say I am in the kingdom? What kingdom? I have to support you, there is no way that I can say that and it be the truth.

We all are subjects of the kingdom under one king. And so how can I break so many of the kingdom rules and still say I am in the kingdom. The question we have to ask is: what kingdom? John says, look, I am your brother in tribulation and in the kingdom and in the patience of Jesus Christ. The what? -- The patience of Jesus Christ. We all ought to be pursuing that -- the patience of Jesus Christ. We ought to be walking in it. Now, if we have already made the seven Spirits of God a part of our lifestyle, we walk in that. What do you mean we are walking in that? Because we are dealing with the seven Spirits, right? The seven Spirits of God (Isaiah 11:2): *spirit of the Lord, spirit of wisdom, spirit of counsel, the spirit of might, spirit of understanding, spirit of knowledge, and spirit of fear of the Lord.* The seven Spirits at the throne, they are always there. He says, "*I…was in the isle that is called Patmos, for the word of God and for the testimony of Jesus Christ."* That is why He was there, for the word of God and for the testimony of Jesus Christ.

Why the word of God and why the testimony of Jesus Christ, because it is in the word of God that the testimony of Jesus Christ is going to be revealed. He is going to be revealed. Look, you will be revealed out of your testimony. I said, "You will be revealed out of your testimony." You are not revealed just because you say, I am. You are revealed once you have a testimony. That is the reason we have to stand in the isle called Patmos until we have the word of God and the testimony of Jesus Christ, because it is only out of that, that we are really revealed. If you do not go through anything, you do not have a testimony. We do not know who you are. We know who God says you are but we do not really know whether or not you stepped into what God said you are yet because you have not gone through anything. We know you went in; therefore we stand at the other end to see if you came out or are you still up in there somewhere. You need to be able to stand a test? So John says, he "…*was in the isle that is called*

Patmos for the word of God and for the testimony of Jesus Christ. I was in the Spirit on the Lord's day,"(this is key) *"I was in the Spirit on the Lord's day, and heard behind me a great voice, as of a trumpet,"* John says *"I…heard behind me a great voice, as of a trumpet,"* wait; see this is one of the things we have to understand, he heard behind him a voice. What this literally means is that where he had gone was pass the voice that he heard. Let us read this again. *"I… heard behind me a great voice, as of a trumpet, Saying, I am Alpha and Omega, the first and the last: and, What thou seest, write in a book, and send it unto the seven churches which are in Asia; unto Ephesus, and unto Smyrna, and unto Pergamos, and unto Thyatira, and unto Sardis, and unto Philadelphia, and unto Laodicea."* This is what I wanted you to notice, he had to turn to see the voice *"And I turned to see the voice that spake with me. And being turned, I saw seven golden candlesticks..;"* he turned to see the voice that he heard and he saw seven golden candlesticks. What are these seven golden candlesticks?

Let us go a little further, take a look at verse 20: *"The mystery of the seven stars (we will get to that) which thou sawest in my right hand (now he is explaining to John), and the seven golden candlesticks. The seven stars are the angels of the seven churches: and the seven candlesticks which thou sawest are the seven churches."* So he had gone up into the kingdom, existing in the kingdom and he says, "I turned." Let us go back to that, verse 10: *"…and (I) heard behind me a great voice, as of a trumpet,"* Verse 12 says, *"And I turned to see the voice that spake with me. And being turned, I saw seven golden candlesticks;"* What he saw behind him was the seven churches. He had gone beyond the church age; gone beyond it. Let me help you out with this a bit, he had gone beyond the church and so he was operating beyond the church.

In order to really hear the voice of Christ, he had to turn back to the church to see what was going on and what Christ was trying to say to him regarding the seven churches. Because the voice was within the church but that is not where he was operating. Remember, Peter operated beyond, that is the reason that Peter said, *"Thou art the Christ, the son of the living God"*. See, he received all of his information differently. He heard, he tapped into the realm of God and understood what this was in the church. So he tapped into that so he had gone beyond where everybody else was. John did the same thing. John had gone beyond then he heard behind him a voice which spake to him. So he turns, he hears Him, *"Saying, I am Alpha and Omega, (I am) the first and the last: and, What thou seest, write in a book…"* Aren't you so glad that he wrote? Look at it, we are reading it right now; we are reading what he wrote. *"…write in a book, and send it unto the seven churches…"* Your mind would be so amazed if you would look back at all of how this word of God, the Bible has been translated, just amazed at all of the different translations that it has gone through in order to get to English so that we would be able to read this for ourselves.

He says I am the first and the last. I am He that was dead but yet I live forever more.

He keeps His word, made sure that all of this word right here in the book of Revelation gets all the way down to us, English speaking folk that came from wherever we came from. In verse 11, He says: *"send it…unto Ephesus, …Smyrna, …Pergamos, …Thyatira, …Sardis, …Philadelphia, and …Laodicea."* Send it to the seven churches. Now when we get ready to get into the seven churches, you are going to find what church you are really in. You are going to find the church that you are really in and then you are going to find the church that we are suppose to be. You may not bear the characteristics of the church that we are really from. The church that we really represent based on what we talk about is the church of Philadelphia, whom He had nothing bad to say about. We will talk about that later. So he says: verse 12: *"And I turned to see the voice that spake with me. And being turned, I saw seven golden candlesticks; And in the midst of the seven candlesticks one like unto the Son of man, clothed with a garment down to the foot, and girt about the paps with a golden girdle. His head and his hairs were white like wool, as white as snow; and his eyes were as a flame of fire;"* His eyes were red, as a flame of fire. And so now watch this. So we get in a little trouble when we start trying to prove that He was black or He was white or He was this or He was that. We get into a little trouble trying to prove that because what John saw was different than what everybody else saw.

It is important for us not to try to figure that out, if John does not talk about it, let us not worry about it. John continues in Revelation 1:15 15 *And his feet like unto fine brass, as if they burned in a furnace; and his voice as the sound of many waters.* (KJV)….as if; they were not burned but as if they had burned in a furnace; and his voice as the sound of many waters… it was not the sound of many waters but as the sound. Verse 16: *"And he had in his right hand seven stars…"* Now we have a little challenge here. What are the seven stars? He explains in verse 20: *"The mystery of the seven stars which thou sawest in my right hand, and the seven golden candlesticks. The seven stars are the angels of the seven churches…"* Now they are the angels of the seven churches. The Greek word for angels is "angelos" which is the same word that is actually used for ministers in this context. In other words those angels that He is talking about, they are the angels, they are the bishops of the seven churches. He says, they are in my hand. This is very important, and this is the reason that I do not put my mouth (talk bad about) on folk because they are in the hand of Jesus. Let us look back into that. "And He had in his (what? In his) right hand (not His left hand)." I am in His right hand, not His left hand. His right hand is symbolic of the greater power. So I am in the hand where there is the greater power. The left hand is symbolic of the lesser power nevertheless it is under the power. Just being in His hand is wonderful.

All I can say, just make sure that you are in one of His hands. So in His right hand He has the bishops of the seven churches and He has the church in His hand. Do not tell me that the church is about over because He still have it in His right hand. Jeremiah had a revelation of this in Jeremiah 18:6 *"O house of Israel, can I not do with you as this potter does?" declares the LORD. "Like clay in the hand of the potter, so are you in my hand, O house of Israel".* (NIV) and he say that we are in His hand. You are in His hand if you are in the church. That is the reason we need to make sure that we are in the church so we can be in His hand. So where are you? In His right hand, are you about to fail? Are you a wretch? Are you a sinner? Now we are not talking about whether or not you sin, all have sinned and come short of the glory of God, but you are not a sinner. But you are in His right hand; look, if you go ahead and take advantage of what is available at the Throne then you will never fail. You are in His right hand. One of the things that He said, in John 10:28: *And I give unto them eternal life; and they shall never perish, neither shall any man pluck them out of my hand.* (KJV) He said that "you shall not be plucked out." You will not be plucked out now you can jump out of His hand, it is difficult but you can get out. You say how you going to get out of His hand? You want to know how. You really want to know -- according to the Book of Revelation, be lukewarm; I will spew you out of my mouth. But wait a minute now, I thought you were in His hand. There is no way to disconnect me from you unless He puts you in His mouth and see that you are lukewarm and spew you out. Because remember He can not let everybody go out of His hand nor can He let anybody go in His hand to take you out. So there is only one way to get you out, put you in His mouth and spew you out; because if you are lukewarm, you want out bad.

In Verse 17 John records: *"And when I saw him, I fell at his feet as dead. And he laid his right hand upon me, saying unto me, Fear not; I am the first and the last: I am he that liveth, and was dead; and, behold, I am alive for evermore…"* I can not imagine what John was experiencing because he is seeing Him in a state of being that nobody else has seen Him. Why was John able to see Him that way? Because he was willing to go to the isle of Patmos, this was a very bad place if someone picked you up and dropped you off at the isle of Patmos, they did not intend for you to come back. Jesus said to John, *"I am alive for evermore, … and (I) have the keys of hell and of death."* That says that He victoriously went down to hell, snatched those keys back from the devil. The devil got those keys back from Adam by all right; he had the keys to death and hell. Jesus went down and He got them back. Triumphed over him in it, the bible says. Again, verse 18: *"I am he that liveth, and was dead; and, behold, I am alive for evermore, Amen; and have the keys of hell and of death. Write the things which thou hast seen, and the things which are, and the things which shall be hereafter;"* Write it. Write everything John, that I am showing you right now. I want you to write it so that everybody knows that I have gotten the keys back. Satan is no longer a owner nor a key holder on this planet; he has a lease on the earth and when his lease is up we are going to cast him off of this earth.

Let's go back to Matthew 16:19; let us take a look at those keys. I have got to start with verse 17 so it will make sense to you, Matthew 16:17 - 19 says this: *"…Blessed art thou, Simon Barjona: for flesh and blood hath not revealed it unto thee, but my Father which is in heaven. And I say also unto thee, That thou art Peter, and upon this rock (upon this kind of revelation) I will build my church; and the gates of hell shall not prevail against it. And I will give unto thee the keys of the kingdom of heaven: and whatsoever thou shalt bind on earth shall be bound in heaven: and whatsoever thou shalt loose on earth shall be loosed in heaven."* You got to make it into the kingdom in order to bind like that, in order to loose like that. You have got to make it in there; otherwise, you do not have keys. It takes a key to bind; it takes a key to loose, but you need to get into the kingdom first. Remember what we said about John; where did he make it to—beyond the church, stepped into the kingdom. So when he stepped into the kingdom, he had the keys. He had access to the keys. So when he looks back at the church… wait a minute now, because he stepped into the kingdom he has access to the keys, he sees the seven Spirits at the throne and when he heard the voice he turned to see the voice. He has marching orders to go back to the church and tell the church about all of this. If we only realize what we have to do to get the kingdom in us, the only thing we have to do is develop in us Matthew, Chapter 5, Chapter 6, and Chapter 7, and we will know how the kingdom works.

Revelation Chapter 2 deals with the seven churches. John had the assignment to carry this message to the seven churches and it became important that he understood that he was dealing with the seven churches. Here is one of the reasons that that was so important: now remember, there were more than seven churches, this is very important to understand. There were more than seven churches in Asia Minor but there were seven key churches that were designed to echo what God was saying. This is very important for us to understand because remember what God had done in the past, He will also do in our day and so we have to identify and understand when or if we are one of those churches that God has in the earth that is a voice to the earth.

He had a strong rebuke for some of them. One of the reasons that there was such a strong rebuke for some of them was because they were designed to be a strong voice to the earth. You know, these were not churches that did not have a voice. One of the things that I think that becomes imperative that as we begin to engage in this, that we understand that when you are part of a church that is a voice to the earth then you are dealing with serious principalities and powers. You are dealing with some of the chief rulers of the heavens that are actually coming after you. It becomes imperative that we really understand what that means and how upset the devil could actually get when you are a chief voice in our time. I believe that my church, Heritage Church International is one of those churches that is a voice in the earth. A church that is saying something in the earth has to make sure that they are accountable with what they say.

Chapter 2, beginning at verse 1 - 7: *"Unto the angel of the church of Ephesus write; These things saith he that holdeth the seven stars in his right hand, who walketh in the midst of the seven golden candlesticks; I know thy works, and thy labour, and thy patience, and how thou canst not bear them which are evil: and thou hast tried them which say they are apostles, and are not, and hast found them liars: And hast borne, and hast patience, and for my name's sake hast laboured, and hast not fainted. Nevertheless I have somewhat against thee, because thou hast left thy first love. Remember therefore from whence thou art fallen, and repent, and do the first works; or else I will come unto thee quickly, and will remove thy candlestick out of his place, except thou repent. But this thou hast, that thou hatest the deeds of the Nicolaitanes, which I also hate. He that hath an ear, let him hear what the Spirit saith unto the churches; To him that overcometh will I give to eat of the tree of life, which is in the midst of the paradise of God."* (KJV) Let us deal with that first church. We really want to take a serious look at the church of Ephesus because one of the things that I think that we are actually going to see is ourselves in many of the different principles that exist in each church. We are going to see a lot of things as we increase in our understanding of the seven churches. And it says, verse 1: *"Unto the angel of the church of Ephesus write; These things saith he that holdeth the seven stars in his right hand, who walketh in the midst of the seven golden candlesticks;"* He holds the seven stars. Remember, according to Chapter 1:20, the seven stars were the angels or the bishops of those seven churches; He has them in His right hand. This is real important for us to understand. If God have them in His right hand, then what that means is we need not to really worry about them because God has them. And this is extremely important for us to really understand.

God has them in His right hand; now just as important as that, Jesus is actually walking through the midst of the seven churches. This might kind of disturb you a little bit because sometimes we, as the people of God, are so double-minded, so moved by things, situations and circumstances; but this might really catch you by surprise that Jesus was still walking in the midst of the seven churches even though He revealed what was wrong with them. Now that ought to give us some sense of consolation, but most of us would think after seeing all that, that is wrong with the church, no way in the world is Jesus still there. But the bible says that He has got those bishops in His hand, in His right hand -- His right hand symbolic of the greater power.

If we are really going to understand the Book of Revelation, one of the key things that we are going to have to do is make sure that we understand that the Book of Revelation is written in many symbols, in symbolism. It does not mean that you can not take the Book of Revelation serious it just means that you are going to have to put on your God-understanding in order to really grasp what it is talking about because the natural man is not going to be able to get this. We actually have to question almost everything that we read in the Book of Revelation and look closely at it and take a close look at it and make sure that we understand what that symbol is. We are going to have to really deal with some things very seriously and identify symbolically what John is talking about. A couple of the symbols that we have already found were the star and the candlestick. Some of the symbolism we actually skipped so let us cover one of them now and that is God's numbering system. Note that when God deals with this particular book He also deals with the numbering system. So if we will take a look in verse 4 of Chapter 1, it says this: "John to the seven churches…" John saw how many churches? -- Seven. Seven is that number of completion or that number of perfection. So we have seven churches; we have seven spirits; we have seven golden candlesticks; we have seven starts; and so now we are going to have to really take a look at that and make sure that we are examining that really closely because if God is coming up with all of these sevens apparently He is trying to say something.

Let us go back to Chapter 2. So He says, look, I have got them in my right hand. I have the leaders of these churches in my right hand and if they are in the right hand of God--symbolizing the greater power of God--then what that means is that nothing is going to jump out of His hand or none of them are going to get so far out of line that God does not have them. Then He is walking in the midst of the seven churches which mean that I have them. I am in the midst of them. Because now remember earlier in this book, we talked about how John had gone pass the church and heard behind him somebody that was still in the church. That was Jesus, he heard the voice of Jesus, Jesus was still in the church but John had actually gone pass the church.

Do you realize a lot of times we actually do that? We go way pass what Jesus is still dealing with. Some of us get so deep that a lot of times we go way pass what we really need to go pass and God is still dealing with the church about those particular things. He is still dealing with the things that you actually want to go pass. Because it is easy to go pass things, I mean that is real easy, because then we do not have to deal with what we go pass.

Chapter 2:2 - 3: "*I know thy works, and thy labour, and thy patience, and how thou canst not bear them which are evil: and thou hast tried them which say they are apostles, and are not, and hast found them liars: And hast borne, and hast patience, and for my name's sake hast laboured, and hast not fainted.*" So He is saying, look, I realize that you have done all of that; I realize that you have good works, you really do church of Ephesus. Remember this, the church of Ephesus was dealing with, they were located in one of the major areas where there was tremendous pagan activity. Now that sounds kind of like where we are, dealing with a lot of pagan activity. In the area where we live presently, they celebrate everything. I mean they celebrate every-thing—during Halloween they have little pumpkins outside, lights in them, all kinds of pagan activities: St. Patrick's Day, everything is green; everybody is in green except for us. I mean they celebrate absolutely everything, you have not seen a street that is lit up like our street during Christmas. I mean lights outside during Halloween season all of that. We are also in the midst of a pagan society. If we really tell the truth about it, when we erect our green Christmas trees during Christmas we are participating with a pagan event. When we do the Easter egg hunts that is pagan all the way.

I know we try to cooperate with how things are in this particular day that we live and that was exactly what the church of Ephesus had to deal with. However, one of the things that they were applauded for was because they hated the deeds of the Nicolaitanes. They hated their deeds. They hated evil. They absolutely hated it. It is amazing that you could hate something so bad which is evil and you have left your first love? I wonder, if it is possible that the things that we feel that are wrong with everybody else have distracted us and we never noticed that possibly our giving attention to what is wrong with them has caused us not to focused on what we really need to be focused on. They had literally left their first love. Jesus says, "nevertheless I have somewhat against thee…" It is good that you hate those things, all of those things. I applaud you on those particular issues. You are in this pagan society and you are wrestling with some things. Anytime you are in a pagan society you wrestle with things because everybody that you know is engaged in particular pagan events.

They hate the deeds of the Nicolaitans. Now let us see if we can talk just a bit about the Nicolaitans. The Nicolaitans comes from a Greek word, it is a compound word: one portion of that word is nico meaning "overcome"; and the other word laitans meaning "lay" people. So what they actually wanted to do was to lord over people; they wanted to control people; this was actually their practice, this is what they practiced every single day. The very deeds that they practiced the church of Ephesus really did hate. But watch this. Verse 4: *"Nevertheless I have somewhat against thee, because thou hast left thy first love."* So in other words you have something church of Ephesus that you really need to repent of, you all need to come back in line. Sometimes we can zero in so much on somebody else's thing that we start to shift and sway from what the real deal is with us, and so their issue was they left their first love. They had veered off course from what they were really called to do. What their real assignment was, they had veered off course of that. We are talking about the church of Ephesus.

We are talking about a church having to deal with the Ephesians goddess Diana. She was a strong force in that particular land, so they had to deal with some things. They had to put up a strong guard against them. As we go down toward the end and pick up from verse 4: *"Nevertheless I have somewhat against thee, because thou hast left thy first love."* Verse 5: *"Remember therefore from whence thou art fallen…"* He is bringing them back in line. He is giving them a specific plan as to come back in line. God will never leave you out there without a plan of action to come back in line. Read (verse 5): *"and repent, and do the first works…"* They have given me instructions to repent, turn from what you are doing. The quickest way to really get right with God is admit it, quit it, get rid of it; that is the quickest way to repentance. That is the quickest way to do the repentant work – admit it, quit it, get rid of it, whatever it is.

Let us go a little further, (verse 5) "or else I will come unto thee quickly, and will remove thy candlestick out of his place…" Candlesticks – symbol right? What is the candlestick? The church. Now watch this: "or else I will come unto thee, how? Quickly! And will remove the church out of his place." That is serious. Now we need to go back and understand, what does that really mean? Right now they are a voice in the earth; right now they have influence; right now they have such authority and such power with God that God is saying, look right now you are a major voice in the earth but if you do not repent and deal with this particular area, then I am going to have to move the church of Ephesus out of your place so that it is no longer a voice. Let us go on, (verse 5) "…*except thou repent.*" Verse 6: "*But this thou hast, that thou hatest the deeds of the Nicolaitanes, which I also hate.*" Verse 7: "*He that hath an ear, let him hear what the Spirit saith unto the churches…*" Did you notice that He would say that to every church? "*He that hath an ear*" – I want to bring you back into something now. "He that hath an ear," what? Let. The word let once again is a word of permission. If information is being withheld, it is because you have not been allowed that level of information. This is the reason we can not set around and argue with people that do not understand what you understand.

Once you see that people do not understand what you understand just say "alright." What does that mean? Only you really know the meaning of that; because what they think that you are saying is "it is okay, now I understand what you are saying." But what you are really saying is "okay, I understand your ears are not on. You can not hear what I am saying." This is very important -- "He that hath an ear" let. So, it is apparent that they do not have an ear. Everybody does not have an ear to hear what you are saying. Everybody does not have an ear to hear what you are hearing. And that is the reason that some people could stay in dead, dried up places and be content with where they are, and you can not figure out why they are still there. They stay because their appetite is being satisfied. They do not hunger for more. They do not have an ear to hear more.

Let us go further, verse 7: "*let him hear what the Spirit saith unto the churches; To him that overcometh will I give to eat of the tree of life, which is in the midst of the paradise of God.*" Verses 8 - 11: "*And unto the angel of the church in Smyrna write; These things saith the first and the last, which was dead, and is alive; I know thy works, and tribulation, and poverty, (but thou art rich) and I know the blasphemy of them which say they are Jews, and are not, but are the synagogue of Satan. Fear none of those things which thou shalt suffer: behold, the devil shall cast some of you into prison, that ye may be tried; and ye shall have tribulation ten days: be thou faithful unto death, and I will give thee a crown of life. He that hath an ear, let him hear what the Spirit saith unto the churches; He that overcometh shall not be hurt of the second death.*" This is good. Now if you notice, He had nothing bad to say about the church of Smyrna. Do you want to know why? Smyrna by its name comes from the word "myrrh" and the only way, myrrh like the ointment, to get the fragrance out of myrrh is for myrrh to be crushed, there is no other way to get the fragrance. But Smyrna went through what it had to go through, came through to the other side where now they are giving off a fragrance based on what they have gone through. Anytime you make an excuse for why you are like you are, you are refusing to be crushed. What you are going through, go on through it; because when you come through that God has something for you. But a lot of us make excuses "I am the way I am is because." Some Christians will even lie to protect themselves. Let us go back and see if we can highlight some particular things in here; verse 8: "*And unto the angel of the church in Smyrna write; These things saith the first and the last, which was dead, and is alive;*" Was dead and is alive—that must be talking about Jesus. Now watch this, "I know thy works, and tribulation," I know what you are going through. I know your works and I know what you are going through. Does not that just kind of make you feel better on the inside when somebody knows what you are going through? Jesus says, look I know your works and I know what you are going through, I know your tribulation, "and poverty, (but thou art rich) and I know the blasphemy of them which say they are Jews, and are not, but are (of) the synagogue of Satan." Now watch this, this is interesting, "and are (of) the synagogue of Satan", a synagogue which is where the Jews actually have their fellowship. In other words the synagogue, a place of fellowship but it is a synagogue of Satan, in other words a place that Satan is actually ruling the fellowship.

And so now the question is how do we really know when Satan is ruling the fellowship? Because of what comes out of it. This is how we know. We know that he is ruling the fellowship because everything that he does—steal, kill and destroy—and so that is what really comes out of the fellowship where he actually rules. This becomes somewhat important, because it was actually believed that the synagogue of Satan was where people actually gathered and they put a certain force on people to come to a point where they are actually working for their salvation rather than believing for things by faith. Now that sounds familiar!

But now can I remind you just for one moment that, God's hand is on this church, Smyrna. That God's hand is on this church which means that they are -- let us go back to that. Verse 9: "*I know thy works, and tribulation, and poverty, (but thou art rich) and I know the blasphemy of them which say they are Jews, and are not,*" the blasphemy--they blasphemed. They are coming against you richly, they are coming against you in every way that they possibly can. They are throwing every single thing that they can at you, every level of persecution, every thing that they could possibly throw at you they are throwing. And guess what? The church of Smyrna is only receiving this as another level of crushing. So they never do take a break from being able to bounce back out of this thing because then everything that they are doing they are doing this as unto the Lord. And they know that everything that they are going through is for the glory of God. Well, we seem to be suffering some level of poverty here but this is for the glory of God; and then God comes by and speaks a word in that place and says, "But thou art rich." And so how they actually viewed what was their lack God is saying, no, that is not who you are. You are actually rich. Then He goes right on from that and He says, "I know the blasphemy of them which say they are Jews, and are not, but are the synagogue of Satan. Fear none of those things which thou shalt suffer: behold, the devil shall cast some of you into prison, that ye may be tried;" Whatever prison that you are in, whatever prison that you are confronted with it is only to be tried.

I know it does not feel good, it never feels good. It is only so that you would be tried. Job was tried to same way. Job was hit with nine different diseases at the same time, now if that is not a prison I do not know what a prison is. He was hit with nine different diseases, all at the same time but yet the bible says that he had his integrity. He lived through all of that. Many times we do not think we are going to live through what we are going through but somewhere along the line you have to still keep your face to the face of God. What they were actually going through at this particular point was a crushing. So now every time you are crushed you are giving off a fragrance that goes up before God but when you refuse to be crushed, when we refuse to go through that crushing then what that means is that we give off no fragrance to God; we walk by, God does not even smell us. Have you ever walked by somebody and you just want to ask them "what is that that you are wearing"? You just wanted to ask, what in the world is that that you are wearing, that smells good? So when you walk by and you are part of the church of Smyrna you are giving off a particular fragrance God stops you as you are walking by, wait a minute what is that you are wearing? What in the world is that that you are wearing? It can only come through tribulation, persecution and all of that good stuff.

You can never get it outside of that. Did you notice that before Jesus was every crucified that He went into Gethsemane the place of crushing? Before He was ever crucified, why, because anything that is going to be sacrificed it has to go through that, it has to go through a preparation period. It has to have a certain fragrance about it. Otherwise it is not ready to be sacrificed. That was interesting to me, anyway. He says something else to them, "Be...faithful unto death." Be faithful, what does it mean to be faithful? Stay the course, be totally committed, and be full of faith. Do not falter; stick with what you are going through. What you started before you start going through, stick with that. Do not back up because of what you are going through, be faithful unto death. Now that is an interesting way to put it though, you know that, right?

Because "be faithful unto death" means that there is a dying associated with being faithful. Have you ever had to be faithful doing something that you really did not want to do? That was is a little difficult. It was okay being faithful to that thing as long as it was convenient, but when it became inconvenient it begins to press you and that is when fragrance start coming off of you because now it is taking a little more to do this thing now because this thing is no longer convenient. It was alright when there was no pressure on it.

When you start speaking the word of God and the condition of your life is normal you have not proven to be faithful. For instance, at the point of your confessing the word of God over your life you have no problems that you can identify, all your bills are paid every month on time, your body is healed, you are doing well in all of those things. You do not know that you are really faithful until after the pressure is on your body and it begins giving you problems; your finances are no longer comfortable. All of these are now giving you problems. If you still tithe in the midst of this financial crunch then you know that you are faithful. If you still believe God that you are healed in spite of what you are experiencing in you body then you know that you are faithful. If you do not have some trying moment like these, we do not really know that you are faithful. We do not know for sure; we would like to believe that you are but faithfulness really does not show up or it is not really magnified until you are going through an inconvenient situation.

If you are still reading your Bible and your body is wrecked with pain and you are still reading the word of God, oh yea you are faithful, you are a faithful word reader. You are faithful to it. If you are confessing the word over your body, you are faithful. Your body is making this inconvenient right now, but you are faithful. All God is really saying at that particular point is, "I can count on you to really do this even though things are not convenient for you to be doing this right now."

Things were not convenient for the church of Smyrna, but that is the time that you will know whether or not you are faithful, so the church of Smyrna was a faithful church. Are you faithful? Now let us qualify that, are you faithful to the Lord? God came and was walking in the midst of the seven churches checking out the level of faithfulness. He says be faithful unto death; be faithful until you die to you. Read on, 2:10: "*...and I will give you thee a crown of life.*" I will give you a crown of life. Verse 11: "*He that hath an ear, let him hear what the Spirit saith unto the churches; He that overcometh shall not be hurt of the second death.*" He that overcometh! See, because according to Hebrews 9:27 *And as it is appointed unto men once to die ...* (KJV). It is appointed unto man once to die, but he shall not be hurt; he shall not experience pain in the second death. If you die to death now, then the second death will not be painful. If you do not die to death now, then the second death is going to be painful.

Let us go further, Revelation 2:12 "*And to the angel of the church in Pergamos write; These things saith he which hath the sharp sword with two edges;*" Verse 13: "*I know thy works, and where thou dwellest, even where Satan's seat is:*" Wait a minute, Jesus is talking about Satan's seat again. At first it was the synagogue of Satan now it is Satan's seat. So Satan actually has a seat in this church, this church of Pergamos. *"and thou holdest fast my name, and hast not denied my faith, even in those days wherein Antipas was my faithful martyr, who was slain among you, where Satan dwelleth. But I have a few things against thee, because thou hast there them that hold the doctrine of Balaam, who taught Balac to cast a stumblingblock before the children of Israel, to eat things sacrificed unto idols, and to commit fornication."* They were actually taught to commit fornication. Now if you limit this to two single people carrying out a sexual act, you really missed the boat big time. Let's go over to Matthew, I want to show you this in Chapter 19. Let us start at verse 4: *"And he answered and said unto them, Have ye not read, that he which made them at the beginning made them male and female, And said, For this cause shall a man leave father and mother, and shall cleave to his wife: and they twain shall be one flesh? Wherefore they are no more twain, but one flesh. What therefore God hath joined together, let not man put asunder. They say unto him, Why did Moses then command to give a writing of divorcement, and to put her away? He saith unto them, Moses because of the hardness of your hearts suffered you to put away your wives: but from the beginning it was not so."* Verse 9: *"And I say unto you, Whosoever shall put away his wife, except it be for fornication, and shall marry another, committeth adultery: and whoso marrieth her which is put away doth commit adultery."* (KJV)

Okay now wait a minute. How can you commit fornication if you are married? I mean really think about this a minute now because either this is wrong or somewhere along the line our thinking has been wrong. Because what we said was if you are married it is adultery, it is not fornication; but except for the cause of fornication then what? "Whosoever shall put away his wife, except it be for fornication, and shall marry another, committeth adultery: and whoso marrieth her which is put away doth commit adultery." So the thing is "fornication" and fornication is really an umbrella of things. Adultery is one of the items under that umbrella. Let us go back to Revelation 2:14: *"But I have a few things against thee, because thou hast there them that hold the doctrine of Balaam,"* They hold the doctrine of Balaam, who what? "who taught Balak to cast a stumblingblock before the children of Israel, to eat things sacrificed unto idols, and to commit fornication." Now, there are two items that Jesus has a major problem with here: they are teaching them to eat things sacrificed to idols, and to commit fornication. Whether this is physical fornication or spiritual fornication they are taught to walk on both sides of the line. They are taught to be unfaithful to God.

What is Jesus talking about here, fornication; if you really get down deep into what it really is, it is being unfaithful. It means that you are not living a life that you are committed. So "Why would eating things sacrificed to idols be a problem" -- that sounds like a spiritual issue. It is a physical act but a spiritual sin. Because you can eat what you want to eat, right? That is true for us that have no conscience, so we just eat with anybody; and sometimes we eat things that we are not supposed to eat. As a matter of fact, if we go over into the book of Acts it will tell you what you ought not to be eating according to the New Testament. You ought not to eat things that are strangled. That is what the book of Acts says, Chapter 15:29: *"That ye abstain from meats offered to idols, and from blood, and from things strangled, and from fornication: from which if ye keep yourselves, ye shall do well. Fare ye well."* (KJV) *"and from things strangled, and from fornication: from which if ye keep yourselves, ye shall do well, Fare ye well."* Get out of here is what he is saying; in other words, do not listen to the Nicolaitanes. Do not listen to people that are telling you to walk by the law. Here is the deal, keep yourselves from meats offered to idols and from blood and from things strangled and from fornication; if you keep yourselves from those things you shall do well. He mentioned nothing about keeping the Sabbath, even though you need a Sabbath, he did not mention about keeping the Sabbath. He did not mention anything else, he says if you do those things right there you are going to be alright. He did not mention circumcision or being circumcised, He did not mention any of those things, but He did say if you do these things you are going to be alright.

Let us go on, Revelation 2:15: *"So hast thou also them that hold the doctrine of the Nicolaitanes, which thing I hate. Repent; or else I will come unto thee quickly, and will fight against them with the sword of my mouth."* I will fight against whom? The Nicolaitanes, therefore, if you are a part of them then I will fight against you even though you are part of the church. Remember Satan's seat is there and so Satan promotes the Nicolaitanes and their deeds and their work. Rebellious acts are a part of what the Nicolaitanes do. People that cast stumbling blocks before other people so that they would fall is the same thing -- that is an act of the Nicolaitanes. I mean if you are messed up do not mess other people up. Do not cause problems for other people just because you are experiencing some challenges. Do not make other people fall down because you fell down. And that is what that is all about. Revelation 2:17: *"He that hath an ear, let him hear what the Spirit saith unto the churches; To him that overcometh will I give to eat of the hidden manna..."* He that overcometh I will give manna that is hidden; but it is contingent upon your overcoming. Overcoming what? Whatever it is that you go through or whatever you are going through at this moment. Receiving the hidden manna is contingent upon you overcoming whatever your situation happens to be.

You are not going to get in a prayer line and receive the hidden manna, nor are you going to receive it by the laying on of hands. You receive that hidden manna by way of overcoming what you are going through or what you have to go through or what you have gone through and you overcame it. So this is the reason that some people never ever press through into that next place where they come into this hidden manna. When you open your bible to a particular page all kinds of things jump out at you, this is revelation that you have never seen before but, somebody else opens to the same page and they do not see what you saw, they only see it when you say it; you know why, because what you received is hidden manna.

When you or I make a decision and say that I am overcoming this challenge, we position ourselves to receive the hidden manna. If you are like me, you will make the decision to overcome every challenge because we want hidden manna. We want some hidden manna. We want to hear God say some revelatory things to us. We do not want Him to have to say to us what He said to the disciples and to the apostles, "*I have yet many things to say unto you but you can not handle it right now.*" As He did in John 16:12 I have yet many things to say unto you, but ye cannot bear them now. (KJV) Why? They had not qualified for it. You have got to qualify for the manna that is hidden. You do not get that just because you have a bible. You do not get that just because you go to a word church that teach and preach the word of God fervently like yours or mind, you do not get the hidden manna that way. You get it because you have accepted the challenge of overcoming whatever you are going through right now, you accepted it as a challenge. You are not going to make an excuse for quitting or giving up, "well the devil just after me." No, you do not care about that, accept this as a challenge and be determined that you are going to overcome this.

I can not tell you how many things rose up in my life and in my private place I looked right at that thing and I said, "I am going to overcome this thing." Everybody has something that they have to overcome, however, if you belong to a church that offers you the opportunity to tell your story in testimony service, let me tell you something you do not have to stand up in testimony service and tell them your challenge; as a matter of fact you better not say it in a testimony service until you have settled it in your spirit, then you can testify about it. You get in your private place and you say, "This demon of pain I will overcome you. This demon of this, whatever the challenge is, I will overcome you." You make up your mind and you refuse to move and now God says, "I have something for you. I will cause you to tap into hidden manna." Now that might not mean much to a lot of people but it means so much to me. Hidden manna, you know what that says to me. That says, that there are some things that God wants to say to the body of Christ that He can not say, and He can not say it to them because they have never overcome what they go through. What is it that you go through? Overcome that thing.

Do you realize that this is what God said, 1 John 5:4: "*For whatsoever is born of God overcometh the world: and this is the victory that overcometh the world...*" (KJV) Wait a minute. Some people that find it difficult to overcome things, I do not care what the thing is, they find it difficult, they say "I just can not overcome this one," well, wait a minute, are you born of God? We are believers of God and are born of Him, this positions us to overcome things. Let me tell you something; believers ought to be able to overcome things. So if we are born of God and we are not overcoming in a particular area, it is because we have not settled it. Take note of this, we do not automatically overcome things just because we are born of God. I am telling you right now, overcoming is not automatic just because you are born of God. You have to settle that in your mind and say I am overcoming this challenge. This is the way that I overcame so many things in my life. I settled it in my private place. This is the point where you come face to face with you, you do not have any thing to prove to anybody, you come face to face with you in that private place – it is nobody there but you and God. If you get up in that private place and say, "No I am not defeated, I will overcome this. Oh yes I will; I will overcome this thing." You start to talk to it, saying "no I am not giving up, I am going to overcome you in the Name of Jesus" and, then before you know it, your saying "I am going to overcome you" becomes "I overcome you right now in Jesus' Name. I take authority over you. You are under my feet." So that ends up becoming a reality on the inside of you and you start to triumph over that challenge. Do you realize that is what we are really talking about now; we are talking about the Christ that triumphed.

The next church John mentions is the church of Thyatira, a sweet smell sacrifice of labor. This is basically what Thyatira actually means. However, their negative characteristics were that they had false teachings and doctrinal corruption; they had false teachers. Let us go to that, Revelation 2:18, because Jesus had particular complaints about this church. Beginning at verse 18: "And unto the angel of the church in Thyatira write; These things saith the Son of God, who hath his eyes like unto a flame of fire, and his feet are like fine brass;" (KJV) Let me stop you right there for just a minute. Because one of the things that we said, that if you are going to understand the Book of Revelation it means that you and I are going to have to really understand that a lot of it is written in symbols, so when it comes down to the Book of Revelation you have to pay attention.

You have to pay very close attention because some words we hear so much that it is easy for us not to hear it when it is actually read. Read verse 18 again, let me show you that: "*And unto the angel of the church in Thyatira write; These things saith the Son of God, (saith the who? Son of God) who hath his eyes like unto a flame of fire…*" Okay now watch this now. "…Who hath his eyes like unto a flame of fire…" They are not a flame of fire but they are like it. Not as a flame but like a flame. As soon as we think about that the first thing that we do is go toward color and that is not what it was at all. Let me ask you this question: "What is a fire like? What is a flame of fire like? Number 1, it is piercing; Number 2, a flame of fire is intimidating; so he had eyes like a flame of fire, not as a flame of fire but like a flame of fire. Let us not draw our attention to the color more than we actually look at the very characteristics of that fire or the very effects of that fire. Let us go a little further, "…*and his feet are like fine brass;*" Verse 19: "*I know thy works, and charity, and service, and faith, and thy patience, and thy works; and the last to be more than the first.*" "…*and the last to be more than the first*" so, this is a serving church. This is a serving church; they have a sweet smell, a sacrifice of labor. But then He goes on to say, "***But I have got some stuff against you.***" Verse 20: "***Notwithstanding I have a few things against thee, because thou sufferest that woman Jezebel, which calleth herself a prophetess, to teach and to seduce my servants to commit fornication, and to eat things sacrificed unto idols.***" This is so important because He says, "Okay, here is the complaint that I have: because you suffer that woman Jezebel to teach." Let us cover what it does not mean and then let us cover what it means. What it does not mean, that a woman can not teach; because when you really think about this, it is not even dealing with gender at all, it calls it a woman because it is reproductive. It reproduces itself and gender does not matter.

Male or a female, it reproduces itself. We are going to have to look at this very seriously; one of the things that this particular scripture deals with is usurping authority. Our thought process has normally been that a woman should not teach nor to usurp authority over a man. Well, the word "usurp" really means "to take." It did not really say anything about a woman could not exercise authority, it says you can not take it. Well neither can a man usurp authority; a man is not suppose to take authority either. See, authority is not something that is taken; authority is given. So when it comes down to what God actually desire to do in the church, women are not excluded. God desires to use males and females in the church. Why? Because He wants to create that balance; so a woman should not take authority and a man should not take authority.

So when it comes down to this woman Jezebel, we are not talking about what is commonly thought, her spirit was not that of a loose woman, Jezebel represents a reproducing seductive spirit. This spirit is not male or female, but that is what she actually represented; someone that actually seduced people in order to sway them in their direction. Watch this now, because a lot of us are actually in danger of this right here. I wonder if you know anybody or maybe even yourself challenged in that particular area where you would like to seduce someone, whatever it takes, in order to actually go in your direction. This is a particular spirit that you have to look out for in the church because sometimes it means that wants to do things their way and override the authority set in the church. Let me give it to you this way. Jezebel was someone that actually seduced leadership, mature leaders selected to help the pastor. She did not go after babes; she went after some of the key people in leadership and used her seduction in order to drive them in the direction that she wanted them to go in order to carry out her own ideas.

So in other words, this church was actually guilty of that and was in danger of setting up a church within the church. A Jezebel lead group of her, (reproducing spirit), own within the church; that is one of the spirits that you actually have to look out for in the church. How do you recognize the Jezebel spirit? They will start gravitating to leadership rather than the other people and then use seductive ways inserting a method to breakdown leadership and move them in their own direction away from the key leadership in the church. Once that happens, they would be recognized and establish their own leadership and then lead that whole thing in another direction. And so now that thing is very alive in church. So when it came down to this particular church, the church of Thyatira, He says, "*This is what I have against you: because you suffer her to teach.*" I am going to let that sink in for a few minutes. So in other words, "you suffered her to teach." I am saying "her" but please remember what I just got finish saying, it is not necessarily a "her." This is one of the reasons it requires strong leadership. Church requires strong leadership. Church requires leadership that has no problem with rebuke. Because now understand this, this is how Jezebel slides in – where there is no rebuke. Where there is no rebuke; where there is no direction; where there is no correction; where there is none of that, then Jezebel is able to slide in; that spirit of Jezebel is actually able to slide in and it is the whole spirit of Jezebel, is able to slide in where there is not strong leadership.

Remember King Ahab, Jezebel's husband, he was the king the person that should have been leading and controlling things, but Ahab did not display strong leadership. Every, every Jezebel (male or female) needs an Ahab, a person that lacks strong leadership. Any time the spirit of Jezebel is trying to move forward it looks for a weak leadership and when it does not find weak leadership, it moves on because then that spirit is unable to do what it wants to do within that particular group. It moves on to another location; so, we have to make sure that we are actually prayerful about our reasoning for actually wanting to move on. And I am telling you this seductive spirit is also a key and we have to watch out for it because now, this is something that is actually dealt with in the seven churches.

Let us see if we can come to an understanding of where we are. Why does God think it so important to actually deal with this. Because now remember, we are in Day 6, the 6 dispensation of God? Remember that 1000 years is as one day in the Lord, 2 Peter 3:8 8 *But, beloved, be not ignorant of this one thing, that one day is with the Lord as a thousand years, and a thousand years as one day.* (KJV) We are in Day 6; Day 1 was a Day of Innocence. We have Dispensation, number: 1, 2, 3, 4, 5, and then the Grace Dispensation is Dispensation or Day 6. Day 7 is about to come, we do not know the day or hour, only the Father knows that, but we know that we are in a particular age; right now, the church age which is the Dispensation of Grace. The next age that is actually coming is the Great Tribulation. God says in the book of Revelation, "*Look, I want to make sure that I deal with the church.*" Remember the word of the Lord came from Jesus as John heard Him behind him but he had already moved into a kingdom age. John heard the voice behind him coming from the midst of the seven churches and God says, "Look, I need you to get this message to them." Now, this is one of the messages that He wanted to make sure that got to the church. I wonder if you checked yourself out, where would you find yourself in the church, which one of the seven churches can you say, "this is what I need to deal with"? If you took an inventory of what Jesus was telling John especially of His concerns, where would you actually find yourself.

Jezebel did not want strong leadership, she wanted to seduce people; well let us take a look at the leadership. God had a problem with the leadership because His complaint against them is "you let her teach." He says, "You let her teach." In other words, you did not have to let her teach -- teach, instruct, lead, give her influence. If you are the key leader, it is up to you whether or not you give that person influence or not. You actually sanction them within the church. You actually give them authority so they can operate. If it is a spirit of Jezebel, once again, whether it is male or female you can recognize it by the approach used to seduce leaders. For example, I had an incident that happened in my church that I had to deal with immediately. Someone actually sent out an email to as many people as he had an email address to in the church and it was all about this seductive spirit, he used the email as a means to protect himself in order to soften the blows of the rebuke that he received. He sent to everybody thinking that everybody knew about the rebuke, but I simply do not operate that way; I did not tell anyone about his rebuke, if I rebuke someone, if it is not something that needs to be a public rebuke, I do not rebuke publicly. I correct a lot of people and it is all behind the scene and if you were not there you would never know about it nor will I tell you.

If you do not have a need to know you will not be there because each one is going to be private. He sent that email out to people who had no idea what he was talking about. Because he did that I needed to send out an email to everybody that I think he sent it out to. Why? Because when this happens the Pastor needs to go ahead and deal with it so that everybody sees the correction on the screen. When you are in a position of leadership, you have been given the space to teach whether you do that in the pulpit or not. In other words, you have been given influence. To give somebody that level of influence and then let them have the floor is to allow them or their voice to be heard regardless of whether it is correct or incorrect. And so God says, "I have got some problems with you, Thyatira. You suffered her to teach. You suffered her to have influence and you did not correct her when she did. When she said what she said, you did not correct her." He says, "I have some what against thee." The word "suffer" in this context really means "to allow." You allowed it. So, I wonder what is it that we actually allow that God says we should not allow.

Let us go a little further; Revelation 2:21: "*And I gave her space to repent of her fornication; and she repented not.*" This is something that we have to see – "*...gave her space to repent...*" Now remember this, a rebuke that comes always lends space to repent. That is the reason for a rebuke because then you have space to repent. Why? When the rebuke comes, you have space to repent and if we make sure that we do not get offended by a rebuke then most of the time, nine times out of ten, you will make the right decision.

If you get offended by a rebuke, nine times out of ten, you are going to make the wrong decision. But now understand this, you have to be honest with yourself and say, "I am offended" and be able to go back to the person that corrected you and say, "I am offended" because then if you go to them personally then the whole thing can be ironed out. Remember, you must go back to that person privately, nobody else just that person because that is the person that you have the problem with, you can work it out. You should work this out before we give our next tithe or offering. We are commanded by Jesus to do this in Matt 5:23-24 *Therefore if thou bring thy gift to the altar, and there rememberest that thy brother hath ought against thee; 24 Leave there thy gift before the altar, and go thy way; first be reconciled to thy brother, and then come and offer thy gift.* (KJV) If you do not go back to them you are going to end up spewing or spitting up on somebody else—vomiting on somebody else all of your offense. Now God says, "do not let her teach." Why? "Because she is going to vomit; do not let her teach." We want to rush to leadership but I am telling you that is not a place you want to rush to because it requires sacrifice on your part. God says we, are the ones, we the leadership are the ones that are beaten with man stripes. According to Luke 12:47: *And that servant, which knew his lord's will, and prepared not himself, neither did according to his will, shall be beaten with many stripes.* (KJV) Everybody is going to get whipped but we get whipped with many stripes. Verse 22: "*Behold, I will cast her into a bed, and them that commit adultery with her into great tribulation…*" We are talking about seduction -- right? All of those that are seduced are going to go down with Jezebel because she should be cast into a bed with all of those that where seduced by her because they permitted this abduction, they knew of their seduction and they got in the bed with her, therefore, all of you got to go down. He says to the leader, "get rid of all of them." If you do not get rid of them they are going to go out and seduce somebody else.

Let us go a little further, "…*except they repent of their deeds. And I will kill her children with death…*" I will kill her what? Her children have to be killed. She reproduced, they have got to die; all of her children have to die. You have to know those that you labor among because you want to make sure that you are not one of her children.

Remember, we were talking about the next age. The next age is Great Tribulation. Just prior to Great Tribulation all of those that are in safety with God are raptured out -- The Great Snatch; so all of that are raptured will be gone and everybody that did not leave goes right into Great Tribulation. So, those that were cast in the bed with Jezebel stayed on the earth and were ushered into Great Tribulation; all of those that were not involved with that were raptured out. Are you going to be left behind? The Holy

Ghost is not going to be here to help you. God is not going to call each and every one of you by name, He is going to call the Holy Ghost home and everybody that has the Holy Ghost in them—Snatch! I mean just like that you will be gone. That is what it is called, the Great Snatch, the Rapture; it means that everybody that has the Holy Ghost on the inside of them at that particular time – Snatch! If they are flying an airplane, snatch; if they are driving their cabs, snatch; if they are driving their car, snatch; they will leave. You do not want to be here with the ones left behind. God has given space to repent, "I have given her space to repent; I have given her space to repent but she repented not." So when the season changed and she was left behind and everybody else that was involved in her seduction were left behind.

Let us go a little further, verse 23: "*and all the churches shall know that I am he which searcheth the reins and hearts: and I will give unto every one of you according to your works.*" Verse 24: "*But unto you I say, and unto the rest in Thyatira, as many as have not this doctrine…*" Have not this what? Doctrine! The word "doctrine" means "teaching." They are setting under that teaching and they already understand that it is seduction. How would they know that it is seduction? Here is how they actually know that it is seduction -- because God is a God of order. Look, God sets authority in place and what actually happens is the enemy comes in to disrupt that order, to disrupt that authority, sway people from following the order of the house. So how is it that people just automatically follow something other than the order of the pastor? They are able to follow that because they have to take their attention off of the authority that was set in the church. Now some other person is operating as an authoritative head and people are following that which is divide-vision. Now the new vision is separated from the vision that God originally set. The church is now divided into two separate groups and we now have a church within the church.

Understand that that is seduction; they have been seduced to follow someone else. Remember what He says in the Book of Galatians, Chapter 3: "*who hath bewitched you that ye should not obey the truth…*" (KJV) In other words, who seduced you that you should not obey the truth, who seduced you? Let us go back, Revelation 2:24: "*…and which have not known the depths of Satan, as they speak; I will put upon you none other burden.*" Verse 25: "*But that which ye have already hold fast till I come.*" That which you have already hold fast till I come; God is not so unfair to…He says, "look, whatever part you already understand just hold that. No, you will not under-stand every thing; no, you do not have all of the answers but here is what I want you to do, whatever you have hold on to that." Read, verse 26: "*And he that overcometh, and keepeth my works unto the end, to him will I give power over the nations: And he shall rule them with a rod of iron…*" Jesus is talking to the church, those that over-come and keep his works to the end He will give power over the nations.

This last church is found in Revelation 3:14 - 22: "*And unto the angel of the church of the Laodiceans write; These things saith the Amen, the faithful and true witness, the beginning of the creation of God; I know thy works, that thou art neither cold nor hot: I would thou wast cold or hot. So then because thou art lukewarm, and neither cold nor hot, I will spew thee out of my mouth. Because thou sayest, I am rich, and increased with goods, and have need of nothing; and knowest not that thou art wretched, and miserable, and poor, and blind, and naked: I counsel thee to buy of me gold tried in the fire, that thou mayest be rich; and white raiment, that thou mayest be clothed, and that the shame of thy nakedness do not appear; and anoint thine eyes with eyesalve, that thou mayest see. As many as I love, I rebuke and chasten: be zealous therefore, and repent. Behold, I stand at the door, and knock: if any man hear my voice, and open the door, I will come in to him, and will sup with him, and he with me. To him that overcometh will I grant to sit with me in my throne, even as I also overcame, and am set down with my Father in his throne. He that hath an ear, let him hear what the Spirit saith unto the churches."* (KJV) Let us go back through that, now this is the church of Laodicea and I think there are some very important things that we should really gather from this particular book. Now remember as it pertains to the seven churches, one of the things that I think that is going to be very important for us to understand is that God wants us to get a glimpse of where we are. I am going to say that one more time, God wants us to get a glimpse of where we are; this place is heaven and this is all about 'A Glimpse of Heaven' we will talk more about that in the next chapter.

God is actually dealing with these churches speaking into the church what the problem is, what He really praise them for and what He has against them so that they can actually correct the wrong and move forward in position so that they are not left behind. One of the things that I think that we really do need to understand is that God does not want to leave anybody behind, His grace and His mercy endureth forever (Psalm 106:1); and we want to make sure that we are positioned because some of us may not know if we are positioned right now to go to heaven. Believe me we want to make sure we are ready. Paul dealt with this when he dealt with the fruit of the spirit but then he also dealt with the works of the flesh in order to show us where we are, some of the things we have challenges with and then what God actually expects of us. As we look closely at this church of Laodicea we see some things that God is concerned about. So let us go back to Revelation 3:14: *"And unto the angel of the church of the Laodiceans write; These things saith the Amen, the faithful and true witness, the beginning of the creation of God; I know thy works, that thou art neither cold nor ho I would thou wast cold or hot. So then because thou art lukewarm, and neither cold nor hot, I will spew thee out of my mouth..."* He jumps right into it with this church. He says, "Look, you are neither cold nor hot. As a matter of fact, you are lukewarm and because you are, I will spew you out; I will spit you out of my mouth. We are the body of Christ and not only do we dwell in God, we live in God and God also lives in us. But now what God is actually saying, if you being lukewarm do not pull it together, I am going to have to spit you out. He says, *"I would rather have you cold or I would rather have you hot.* One or the other, at least then I will know what to do with you. But when you are lukewarm there is only one thing to do and that is to spit you out."

Let us go back and remember where we actually are. Remember John is telling us about things that are past, present and future. At this point we are dealing with the seven churches, we are actually talking about the end of this dispensation, the end of the 6 day, and this is the tine when the Rapture is to take place. The Rapture takes place; we are snatched out of the earth and are in heaven. But then there is something happening on earth at the same time you are in heaven. There is something actually taking place in the earth while we are in heaven and enjoying ourselves.

It is amazing that He deals with this issue first, right out of the gate, He deals with this church being a lukewarm church. In other words, dealing with this church as a church that has particular issues that they really have not pulled together; this becomes extremely important for us to actually understand. So now what we are actually seeing is that this church is a lukewarm church, they are not the church that is hot and on fire. That is not who they are; this church is actually lukewarm. This church is voluntarily and habitually operating in sin, in flesh; know they are in the flesh and will not change. So this is very important for us to understand because how many of you reading this book knows that some of us have been there or some are there right now.

How many of us know that it is only by the grace of God that we are not operating voluntarily habitually in sin right now, it is only by His grace that we are not. So this does not give us a reason to look down on other people, because if we are not there, what this says is we have overcome and we talked about that in the last church, church 6, the church of Philadelphia. This is very important to understand—wherever you are in your mind, wherever you are in your level of being lukewarm, it means that there is only one thing that we really need to do, that is admit it and quit it. There is no long drawn out thing that we need to do, just admit it and quit it. The church of Laodicea are a lukewarm church and He says to them in verses 15 - 17: *"And unto the angel of the church of the Laodiceans write; These things saith the Amen, the faithful and true witness, the beginning of the creation of God; I know thy works, that thou art neither cold nor hot: I would thou wast cold or hot. So then because thou art lukewarm, and neither cold nor hot, I will spew thee out of my mouth. Because thou sayest, I am rich, and increased with goods, and have need of nothing; and knowest not that thou art wretched, and miserable, and poor, and blind, and naked:"* Take note of this, this is important to see because it sounds like somebody has a confession of faith but are not really walking their faith out. They are saying one thing about themselves but that is not really how things are. We really have to understand the difference, there is going to be a difference between us actually operating in faith and calling those things which be not as though they were, than us just pretending that we are walking in faith but what we are doing is just putting on a show for people. Do not put on show, be real. We must know the difference between walking in faith calling those things which be not as though they were, and putting on a show as if you owe me something. You do not owe me anything. You do not owe me an explanation nor do I owe you an explanation, therefore if I am messed up and you are messed up we are just messed up. We have to just be real. I need you to really understand the difference though. Let us say for instance you as an individual trying to walk faith out and you know that you are messed up, well, you do not have to go around broadcasting your problem because you are going to have what you say. Since you are going to have what you say then you do not want to go around broadcasting that particular problem, because you are creating your tomorrow. So that is not what you want to do but here is what you actually want to do--you want to make sure that you are declaring what it is that you are believing for.

You are not just saying this so that people will think that you are alright; because that is the spirit of pride. You are not verbalizing your solution because you want people to think that you are alright, you are saying this because "I believe that my change has come." This is very important to understand, because when you are walking your faith out you are creating your tomorrow to be the solution not the problem. But if you are just trying to cover it up you are not creating anything for tomorrow, you are not even bringing in the change, you are just trying to cover up some things that you have going on. We have to really understand that we must not even try to pretend. Why? Because people that are pretenders never create a positive tomorrow! Let us go a little further, verse 18: *"I counsel thee to buy of me gold tried in the fire..."* Let us remember who He is talking to first. He is talking to people that are lukewarm and He says, "You need to make a purchase. I counsel thee to buy of me gold tried in the fire; Buy of me some stuff that is of me; buy some stuff of me that is tried already in the fire." What does He really mean by that?

Now if you do not have the answer, you need to buy into somebody else's program that works. In other words, most of the time when somebody is walking around lukewarm it is because they bought into somebody's program that was lukewarm. They are the kind of people that they hang around. I like the way Mike Murdock says it "show me your friends and I can predict your future." We become cold and lukewarm and all of that, because our friends are cold and lukewarm. We become gossipers because our friends are gossipers (people who talk about people) and if we do not get away from them we are going to be messed up. You may not be a person that gossips but if you do not deliberately get away from people knowing that they are gossiping then you will be messed up just as they are messed up. When you realize that they have all of these kinds of issues and you do not get away from them; then, that same spirit you have fellowshipped with before you know it, you are talking about people too.

He says, buy stuff of me that is already been tried. Find some people who have accomplished what you are trying to get done. If you just need to be around people, get around people that will not smile at your sin, people that will rebuke you whenever you are operating in gossip. Do not gather together as many 'yes' people as you can gather together, grab a hold of someone and fellowship with someone that just will not let you be like that. Let us go on, verse 18: *"that thou mayest be rich; and white raiment, that thou mayest be clothed, and that the shame of thy nakedness do not appear..."* that the shame of (your) nakedness do not appear, it is difficult being around people that challenge you and you just remain the same. This is difficult because you need to choose people that challenge you, people that push you to the next degree; not people that will talk behind your back, people that will tell you in your face, you know that is wrong. I mean just point blank, "That is wrong; I understand what you are saying, I understand where you are right now but that particular thing that you are doing is wrong. I just wanted you to know just in case you do not know."

These kinds of people are actually going to push you to the next place and you should be that kind of a person to someone else. But when you have people around you that are trying to rub over your little errors and rub over your issues, guess what is going to happen—they are literally spoiling you. God is concerned about His people and He is going to charge us when we get to heaven for not correcting people when we knew that they were wrong.

Take a look in Ezekiel 3:18-21 *18 When I say unto the wicked, Thou shalt surely die; and thou givest him not warning, nor speakest to warn the wicked from his wicked way, to save his life; the same wicked man shall die in his iniquity; but his blood will I require at thine hand. 19 Yet if thou warn the wicked, and he turn not from his wickedness, nor from his wicked way, he shall die in his iniquity; but thou hast delivered thy soul. 20 Again, When a righteous man doth turn from his righteousness, and commit iniquity, and I lay a stumblingblock before him, he shall die: because thou hast not given him warning, he shall die in his sin, and his righteousness which he hath done shall not be remembered; but his blood will I require at thine hand. 21 Nevertheless if thou warn the righteous man, that the righteous sin not, and he doth not sin, he shall surely live, because he is warned; also thou hast delivered thy soul.* (KJV) and see is it not so. I can not allow people to stay around me and just be wrong and I know they are wrong; you know I have got to say something. That is true for you also; you are going to have to say something. Once you identify that they are wrong it is even wrong for you to suspend the friendship and not tell them that they are wrong. "No, you are wrong. If you do not want to be my friend after this that is fine but you are wrong. You can make the call on that, I am not going to abandon you because you are wrong, I am going to help you because you are wrong." I am going to help you if you want my help but you are wrong." That will get you in trouble, will it not? That will turn up the heat in your relationship, regardless of what kind of relationship you have

184 | Bishop R. S. Walker

going on that will turn up the heat on it, because everybody's flesh likes people that agreed with them.

Everybody's flesh like people that will agree with them, but your spirit does not like what you are doing. Your flesh loves it so you say to people —just agree with me. Let us go back to Revelation 3:18 *I counsel thee to buy of me gold tried in the fire, that thou mayest be rich; and white raiment, that thou mayest be clothed, and that the shame of thy nakedness do not appear; and anoint thine eyes with eyesalve , that thou mayest see.* (KJV) Let us go back to anoint thine eyes with eyesalve. Now salve is basically a medicine, it is something that cures; but isn't it amazing that He said put that in your eyes. Remember this church is actually lukewarm, the church of Laodicea is a lukewarm church and He says, *"Look, here is what you actually have to do, put something in your eyes."* Now Jesus gave the instruction: pluck the eye out; if it offends you, pluck it out (Matthew 5:29). Jesus is actually giving some direction, put eye salve on your eye. So plucking the eye out is not the only remedy. Jesus is not really willing for you to just pluck your eye out because that is not going to do anything with your heart except not give you vision for what we are actually doing wrong. You do have to get vision before you actually do things. You actually get vision for the stuff that you do wrong, you get vision for that before you ever go into it, you get vision for it and then you start feeding that vision by meditating upon that and the more you meditate upon it the more you position yourself to start bringing it to pass.

Meditating upon things and getting visions is what God wants you to use for His glory because that is actually the method of bringing forth a manifestation of what God wants you to have. He wants you to meditate upon what He wants you to meditate upon so that you can start getting vision for it and you can start to getting an image on the inside; once you get that image on the inside then you start to carry out particular things and you start to manifest those things and then before you know it, you have a complete harvest. The devil uses this method the same way.

Jesus says put some eye salve in your eyes and that is going to create a different vision for you. Verse 19: *"As many as I love, I rebuke and chasten…"* As many as I love, I rebuke and I chastise them. I rebuke them and I chastise them if I love them. If we do not get rebuked and chasten by the people that are designed to sharpen us we need to question whether or not they really love us, because if I love you, I am going to rebuke you. Every rebuke is needed. I mean you just do not go around rebuking folks just because you have a position to rebuke. You know that is not why you do it; you rebuke people because they do not see what they are doing. They do not see where they are actually going in participating where they are participating. Verse 20: *"be zealous therefore, and repent. Behold, I stand at the door, and knock: if…"* I love verse 20: *"Behold, I stand at the door, and knock: if…"* If! – this means that you have got to open the door and let Him in, He will not bust down the door. Now I am telling you behold, in other words, "look" I am standing at the door of your heart, the door of your will and I am knocking. If you will open that door I will come in and I will sup with you, I will commune with you, I will fellowship with you and you with Me. He says, I will come in, set down and talk to you.

Can you even imagine that God has actually been trying to get in? He has been knocking on the door of your heart and just wanting in. Do not forget that He was talking to a lukewarm church! Is not that good news! Why do I bring that up, because I do not want you to forget who He is talking to; in other words, He says, even though this church is lukewarm, the church of Laodicea is a lukewarm church, He says, "all hope is not lost for you." He says, "The things that had been going wrong in your life were caused by Me, that was not the devil, that was Me knocking on the door waiting on you to let Me in. The stuff that has been going haywire in your life that was Me knocking on the door. I have been knocking on the door trying to get in. I have been trying to get your attention because I want to come in so that I can fellowship with you."

Chapter 12
A GLIMPSE OF HEAVEN

*L*et us go to heaven and see… what John saw! Revelation 4:1 *After this I looked, and, behold, a door was opened in heaven: and the first voice which I heard was as it were of a trumpet talking with me; which said, Come up hither, and I will shew thee things which must be hereafter.* (KJV) 4:1: "*After this I looked, and, behold…*" He says, "*After all of that I just showed you in the churches, some of the stuff you knew about, some you did not know about, but after this here is what it looks like in heaven.* "*a door was opened in heaven: and the first voice which I heard…*" He mentions the first voice! This is an indication that there are going to be other voices but the first one that I heard "*was as it were of a trumpet talking with me…*" Now wait a minute, we have already heard that trumpet voice over in Revelation, Chapter 1:10: *I heard a voice and it sounded like a trumpet….* "*which said, Come up hither…*" Now wait a minute. The voice that sounded like a trumpet said, "*Come up hither.*" A door was opened in heaven not a window. A door was opened in heaven, why? Because this is the door… see if you are Rapture out at this point, this is a door that is opened in heaven opening to John so that John could come up and see what it looks like in heaven; what goes on in heaven?

HEAVENLY ITEMS LOOKED AS PRECIOUS STONES

Come on let us go and take a look: "*and I will shew thee things which must be hereafter.*" Watch this. Must be where? Here after. Here that is "where" and that is "when." I will shew thee things which must be hereafter. Here after; so that means that he went up and then through the door. And so now let me show you what is going to be here after. Rev 4:2 *And immediately I was in the spirit: and, behold, a throne was set in heaven, and one sat on the throne.* (KJV): Notice what John said "*And immediately I was in the spirit…*" Wait a minute. Did you see what happened? To be absent from the body, the bible says, is to be present with the Lord 2 Cor 5:8 *We are confident, I say, and willing rather to be absent from the body, and to be present with the Lord*

187

(KJV). You may be asking "how did John position himself to do this"? In order to do this you must detach yourself from your flesh because your flesh can not go; as matter of fact your flesh does not even want to go. It really does not, why? The reason that your flesh does not want to go is because it is going to be too painful the change. Your flesh does not want to change, your flesh does not want to go through anything, your flesh do not want to fast, it does not want to wake up in the morning and pray, your flesh does not want to do any of that, all of that is for your spirit. Every bit of that is for your spirit. Your spirit wants to get up in the morning; it is your spirit that wants to fast; it is your spirit that wants to do all those things. And so the cry from that voice of Jesus what sounded to John like a trumpet said, "come up." Once there he writes… "and, behold, a throne was set in heaven, and one sat on the throne." Verse 3: *"And he that sat was to look upon like a jasper…"*

I thought about that, now what in the world does that mean? You know He that was sat on the throne was… Watch this now; John is very clear about this observation: And he that sat was to look upon like a jasper. Now he that sat was to look upon like a jasper; so the same way that you would look at a jewel is the same way you would look at who was sat on the throne. It is amazing. He did not look like a jasper; he was to look upon him like a jasper. How many of you have ever seen somebody with a diamond so huge on their finger that amazed you. You had never seen one like that before and you just kept looking at it. And so that is what it was like for John, when he came up hither the door was opened and he came up before God, he just could not take his eyes off of him. Let's continue with verse 3: *"and a sardine stone: and there was a rainbow round about the throne, in sight like unto an emerald."* Verse 4: *"And round about the throne were four and twenty seats…"* I thank God that John was so detailed in what he saw; this is absolutely amazing to me. He goes in and he looks at the throne and all around the throne was twenty-four seats. Now, verse 4: *"and upon the seats I saw four and twenty elders sitting, clothed in white raiment…"* They are sitting on momentarily because when you come in the presence of God, you just can not sit too long. *"and they had on their heads crowns of gold. And out of the throne proceeded lightnings and thunderings and voices: and there were seven lamps of fire burning before the throne, which are the seven Spirits of God."* Now this is amazing: Out of the throne proceeded lightnings and thunderings and voices: and there were seven lamps of fire burning before the throne, which are the seven Spirits of God.

THE SEVEN SPIRITS OF GOD

Now we have already heard about that, did we not? The seven Spirits of God – are found in Isaiah 11:2 and they are the seven characteristics (Spirit of Jehovah, wisdom, understanding, counsel, power, knowledge and fear of the LORD), these were the seven individual characters of God and they were burning at the altar. Read, verse 6: *"And before the throne there was a sea of glass like unto crystal: and in the midst of the throne, and round about the throne, were four beasts full of eyes before and behind."* Verse 7: *"And the first beast was like a lion…"* We are going to find this in Ezekiel. Remember the vision that Ezekiel had, we are going to find that over in Ezekiel 1:5 – 24 *is what gives the whole understanding of these beasts.* Ezek 1:5-25 *5 Also out of the midst thereof came the likeness of four living creatures. And this was their appearance; they had the likeness of a man. 6 And every one had four faces, and every one had four wings. 7 And their feet were straight feet; and the sole of their feet was like the sole of a calf's foot: and they sparkled like the colour of burnished brass. 8 And they had the hands of a man under their wings on their four sides; and they four had their faces and their wings. 9 Their wings were joined one to another; they turned not when they went; they went every one straight forward. 10 As for the likeness of their faces, they four had the face of a man, and the face of a lion, on the right side: and they four had the face of an ox on the left side; they four also had the face of an eagle. 11 Thus were their faces: and their wings were stretched upward; two wings of every one were joined one to another, and two covered their bodies. 12 And they went every one straight forward: whither the spirit was to go, they went; and they turned not when they went.*

13 As for the likeness of the living creatures, their appearance was like burning coals of fire, and like the appearance of lamps: it went up and down among the living creatures; and the fire was bright, and out of the fire went forth lightning. 14 And the living creatures ran and returned as the appearance of a flash of lightning. 15 Now as I beheld the living creatures, behold one wheel upon the earth by the living creatures, with his four faces. 16 The appearance of the wheels and their work was like unto the colour of a beryl: and they four had one likeness: and their appearance and their work was as it were a wheel in the middle of a wheel. 17 When they went, they went upon their four sides: and they turned not when they went. 18 As for their rings, they were so high that they were dreadful; and their rings were full of eyes round about them four. 19 And when the living creatures went, the wheels went by them: and when the living creatures were lifted up from the earth, the wheels were lifted up. 20 Whithersoever the spirit was to go, they went, thither was their spirit to go; and the wheels were lifted up over against them: for the spirit of the living creature was in the wheels. 21 When those went, these went; and when those stood, these stood; and when those were lifted up from the earth, the wheels were lifted up over against them: for the spirit of the living creature was in the wheels.

22 And the likeness of the firmament upon the heads of the living creature was as the colour of the terrible crystal, stretched forth over their heads above. 23 And under the firmament were their wings straight, the one toward the other: every one had two, which covered on this side, and every one had two, which covered on that side, their bodies. 24 And when they went, I heard the noise of their wings, like the noise of great waters, as the voice of the Almighty, the voice of speech, as the noise of an host: when they stood, they let down their wings.(KJV)

Now let us not talk about what they actually mean yet, because I want to make sure that we are actually getting this part first. What was in heaven? Let us get a glimpse of heaven. Now we have these beasts that are actually there; but these are not literally beasts. They were according to The New Unger's Bible Dictionary CHERUB or cherubim (NASB, "living beings"; NIV, "living creatures") seen by Ezekiel (Ezek 1:5-14; 10), and that of the "four living creatures" in Revelation 4:6-9.

The Twenty Four Elders

These twenty-four elders actually represent us, the saints. Take a look at Revelation 5:9: "*And they sung a new song, saying, Thou art worthy to take the book, and to open the seals thereof: for thou wast slain, and hast redeemed us to God by thy blood out of every kindred, and tongue, and people, and nation;*"(KJV) So now this is actually the twenty-four elders that represent us because they have actually come out of every kindred, every tongue and people and every nation. But there is something else that we actually need to see because there is something that these elders and these beasts are actually manifesting at this point. Revelation 4:7: "*And the first beast was like a lion, and the second beast like a calf, and the third beast had a face as a man, and the fourth beast was like a flying eagle. And the four beasts had each of them six wings about him; and they were full of eyes within: and they rest not day and night, saying, Holy, holy, holy, LORD God Almighty, which was, and is, and is to come.*" So these beasts and these elders are around the throne giving continual praise, bowing down before God continually. It is interesting to note how this is continuous, and if you and I really get tired of worshipping and praising God, we need to go ahead and utilize our time on earth as rehearsal time because the twenty-four elders actually represent us coming from every kindred, every tribe, every nation, and so we are the ones that are setting around the throne worshipping and praising God. Now they are not literally us but they do represent us.

Let's go on to verse 9: "And when those beasts give glory and honour and thanks to him that sat on the throne, who liveth for ever and ever," Verse 10: "T*he four and twenty elders fall down before him*…" The last time we saw the twenty-four elders what were they doing? They were sitting. I am telling you as soon as somebody gets it started with praise and worship they (representing us) fall down. They do not just stand up and praise, they fall down and praise Him; why? Because God is worthy, He is worth that and more. Now I think that after this we are able to get a glimpse of what takes place in heaven and say, okay I see it now.

Do you remember Matthew, Chapter 6:9 – 10: "*Our Father which art in heaven, Hallowed be thy name. Thy kingdom come, Thy will be done in earth, as it is in heav-*

en." (KJV) Then how is the will of God carried out in heaven? Fall down and worship him. That is how his will is carried out. His will is carried out that way. Read, Revelation 4:10: *"that sat on the throne, and worship him that liveth for ever and ever, and cast their crowns before the throne, saying, Thou art worthy, O Lord, to receive glory and honour and power: for thou hast created all things, and for thy pleasure they are and were created."* Wait a minute …thou hast created all things, how many of you reading this book has been created by God? I was created and you were created for His good pleasure. Let me just encourage you just for a minute. If you were created for God's good pleasure, do you think for one moment that God is just going to turn you over to Satan just like that? God created you for His purpose. Do you really think that Satan is going to get an advantage over you just because he wants to? No; you were created for the pleasure of God, for the joy of God. That is why you were created; we were created to give Him glory and for His purpose. We should keep on saying that until that becomes revelation? When we wake up in the morning and I dare you to wake up that morning and say, you were created for His glory. You were created for the glory of God and for His good pleasure.

Would you please answer for me then, why in the world would you stand up in a mirror or wherever you stand up and say, you are just a low wretch, undone…no that is not what God had in mind. You think God created a wretch for His own good pleasure. Did you already get a glimpse of when we behold him setting on the throne; we behold him as a jewel. With the same amazement that we look at some diamonds, emeralds, or jewels; that is how John looked at God just totally in awe of God. Now we have to remember that God said that He created you and me in His image and after His likeness. Notice what Paul wrote in 2 Corinthians 5:1: *"For we know that if our earthly house of this tabernacle were dissolved, we have a building of God, an house not made with hands, eternal in the heavens. For in this we groan, earnestly desiring to be clothed upon with our house which is from heaven :"*(KJV) In other words, after you shed off all of this earthly house. After you shed off of all of this is when you really see what is really in the image of God and after his likeness in the glory of how He created you.

Right now you are looking at you like you look at you but if you only knew what the real you look like you would not talk as bad as you talk about you. Please understand low self-esteem would be out the window, because you would look at yourself and be in awe of God's creation. You would not be able to say the horrible things that you say about yourself, why? Because you would realize 'I am created in the image of God and after His likeness. Look at what God has made.' Understanding this the next time you fellowship with someone you will be able to say you are what God has made and I am what God has made and glorious are we.

WHO IS WORTHY TO OPEN THE BOOK

Let us go on to Chapter 5 because we are going to see some similar things in Chapter 5 Chapter 5:1:4 *"And I saw in the right hand of him that sat on the throne a book written within and on the backside, sealed with seven seals. vs. 2: And I saw a strong angel proclaiming with a loud voice, Who is worthy to open the book, and to loose the seals thereof? vs. 3: And no man in heaven, nor in earth, neither under the earth, was able to open the book, neither to look thereon. vs. 4: And I wept much, because no man was found worthy to open and to read the book, neither to look thereon."* (KJV) I think that this is really important for us to see because John is very conscious of the fact that there is a particular assignment that has to be accomplished within a certain amount of time. I think that that is one of the things that most of us are not conscious of. We feel like we are here on earth with all the time that we need to accomplish what God has in mind for us to do. We feel that we have our entire lifetime to really accomplish things and the truth of the matter is Jesus could come back tonight. I am going to say that one more time and that is the reality of it all -- Jesus could come back tonight so most of us do not really have as much time as we think we do. This earth does not have to be here the length of time that we really think it is going to be here. This becomes extremely important for us to grab and understand. John begins to weep because there is no one apparent that could really open this book and read it.

John realizes that the book actually holds the answers for the time and the place where he exists right then. Now, the real question is who has the ability to open this book and to make known to John (who is in the earth at this time and has now been caught up to heaven to get a glimpse of heaven) what is in the book. John is wondering who is going to open this book because I am not worthy to open it. John wants to know who is worthy to open it. In other words not everybody can take hold of this book and open this book because not everybody is worthy to open it. John asked who is worthy to open this book? verse 5: *"And one of the elders saith unto me, Weep not: behold, the Lion of the tribe of Judah, the Root of David, hath prevailed to open the book, and to loose the seven seals thereof."* So Jesus Christ Himself is the one that is actually going to be able to open this book. Why? Because He has prevailed! Now I think there is a real revelation in that that a certain level of revelation never comes unless we have prevailed. Remember this; you will never come in to a serious sense of revelation until after you prevail. You have to prevail through something. If you are given a particular test in life and you do not prevail, the next level of revelation is not open to you. I think we can really see that in Mark chapter 4, Mark 4:1 *And he began again to teach by the sea side: and there was gathered unto him a great multitude, so that he entered into a ship, and sat in the sea; and the whole multitude was by the sea on the land.* (KJV), we see in this verse that Jesus was teaching to a great multitude, but the great majority of them were willing to leave not really understanding the parables. But the ones that prevailed were able to get an understanding of the great revelation of what Jesus was saying because not everybody was actually called to have this next level of revelation. They all were called, they all were summons to have the revelation of the parables but they all did not answer the call. The ones that answered the call prevailed and when Jesus was alone asked him about the parable. We see that in Mark 4:10-13 10 *And when he was alone, they that were about him with the twelve asked of him the parable. 11 And he said unto them, Unto you it is given to know the mystery of the kingdom of God: but unto them that are without, all these things are done in parables: 12 That seeing they may see, and not perceive; and hearing they may hear, and not understand; lest at any time they should be converted, and their sins should be forgiven them. 13 And he said unto them, Know ye not this parable? and how then will ye know all parables?* (KJV). Those that prevailed received the revelation. Notice verse 11 And he said unto them, Unto you(that prevailed) it is given to know the mystery of the kingdom of God: but unto them that are without, all these things are done in parables. Those that did not prevail will never know the revelation of the parable nor will they ever come into the understanding of what Jesus was teaching them.

And so let us go a little further, verse 6: "*And I beheld, and, lo, in the midst of the throne and of the four beasts…*" Okay now watch this; this is key -- In the midst of the throne. We are ushered right back to the throne. "and in the midst of the elders, stood a Lamb as it had been slain, having seven horns and seven eyes, which are the seven Spirits of God sent forth into all the earth." Now I want to give you a breakdown of some symbols so that we would be able to refer back and forth to these things periodically throughout the time that we are going to be talking about this. First of all, heads equals wisdom; horns equals power; crowns equals dominion; seeds equals people or nations; and so let us lock that in our understanding. What is John seeing? What do the symbols say? So now read that over again, because we are going to have to really take a look at this and see some of these symbols matching them up with some of what John is actually seeing. Remember what we have are 21st century words being seen by a man who really is doing his very best to explain what he is seeing and trying to understand how to articulate what he is seeing. Verse 6: "*And I beheld, and, lo, in the midst of the throne and of the four beasts and in the midst of the elders, stood a Lamb as it had been slain, having seven horns and seven eyes, which are the seven Spirits of God sent forth into all the earth.*" He has seven horns, He has seven powers. This is very important to understand because we also have four beasts.

The Four Horses

Now one of the things that happened was the releasing of four horses. The horse is symbolic of power and we are going to actually see this. This is absolutely amazing because Satan is going to be doing a tremendous amount of things in the time period that he is going to have and even though lawlessness is going to be rampant in this particular period, God is also making sure that He has angels around to make sure that they only go but so far—as far as God would permit them to go.

As we go just a bit further here, notice that we have four beasts in the midst of the elders; verse 7: "*And he came and took the book out of the right hand of him that sat upon the throne. vs. 8: And when he had taken the book, the four beasts and four and twenty elders fell down before the Lamb, having every one of them harps, and golden vials full of odours, which are the prayers of saints.*" He has the golden vials full of odours which are the prayers of the saints. Can you see from this how God really feels about what you are actually praying? This is the reason we can not pray crazy stuff. This is the reason that you never pray the problem, you always pray the answer, and it goes up before God as an odour or as an aroma in His presence. We have to go back to find out who is handling your prayers. Let us go back and find out who is handling your prayers; read verse 6: "*And I beheld, and, lo, in the midst of the throne and of the four beasts and in the midst of the elders, stood a Lamb as it had been slain, having seven horns and seven eyes, which are the seven Spirits of God sent forth into all the earth. vs. 7: And he came and took the book out of the right hand of him that sat upon the throne. vs. 8: And when he had taken the book, the four beasts and four and twenty elders fell down before the Lamb, having every one of them harps…*"

Let's read this slowly because otherwise you will actually miss it. Back it up just a bit, verse 8: And when he had taken the book, the four beasts and four and twenty elders…Okay so the four beasts and the four and twenty elders…fell down before the Lamb, having every one of them harps… who is every one of them—the beasts and the elders. When they fall down they are actually using harps as instruments of worship. They had what else…and golden vials full of odours… full of odours, vessels full of odours and the odours are… the prayers of the saints. But now remember – and I have to keep on saying this because I have to make sure that we keep you in proper alignment with dispensation – at this particular point we are getting a glimpse of what is going on in heaven while at the same time Great Tribulation is on earth. Now we can understand what is happening in heaven during the time of Great Tribulation on earth, the four beast and the twenty four elders are worshiping God with harps and also holding the vials full of the prayers of the saints.

Now remember the only reason that you have a Great Tribulation is because there was a forsaking or a denying of the Savior Jesus Christ at the time when He was actually here. Take a look at Daniel Chapter 9 beginning at verse 20; it is talking about the seventy weeks of years. Daniel 9:20:24 "*And whiles I was speaking, and praying, and confessing my sin and the sin of my people Israel, and presenting my supplication before the LORD my God for the holy mountain of my God; vs. 21: Yea, whiles I was speaking in prayer, even the man Gabriel, whom I had seen in the vision at the beginning, being caused to fly swiftly, touched me about the time of the evening oblation. vs. 22: And he informed me, and talked with me, and said, O Daniel, I am now come forth to give thee skill and understanding.* vs. 24: *Seventy weeks are determined upon thy people…*" (KJV) This is seventy weeks of years that "are determined upon thy people and upon thy holy city, to finish the transgression…" You have got to pay attention to this, to finish the transgression. So now they have transgressed the law of God which means that now they have to enter into this punishment, this time of judgment which was going to be seventy weeks of years. And so we are actually talking about 490 years that they are going to have to go through this particular judgment. Now within this period of judgment they are going to go through they are also going to go through a restoration, they are going to come back and acknowledge Jesus Christ. But there was a stop; there was a postponement in the judgment when they rejected Christ. So their judgment was postponed and they were seven years short of actually fulfilling that. They were seven years short of that which means that now that seven years are postponed until Christ Raptures the Church, the Gentile nation out of the earth.

We can see this better in John, Chapter 1, let me show it to you there. Now remember about 445 A.D. that was when this whole judgment period started and it actually was going to end right at the period where they actually rejected Christ. So we are dealing with 483 years, now the seven years left over for them to actually go through the finishing of this judgment period and a restoration before restoration can kick in. In John, Chapter 1:1- 6, it says this: "*In the beginning was the Word, and the Word was with God, and the Word was God. The same was in the beginning with God. All things were made by him; and without him was not any thing made that was made. In him was life; and the life was the light of men. And the light shineth in darkness; and the darkness comprehended it not. There was a man sent from God, whose name was John.*" Read on, verse 7: "*The same came for a witness, to bear witness of the Light, that all men through him might believe. vs. 8: He was not that Light, but was sent to bear witness of that Light. (Watch this closely) vs. 9: That was the true Light, which lighteth every man that cometh into the world.*" (KJV) John is sent to bear witness of Jesus. In order to keep going with this they have to receive Jesus as the Messiah and God, but when they reject Jesus then we, the Gentiles come on the scene.

The Gentile Nation – To Be Without God

That is when the Gentile nation comes on the scene. Gentile basically means "to be without God." So those, that were without God gets a ticket in now; why? Because the Jewish nation, Israel rejects him, as a nation they do not believe that he is the son of God nor do they believe that he is their Messiah. This is stated in verse 11: "*He came unto his own, and his own received him not. But…*" But, watch this, do not overlook that word but. He came unto his own, (but) his own received him not. Verse 12: "*But as many as received him…*" Now if you are a believer, you are one of the as many. "*as many as received him to them gave he power to become the sons of God…*" How do we know that He is really talking about you and me? Because the children of Israel were already sons through Abraham; so they did not need to become sons, you and I needed to become. Why? Because we were not in God, we had to be engrafted in. In doing so an adoption needed to take place for you and me. The only reason that you and I actually got in with God was because the elect of God rejected God, rejected Jesus Christ Himself. So when they rejected God, then God says, okay, there is a new nation that is on the rise. But God has to be fair, remember the Syrophoenician woman (Mark 7:24-30), well, she was one of us. She was a Gentile, she was without God and so when she came and asks, "Can you heal my daughter?" and then, Jesus says, "it is not your time yet." Why would Jesus tell her that? He would tell her that because the children of faith, the sons of faith through the faith of Abraham were the ones that healing was for; it was not for her or us. And so when they rejected Jesus then God says, "I have to give this to somebody in this season." And so then His grace turned on and His mercy turned on and He gave it to people who did not even deserve it.

THE POSTPONEMENT – THE LAST SEVEN YEARS

There were seven years left over and this was the time that, that seven years were postponed. The seven years of the rest of their judgment was postponed and now they have to go through this period where that is going to be called Great Tribulation. Let us go back to Revelation now remembering that this whole period is a consciousness and awareness that there is a judgment that must be finished. There are people that are left on the earth – now do not think that I have lost my point, we are still talking about those prayers of the saints – John is not talking about you and me because you and I by this time are in heaven. He is really talking about the saints on earth that have decided that they were going to cling to Jesus and that they were going to not reject him this time. Let me give you this part, too, because you and I could not be evangelizers in that particular period when Jesus was here on the earth. We were not the ones to evangelize the Jewish Nation. Remember the time period stopped, because at this particular time God is not going to use Gentiles to win Jews. When the time clock starts back God is not going to use Gentiles to win Jews. If not the Gentiles then who is God going to use? He is going to use key elect people that are going to be the chief evangelizers of the earth. The ones mentioned in Rev 7:1-4 :1 *And after these things I saw four angels standing on the four corners of the earth, holding the four winds of the earth, that the wind should not blow on the earth, nor on the sea, nor on any tree. 2 And I saw another angel ascending from the east, having the seal of the living God: and he cried with a loud voice to the four angels, to whom it was given to hurt the earth and the sea, 3 Saying, Hurt not the earth, neither the sea, nor the trees, till we have sealed the servants of our God in their foreheads. 4 And I heard the number of them which were sealed: and there were sealed an hundred and forty and four thousand of all the tribes of the children of Israel.* (KJV) the one hundred forty and four thousand are really chief evangelizers and these are the people that God puts His seal in their head. Remember the scripture that says that if it was possible even the elect of God would be fooled Matt 24:24 *For there shall arise false Christs, and false prophets, and shall shew great signs and wonders; insomuch that, if it were possible, they shall deceive the very elect.*(KJV). Who are those elect that He is talking about? Well He is not talking about you and I, He is really talking about the chief evangelizers. Why? Because remember in this particular time period on earth what is actually happening. Many of the Jewish nation will be left behind because they will actually go after the anti-Christ because the anti-Christ will be operating with signs and lying wonders. There is going to be a covenant that is going to be made in the first half of Tribulation between Israel and the anti-Christ except they do not know that he is the anti-Christ. Why? Because he is supporting Israel; He is making a covenant with Israel and so therefore he looks like he is for Israel but about a year through the covenant he is going to break the covenant. And so anybody that is actually left behind there is only going to be one way that you can buy or sell anything on the planet and that is to receive the mark in the forehead the "666."

Anybody that actually receives the mark at that particular point they are reprobate and they have no way to get in now. The prayers of the saints are going up to heaven but there is something that is going to happen on the planet at that particular time and anybody that receive Jesus more than likely are going to be beheaded. There will be two choices, one receive the mark of the beast or two be beheaded. If you are a believer you want to go to heaven on the first rapture because you get to keep your head. If you are left behind and you want to be with God you have to reject the anti-Christ, if you do that you are apparently standing up for the Christ. To stand up for the Christ means that you may have to lose your head and lay under the altar because that is where the saints are.

THE BEHEADED SAINTS

The beheaded saints are the martyrs. It is important for us to understand what is happening in the earth at this particular time. So the praying that they have done in the earth and the praying that is going on is going into the hands of the beast that stand before the throne of God and the elders that stand before the throne and those prayers are valuable prayers. Those prayers have an odour attached to them and fulfillment is coming based on their prayers they eventually begin to cry out, "My God, how long? How long O Lord?" Then God based on the blood of the Lamb He washes their garments. Revelation 7: 9; *let me show you what is going to happen: "After this I beheld... After this, John is seeing this... and, lo, a great multitude, which no man could number..."* What did John see? "After this I beheld..." After this indicates a particular time and John was originally talking about the Great Tribulation so after the Great Tribulation there was another Rapture, this next Rapture that takes place with the saints that were coming out of Great Tribulation. So not only do you have the hundred and forty and four thousand chief evangelizers coming up but also a great multitude which no man can number. The hundred and forty and four thousand are numbered, aren't they? John cannot be talking about just them. Therefore out of the Great Tribulation came a number which could not be numbered; in other words, it was a multitude of people. Why? Those who came out of Great Tribulation where people that had decided that they were going to acknowledge Jesus Christ as Lord, they were going to acknowledge Him for who He is and for who He was, and that they were going to hold onto Him even if they got beheaded.

So you remember what happened with Columbine High School, April 20, 1999, Columbine, Colorado where they had to acknowledge that they did not believe in Jesus or they were going to be shot down. And some bold teens made the statement, "Go ahead and shot because I will not deny my Christ." As a result, 12 teenagers and 1 teacher were killed. In addition, 23 persons were wounded. Now you might think that was very bold and it was, but the time will come when people will go into Great Tribulation and they are going to have to acknowledge, 'I believe in Jesus Christ as the Son of the Living God.' And when they acknowledge him as such, they will stand a chance in being beheaded and nearly every one of them they are martyrs beheaded because they will not deny Jesus. And so they will not deny that they know Jesus and because they do not deny him, there are two sides to look at one is from a heavenly perspective and the other from an earthly perspective -- from a heavenly perspective, their prayers become valuable because everybody that is at the throne, in other words, the twenty-four elders they are at the throne and the four beasts or the four angels that are at the throne that are assigned to the throne are handling their prayers. They are handling their prayers in the presence of God after having worshiped God, what are they doing? They are falling down and worshipping him with the prayers of the saints. And so understand this, so when the Tribulation saints are under the altar or they are literally buried there, they get their resurrected bodies at the return of Christ. Let us run on. Let us go back to Chapter 5:9: "*And they sung a new song, saying, Thou art worthy to take the book, and to open the seals thereof: for thou wast slain, and hast redeemed us to God by thy blood...*" Notice this. "By thy blood" that is how He redeemed us back to God.

As people of The Importance of Being Willing To Worship God

God we have to be willing to fall down and worship God. This is my prayer for our church. Pride is too prevalent in our lives. We have to learn to fall down and worship God. Let us go into Chapter 6:1: "*And I saw when the Lamb opened one of the seals, and I heard, as it were the noise of thunder, one of the four beasts saying, Come and see. vs. 2: And I saw, and behold a white horse: and he that sat on him had a bow; and a crown was given unto him: and he went forth conquering, and to conquer.*" (KJV) When the first seal was opened, power was given; now please understand the ability to conquer was given. Where is the church? Rapture out; the church is in heaven. If the church is in heaven; who is on earth? All of those that were left behind! When the first horse is released, remember the horse actually symbolizes authority or power, this horse is released with the ability to authority to conquer the earth.

Do you realize and understand that the Holy Ghost is here in the earth right now? This is the reason that some things cannot be done, Satan cannot do some things. Remember this because when He that now letteth or alloweth be taken out of the way then the wicked one comes we find that in 2 Thess 2:7-12 *For the mystery of iniquity doth already work: only he who now letteth will let, until he be taken out of the way. 8 And then shall that Wicked be revealed, whom the Lord shall consume with the spirit of his mouth, and shall destroy with the brightness of his coming: 9 Even him, whose coming is after the working of Satan with all power and signs and lying wonders, 10 And with all deceivableness of unrighteousness in them that perish; because they received not the love of the truth, that they might be saved. 11 And for this cause God shall send them strong delusion, that they should believe a lie: 12 That they all might be damned who believed not the truth, but had pleasure in unrighteousness.* (KJV)

Who is he that now letteth? Now there are two schools of thought: one school of thought says that that person is the Holy Ghost that is here; the second school of thought is that that is the church that is here. So the church is preventing the devil from doing what he wants to do or the Holy Ghost is preventing it, it does not matter which one really because when the church is out of here so is the Holy Ghost. When the Holy Ghost is out of here so is the church, so it does not matter. When that takes place everybody that is left behind will have to deal with what happens on earth at that time. The first seal that was opened where power was given or conquering ability was given to conquer the earth and everybody that is in it. Remember this is all part of the judgment. This is the seven years, the last seven years of the judgment of Israel. Let's keep track of how many years have already passed, 483 years has already passed, they have already completed that part of the judgment. The next seven years has to be completed. Let us move a little further; because that finishes something that has to come. This is the last chance for Israel but some of Israel will actually go along with the Anti-Christ because they believe in the Anti-Christ because of the favor that he is going to show in the first year of that covenant that they will make together.

We really do need to watch when somebody is rubbing shoulders real close with Israel. We really do need to watch that; because we need to understand now who is this Anti-Christ. One of the ways we are going to be able to tell that we are actually getting near that period where Christ is going to crack the sky and going to call the church home, one of the things we need to watch is the returning of the Jews back to Israel. And can I help you to understand this is happening right now, they are re-gathering in Israel. Read, Revelation 6:3: *"And when he had opened the second seal, I heard the second beast say, Come and see. vs. 4: And there went out another horse that was red: and power was given to him that sat thereon to take peace from the earth…"* Wait. To take peace from the earth! This is very important for us to see because whatever peace is still left in the earth at that time and now remember we are still talking about the first three and one-half years of Great Tribulation. Great Tribulation is actually broken down into two halves, the first three and one-half years is when these horses are actually released. This horse is given the ability to take peace. There is going to be no peace on earth. Remember, 2 Thessalonians 2:7: *"For the mystery of iniquity doth already work: only he who now letteth will let, until he be taken out of the way."* When he is taken out of the way then there is a release of these horses -- horse #1 is sent to conquer the earth, horse #2 is sent to extract peace from the earth, there is going to be no peace on earth. If you are a believer you do not want to be here, so go out on the first Rapture.

Read, Revelation 6:4: *"and that they should kill one another…"* What you and I are actually seeing right now is really only a preview of what is going to happen; and please understand this, right now police are able to do something about lawlessness now but at that time when the spirit of lawlessness actually sets in, police are going to be trying to protect themselves. At that particular point everybody has got to protect their own back except for the ones that has received Christ and then you already know what your issue is going to be. Those that receive Christ and do not deny Him will be noticed and at that particular point when the Anti-Christ sees that you are not bowing then they want to behead you, except you that are reading this book and are in Christ now will not be here; right?

Let us go on, *"and there was given unto him a great sword. vs. 5: And when he had opened the third seal, I heard the third beast say, Come and see. And I beheld, and lo a black horse; and he that sat on him had a pair of balances in his hand. vs. 6: And I heard a voice in the midst of the four beasts say, A measure of wheat for a penny, and three measures of barley for a penny; and see thou hurt not the oil and the wine."* Is it not amazing that he said, "See that you do not hurt the oil; see that you do not hurt the wine." Read, verse 7: *"And when he had opened the fourth seal, I heard the voice of the fourth beast say, Come and see. vs. 8: And I looked, and behold a pale horse: and his name that sat on him was Death, and Hell followed with him. And power was given unto them over the fourth part of the earth, to kill with sword, and with hunger, and with death, and with the beasts of the earth."* Okay, let us go back over that. Now this particular horse that was released notice what happens – can you even imagine; you can not even imagine this – when this one is released literally millions upon millions of people are going to be wiped out. This one carries Death and Hell with him, and he is wiping out people. Power was given unto death and hell over the fourth part of the earth, to kill with sword, and with hunger… How are they dying: with sword, hunger and death. And so these are vehicles that they are going to be wiped out, and that is the reason it is going to happen so swiftly. Because remember, here is one of the things that we really have to understand about this is that when all of this is actually taking place they have to get multitudes of people off of the earth. Think about it this way, how many people AIDS has wiped out; just AIDS alone. With all of that it does not look like the earth has even been dented in its population. But at this particular time, Death is wiping people out through all of these vehicles, these three vehicles that were actually named, wiped out through those vehicles.

Let's go on to vs. 8: *"and with the beasts of the earth. vs. 9: And when he had opened the fifth seal, I saw under the altar the souls of them that were slain for the word of God…"* they were slain for what? The word of God! This is amazing, because you and I have the word of God also and a lot of our bibles just set on the shelf and collect dust. But what they had to do, the word of God was the only ticket in and they knew that this is the only way they can get in so they were holding on to the word for dear life. Remember there is no Holy Ghost here to bring this back to their remembrance, the only thing they have is their own memory. You and I probably take that for granted because when something comes back to our remembrance a lot of times we give our memory credit for that and your memory is not that sharp, that is the Holy Ghost. Think about it you have not read something for years nor have you seen it for years but all of a sudden when it is needed, it pop up right up on your brain.

They were slain for the word of God. Why, because they gathered together in huddles just to read the word, remember the Anti-Christ is doing everything that he is authorized to do at that particular time and he is not allowing too many bibles to be on the earth. Therefore everybody that has one at that time realize that this is the word of God, that Jesus Christ is the way, the truth, and the life and that no man comes to the Father but by him (John 14:6); by this time they actually know that. They are digging in the word with everything that they have but they have no Holy Ghost to give them understanding. They only have the chief evangelizers. It is at this particular point that the chief evangelizers are going throughout the earth and sharing the word and then everybody that receives Jesus at that particular time are holding on to Him because they know that the time is short. They already understand that it is only going to be seven years. Seven years does not seem that long but seven years when you are going through Great Tribulation seems like an eternity.

How To Make Sure That You Leave at the First Rapture

How can we make sure that we are not going to be here? There are many so I am not going to be able to give you all of them but I can give you some of them. Number 1, there are things that we have to let go. Because a lot of what we hold on to you can not get into heaven with that; some people are going to be left behind. One example is harboring unforgiveness toward people? You have to forgive people! You are not going to heaven with unforgiveness in your heart. Some of the people that we want to hold things against, you are not going to heaven with them. Let us run over to Proverbs; I want to show you something over there because see this is something that we really have to let go… Read, Proverbs 6:16: *"These six things doth the LORD hate: yea, seven are an abomination unto him:"*(KJV) Okay, now wait a minute, These six things doth the LORD hate: yea, seven are an abomination… so there are literally seven things I think that we might be able to say that can keep you out of heaven. Seven things that could very well keep you out of heaven: verse 17: A proud look… pride will keep you out. If that is your issue, get rid of it. Admit it, quit it, and get rid of it. If you have pride any levels of pride just go ahead and get rid of it. What is next? a lying tongue… you know some people just lie, I mean stand right in your face and just lie. I mean it does not even matter that you know that they are not telling the truth, they just lie. Some of you lie to yourself, I mean you have just got that good, you just lie to yourself. Read on, and hands that shed innocent blood… there are two different ways that you can shed blood: through talking about people and also through physically killing them. Both shed blood. Read, verse 18: An heart that deviseth wicked imaginations… a heart that divides. You conjure up wicked imaginations. So this is stuff that you have got to get out of you because six things that the Lord hate; He hates it. So now wait a minute, do you think you are going to get in heaven with stuff that He hate? I mean you got your pocket filled with stuff that God hate and you think you are coming in, no. Read on, feet that be swift in running to mischief… people that are swift in stirring up stuff. That will keep you out of heaven.

Now understand this, all that we have just finished talking about every bit of that will keep you out of heaven. None of these things are found in heaven so how can you go with it in you. If you are stirring up all kinds of trouble in the church, and stirring up all kinds of trouble at home, and stirring up all kinds of trouble on the job -- God says, *"You are in jeopardy of missing this first flight out, the first Rapture."* How can you be snatched out of the earth with things that God hates living in you, those things cannot exist in heaven, they can only exist on the earth. You are in jeopardy of missing this first flight out and you can not love mischief so much that you are willing to stay here and go through Great Tribulation. It is not worth it. See some people have been doing this so long it has become part of them and if that is true of anyone that means that every single time that they get the thought of doing this they actually have to fast and pray, turn over your plate, battle against your flesh and come up against this stuff. Read, verse 19: *A false witness that speaketh lies*… in other words, please understand this, God wants each and every one of us to be a witness. But some of us are being a false witness and we lie. God says, "I hate that. I hate false witnesses; no, do not be a false witness that speaks lies." One more: and he that soweth discord among brethren… You know that that right there uses some key words there. Notice, discord is something you sow and anything you sow, guess what happens – a harvest comes up.

You get a harvest on what you sow. But God hates that, he that soweth discord among brethren. If you are a believer this passage is talking about your sister and brothers in Christ. There are not sister-rends, there are only brethrens because there is no gender in Christ. God sees us as brethren; that means brothers and sisters in Christ. That is who we are and we are not to be sowing discord among the brethren because God hates it and people will end up in Great Tribulation that do things like that.

Chapter 13
GREAT TRIBULATION: WILL YOU BE LEFT?

*W*e need to find out some things so let's go into Chapter 9 and start reading from verse 1, Revelation 9:1-5: *"And the fifth angel sounded, and I saw a star fall from heaven unto the earth: and to him was given the key of the bottomless pit. And he opened the bottomless pit; and there arose a smoke out of the pit, as the smoke of a great furnace; and the sun and the air were darkened by reason of the smoke of the pit. And there came out of the smoke locusts upon the earth: and unto them was given power, as the scorpions of the earth have power. And it was commanded them that they should not hurt the grass of the earth, neither any green thing, neither any tree; but only those men which have not the seal of God in their foreheads. And to them it was given that they should not kill them, but that they should be tormented five months: and their torment was as the torment of a scorpion, when he striketh a man."* (KJV)

One of the key points that we need to remember regarding this was that there was no authority given to hurt anything until after the elect of God were sealed; those that had confessed, those that had made their commitment to God were then sealed, at that particular time. They were sealed and then there was a releasing of things that were going to hurt the people that were left, God released these angels to do whatever they were going to do in the earth. Also important for us to see is that a third of everything was actually being destroyed; a third of everything was being destroyed. Let's go just a little bit further in here. Verse 4: *"And it was commanded them that they should not hurt the grass of the earth, neither any green thing, neither any tree; but only those men which have not the seal of God in their foreheads."* Only those that did not have the seal were the ones that were not covered. Only the ones that did not have the seal of God in their foreheads were the ones that were not covered which mean that in this particular period, they then were wide open for the enemy to destroy. Now one of the things that we are going to actually see in this as we engage a little further in this particular chapter is the level of wickedness and the level of evil that actually came in the earth and that the people at that particular time embraced, it was so tremendous that there was no lifting up, regardless of what they saw that took place they still did not believe.

THE SEAL OF GOD

Here is one of the things we have to remember, there was no Holy Spirit there in the earth at that particular time to bring conviction. Selected people had the seal of God on them or on their foreheads and in addition to that there were also people that were inspired by the Holy Spirit those were the chief evangelizers. They were inspired by the Holy Spirit; they were led by the Holy Spirit but those that had already rejected Christ there was no Holy Spirit to bring them under conviction. It was just cut and dry – do you believe in Jesus? Those that are in the earth at that time are now depending on what they remembered before the church left, because their minds did work to their advantage before the church left; their memory of what was deposited about God did not work.

Their memory still has all of the information that was given them while the church was in the earth. All of that is still in their memory bank but there was no Holy Spirit to bring all things back to their remembrance, there is no Holy Spirit to show them things to come; and there is no Holy Spirit to do any of that because the church left the earth with the Holy Spirit. It actually gets better than this in verses 5 - 10: "*And to them it was given that they should not kill them, but that they should be tormented five months: and their torment was as the torment of a scorpion, when he striketh a man. And in those days shall men seek death, and shall not find it; and shall desire to die, and death shall flee from them. And the shapes of the locusts were like unto horses prepared unto battle; and on their heads were as it were crowns like gold, and their faces were as the faces of men. And they had hair as the hair of women, and their teeth were as the teeth of lions. And they had breastplates, as it were breastplates of iron; and the sound of their wings was as the sound of chariots of many horses running to battle. And they had tails like unto scorpions, and there were stings in their tails: and their power was to hurt men five months.*"

Their power was to actually hurt men five months. Now what we are actually seeing now is the reason that they were released in the earth. Remember this whole period is a Judgment period; and that is the thing that we don't want to forget. This whole period was a Judgment period but in addition to that this was God's mercy that was actually showing up in the earth to make sure that those that were willing to take this second chance would then be saved, they would be rapture out at this next Rapture. This is key for us to really understand. Read on, verses 11 - 15: "*And they had a king over them, which is the angel of the bottomless pit, whose name in the Hebrew tongue is Abaddon, but in the Greek tongue hath his name Apollyon. One woe is past; and, behold, there come two woes more hereafter. And the sixth angel sounded, and I heard a voice from the four horns of the golden altar which is before God, Saying to the sixth angel which had the trumpet, Loose the four angels which are bound in the great river Euphrates. And the four angels were loosed, which were prepared for an hour, and a day, and a month, and a year, for to slay the third part of men."* The third part of men, a third of all men at this particular point; remember what we talked about, from Thessalonians, that he that now letteth when he be taken out of the way then the wicked one comes. Now what we are actually seeing with our very own eyes are particular angels that were held back, that were actually held back so that they could not do what they were purposed to do. Read that part again so we can see them coming out the sea, verses 13 – 15: *"And the sixth angel sounded, and I heard a voice from the four horns of the golden altar which is before God, Saying to the sixth angel which had the trumpet, Loose the four angels which are bound in the great river Euphrates. And the four angels were loosed, which were prepared for an hour, and a day, and a month, and a year, for to slay the third part of men."* They were prepared to do this; in other words, not only did they have purpose to do this, they were actually prepared to wipe out a third of all men or mankind that were actually in the earth. Read on, verse 16: *"And the number of the army of the horsemen were two hundred thousand thousand: and I heard the number of them."* Now this is important for us to see, two hundred thousand thousand, of course we understand that is 200,000,000 (two hundred million). Okay so now we are talking about 200,000,000 people were wiped out. When we understand this then we understand what we are marching up to. These future events are document in the Bible because none of us in Christ that are reading this book want to be here when these things occur. One of the things that we need to understand is that during this battle period nothing really comes in just by surprise, all of this is building up to the next event.

THE RIVER OF BLOOD

One of the things that we need to remember is that later on we are going to see where blood was as high as the horse's bridle. In order to get that much blood there is going to have to be a lot of death. In other words, for those that are left on the earth this is what they are going to experience. Can you imagine trailing through so much blood that you can swim in it? This is the level of battle here. This tremendous number of people is literally being wiped out at this particular time and the blood is high as the horse's bridle. we are gong to see this, verses 17 - 20: *"And thus I saw the horses in the vision, and them that sat on them, having breastplates of fire, and of jacinth, and brimstone: and the heads of the horses were as the heads of lions; and out of their mouths issued fire and smoke and brimstone. By these three was the third part of men killed, by the fire, and by the smoke, and by the brimstone, which issued out of their mouths. For their power is in their mouth, and in their tails: for their tails were like unto serpents, and had heads, and with them they do hurt. And the rest of the men which were not killed by these plagues yet repented not of the works of their hands..."* Out of all of this, it is extremely important for us to understand that through all of this trouble, all that they had seen and all that had transpired these people still would not repent.

There was a development of a hardness of the heart on the inside of the people on the earth at that particular time. It is going to be difficult to repent in this time. In this particular time period repentance is not going to come easily. This is one of the reasons when we think about the ability that we actually have to get it right in our hearts right now, we want to do that quickly because it is only a matter of a decision right now. But at that time they have so much evil working against them that it will be really difficult to even pull it together. You will want to pull it together and won't be able to.

People that are born during this time period will actually see every bit of the things that are happening, they won't remember what has been preached, what has been taught, but they are going to have whatever material you see available right now, they will still have all of that there. With all of the materials available they will not turn their hearts to God. Remember at this particular point you are going to have a hundred and forty-four thousand people on the earth that are evangelizing the earth but none of them will be hurt because they have the seal of God in their foreheads, so these people are actually marked by God.

THE DIFFERENCE BETWEEN THE MARK OF THE BEAST AND THE MARK OF GOD

Now remember, there is a difference between the mark of the beast and the mark of God, they are two different things. So these men are actually sealed by God and so therefore the enemy could not touch them if they wanted to. What we actually see is the hardness of heart in these particular people, remember in previous Chapters we talked about Revelation chapters 1 and 2 and what we actually covered was the message that went out to the seven churches. After God had pleaded with the seven churches he said to them told them specifically what he had a challenge with or where their problems were, dealt with them specifically about those things and then after dealing with them about those things they had the opportunity to repent and one church he says well look you saw that incorrect teaching and you let her teach which you ought not to allow her to teach. Then, he said I gave her space to repent of her adultery and she repented not. Then right after that particular period the season changed, the whole dispensation changed which means that then Great Tribulation went in and grace was off of the earth. Now with grace off the earth and with Holy

Spirit off of the earth, everything that we have right now to enjoy was at that point off of the earth and none of that that was going to aid people in moving them toward salvation.

Let's go a bit further. Read, verse 20: *"And the rest of the men which were not killed by these plagues yet repented not of the works of their hands, that they should not worship devils, and idols of gold, and silver, and brass, and stone, and of wood: which neither can see, nor hear, nor walk: Neither repented they of their murders, nor of their sorceries, nor of their fornication, nor of their thefts."* Let's get this picture, this is real important. At this particular time, witchcraft, sorcery and all of that is going to be on the rise. And so what we are actually seeing right now today is only a preview of what we are going to see or what people are going to see, now of course we will be in heaven so we will get a birds eye view. But from where people are actually going to experience in the earth witchcraft and Satan worship will be on the increase. Serving God and worshipping God will be on the decrease. This is another reason you don't want to be here. Satan worship is going to be on the high. Now here is one of the things that I think will be good for us to understand that if we notice it is very important, we Christians almost have to apologize for everything we do and believe.

Right now, you can't read your bible in a lot of government places; you can't pray in school, we can't say the name of Jesus or talk about Jesus but other religions can say the name of their gods with no problem. Nobody will bother you when you talk about people like Buddha, you can't do many of the things those other religions are free to do. We cannot teach Jesus in the school systems but we can teach about all of the others. Now we are faced with homosexuality being on the increase and same sex marriages and different things like that. You almost have to be blind not to see where this whole system is going. Now watch this now, so the whole system is actually going in this direction now, can you imagine what it is going to be like at that particular time? Satan worship is going to be on an increase and Satan worship is going to be common. It is going to be a common practice. It just going to be common to bow down and worship Satan, remember that was his major objective with Adam, and when he was confronted with Jesus in the wilderness that was his major objective. Why? To move Adam and Jesus to a place where there would be Satan worship.

If we look at some of the images today we are also going to see that there is that the whole system is getting set up for this. The wearing of these skulls, you see those, right? The skeletons on people's clothes, all of this is a preview to get people ready and accustomed to these things. For instance, what we call the little peace sign, you know that little three little fingers that are pointing down with one arrow pointing up which is a symbol of the antichrist; are you understanding that? People wear this kind of stuff and then wonder why they actually attract demonic influences? All of these things actually attracts that whole demonic picture, all of these items attracts demonic influences and that is why we don't understand that everything is moving in that direction preparing people to accept the symbolism so that it will not seem so bad when we have to deal with the real thing. Why? So that Satan worship will be on the increase. Halloween, different things like this, all of this is moving you toward a place where it is common to worship Satan. And we talked about Halloween, really just a day that was actually set up to counteract the day prior to that which was All Saints Day, All Saints Eve and so now understand this now, then Satan has to set up a day just one day after that to utilize that day as a day where he would be worshipped. One day we will go into all of that what the jack-o'-lantern mean and where it originated and all of that and necromancers and all of those kinds of things but every bit of it is actually Satan worship and these are things that we really need to understand because all of this is really just setting the stage for that which is to come.

Now, as we practice these things, you can run a test on this to see how this actually causes a persons heart to become hard in these particular areas. Run a test on this when you see someone, make sure you know them, that actually wears these different symbols watch and see how attached they are to them and watch to see the rejection that you experience when you begin to tell them how demonic it really is. If you can imagine right now the level that you are experiencing that right now and then imagine that 100 times worse in the time of Great Tribulation when Satanism and Satan worship is on an increase then you are going to have just like today you have a majority of people that surround our lives that somehow knows about God and somehow are in relationship to God. In that particular day, it is going to be just the opposite, everywhere you go somebody is going to be in relationship with the devil; why, because he would be the dominant factor in that particular day.

Let's go onto the next chapter. Let's check out the opening of the little book, Chapter 10:1 – 11: *"And I saw another mighty angel come down from heaven, clothed with a cloud: and a rainbow was upon his head, and his face was as it were the sun, and his feet as pillars of fire: And he had in his hand a little book open: and he set his right foot upon the sea, and his left foot on the earth, And cried with a loud voice, as when a lion roareth: and when he had cried, seven thunders uttered their voices. And when the seven thunders had uttered their voices, I was about to write: and I heard a voice from heaven saying unto me, Seal up those things which the seven thunders uttered, and write them not. And the angel which I saw stand upon the sea and upon the earth lifted up his hand to heaven, And sware by him that liveth for ever and ever, who created heaven, and the things that therein are, and the earth, and the things that therein are, and the sea, and the things which are therein, that there should be time no longer: But in the days of the voice of the seventh angel, when he shall begin to sound, the mystery of God should be finished, as he hath declared to his servants the prophets.*

And the voice which I heard from heaven spake unto me again, and said, Go and take the little book which is open in the hand of the angel which standeth upon the sea and upon the earth. And I went unto the angel, and said unto him, Give me the little book. And he said unto me, Take it, and eat it up; and it shall make thy belly bitter, but it shall be in thy mouth sweet as honey. And I took the little book out of the angel's hand, and ate it up; and it was in my mouth sweet as honey: and as soon as I had eaten it, my belly was bitter. And he said unto me, Thou must prophesy again before many peoples, and nations, and tongues, and kings." (KJV) Let's talk about all of that. Now here we are entering another period because now remember during every shift there is always the release of a prophetic voice. Through every shift there is always the release of another prophetic voice. Now in this particular period, what we are actually going to see is a shift where time will be no more and what we are dealing with is the fact that they are out of time. Now at the end of this particular period right here, he is saying to John, okay here is what you are going to have to do. You are going to have to prophesy now. You are going to have to prophesy but now understand this, this particular period he was urged to not only take the book but eat it all. In other words, eat the whole roll at this particular point; eat the entire roll, why, because now this person is now going to have to speak prophetically to a nation of people who already have not heard God.

So they heard him speak, they heard his words but they did not yield to the voice of God and so now, there is going to be the release of a prophetic voice in order to close out another period. This prophet now is going to begin to speak and we are getting ready to be introduced to two prophetic witnesses each with a prophetic voice in this particular time period that is going to introduce miracles, signs and wonders that are from God. Remember the next thing that must be seen is a witness from God that these voices are undoubtedly the voice of God.

When we enter this next period in Revelation chapter 11, we are going to see the release of a prophetic voice; we also are going to see two prophetic witnesses that are going to rise up. And now this is the thing that will get you, after all that you have already heard, after all that you have already seen, now two prophets show up in the midst of all of this. Now after they have already seen lying wonders and after they have already seen the hand of the devil move, they have already seen the release of the angels, they have already seen a third of all of men wiped out, they have already seen famine, they have seen a third of all of the vegetation, sea and everything else totally wiped out; now two prophets show up. And these two prophets are going to show up with the power of God on their life and they must show up with signs and wonders. Not signs and lying wonders but this time these two need to show up with signs and wonders.

Let's take a look at that, Revelation chapter 11:1 – 4: "*And there was given me a reed like unto a rod: and the angel stood, saying, Rise, and measure the temple of God, and the altar, and them that worship therein. But the court which is without the temple leave out, and measure it not; for it is given unto the Gentiles: and the holy city shall they tread under foot forty and two months. And I will give power unto my two witnesses, and they shall prophesy a thousand two hundred and threescore days, clothed in sackcloth. These are the two olive trees, and the two candlesticks standing before the God of the earth."* We better take this a little slower. These two prophets that showed up at this particular time are recognized as God's witnesses that will come in the earth. And this is actually the period of what is going be introduced and called Satan's Christmas. It is going to appear to be Satan's Christmas because these are the last two witnesses that are going to appear as if he is now defeated God himself. Now, he did not defeat Jesus and now at this particular period he is going to need to defeat somebody that God sent. These are the two witnesses that he understands that are definitely from God.

There are two schools of thought about who these witnesses are: one school of thought says that these two are Elijah and Enoch, the reason is because they are the only two that did not have a natural death and so now Enoch walked with God until he was not; Elijah went up in a whirlwind, so they were the only two in the Old Testament that did not have a death; now the second school of thought is that this is Elijah and Moses. We don't really want to debate about whom we think they are because the bible really doesn't say and so therefore all of this is really just going to be speculation. But there is a reason and I don't even debate that; and one of the reasons that I don't is because it could be either or. Because now in Matt 17:2-3 *And was transfigured before them: and his face did shine as the sun, and his raiment was white as the light. 3 And, behold, there appeared unto them Moses and Elias talking with him.* (KJV), we find that when Jesus was transfigured who showed up? Elijah and Moses, so, they were the two that actually showed up at that particular time and during the period of Transfiguration. Now then it could be Elijah 2 Kings 2:11 *And it came to pass, as they still went on, and talked, that, behold, there appeared a chariot of fire, and horses of fire, and parted them both asunder; and Elijah went up by a whirlwind into heaven.* (KJV) and Enoch Gen 5:24 *And Enoch walked with God: and he was not; for God took him.* (KJV) because those are the only two in the bible that did not have natural death, bible says, it is appointed unto man once to die; so everybody has to have a death. But I don't want to focus on that part, I want to focus on the part that they are witnesses; that they are witnesses regardless of which two it is they are witnesses that are now going to present one of the last manifestations on the earth that actually comes from God.

THE TWO WITNESSES OF THE GREAT TRIBULATION

Remember this period is still Great Tribulation and this is still the first half of the Tribulation. Now in the second half of the Tribulation things just go crazy. The second half of the Great Tribulation is a period within itself because then we are talking about the battle of Armageddon and where it actually took place, how it took place, and all of the people that were slain in that particular time period and then Jesus comes back on the earth with what I call His "Triumphal Entry". When He comes back in He settles the score once and for all in direct opposition against the enemy. Now let's go back to Revelation chapter 11 verses 3 - 5: *"And I will give power unto my two witnesses, and they shall prophesy a thousand two hundred and threescore days, clothed in sackcloth. These are the two olive trees, and the two candlesticks standing before the God of the earth. And if any man will hurt them, fire proceedeth out of their mouth, and devoureth their enemies…"* these are literally going to be some awesome witnesses. We are talking about witnesses that show up with evidence; that is what you are going to be looking at with these two prophets.

These two witnesses are people that when you hurt them, fire comes out of their mouth. In other words, words comes out of their mouth that devours and so they can not be hurt by the power of the enemy, but that is the reason it is going to seem like Satan's Christmas because when they finish their assignment then Satan will be able to kill them, so he thinks, notice in this passage what happens Rev 11:7-12 *And when they shall have finished their testimony, the beast that ascendeth out of the bottomless pit shall make war against them, and shall overcome them, and kill them. 8 And their dead bodies shall lie in the street of the great city, which spiritually is called Sodom and Egypt, where also our Lord was crucified. 9 And they of the people and kindreds and tongues and nations shall see their dead bodies three days and an half, and shall not suffer their dead bodies to be put in graves. 10 And they that dwell upon the earth shall rejoice over them, and make merry, and shall send gifts one to another; because these two prophets tormented them that dwelt on the earth. 11 And after three days and an half the Spirit of life from God entered into them, and they stood upon their feet; and great fear fell upon them which saw them. 12 And they heard a great voice from heaven saying unto them, Come up hither. And they ascended up to heaven in a cloud; and their enemies beheld them.* (KJV)

But he cannot really hurt them; after they are killed they are going lay on the earth for three days and have a resurrection just like Jesus did. Let's go back to verses 5 - 7: *"And if any man will hurt them, fire proceedeth out of their mouth, and devoureth their enemies: and if any man will hurt them, he must in this manner be killed. These have power to shut heaven, that it rain not in the days of their prophecy: and have power over waters to turn them to blood, and to smite the earth with all plagues, as often as they will. And when they shall have finished their testimony, the beast that ascendeth out of the bottomless pit shall make war against them, and shall overcome them, and kill them."* This where it gets real good because remember these witnesses are from God. Through this whole period, anybody that hurts them, fire comes out of their mouth. They get devoured, they must die; why, because they have touched God's anointed. This is where this whole portrait of what is happening during this time of the Great Tribulation comes to light. We actually see in this our grace dispensation because we have witnesses that are prophets and when someone touches one of these prophets in this our hour today, they get the same penalties, but they come in process of time because at this time you are dealing with the Grace Dispensation where they have time to repent.

You have to realize that the only people that are trying to touch these prophets are the people that come straight from the spirit of the enemy, himself. So remember, it is the spirit according to Ephesians, it is the spirit that works in the children of disobedience. Go back, read that one part again, verse 7: "*And when they shall have finished their testimony, the beast that ascendeth out of the bottomless pit shall make war against them…,*" the beast comes out of the bottomless pit, makes war against these two witnesses, why, because these two witnesses are a threat to him; out of all that he stirred up all of this time he now has someone that is really a threat to him because now remember, the hundred and forty-four thousand chief evangelizers are really not that much of a threat to him; on one hand they are because they are bringing people to Christ but on the other hand they are not because they are not ones that are actually doing signs and wonders. The chief evangelizers are getting the message out that Jesus Christ really is Lord. Now what shows up is a manifestation of what the hundred forty-four thousand chief evangelizers were actually proclaiming. These two witnesses are the manifestation of the fact that Jesus Christ is Lord. They show up with power; now remember it says in verse 3: "*I will give power unto my two witnesses…*" they are going to show up with dunamis (power) but they are also going to show up with exousia (authority power). So, they show up with power, show up with ability and they literally do some of the signs and wonders that we have been wanting to see in our day.

Chapter 14
THE REALITY OF HEAVEN

The bible says, "*In a moment, in the twinkling of an eye, at the last trump: for the trumpet shall sound…*" (1 Corinthians 15:52 KJV), it is going to be that quick. When the church, those that are saved are called out of the earth there is not going to be any time at all to repent, none. That is the reason this is the time period where we have the opportunity to repent. This is the time that we live the best life that we can possibly live for the glory of God. That is what we do right now today. Let's us assume that you die before the Great Snatch (the rapture of the church); there will be some people that will be left behind and now they want to pray. It will be too late to pray at that particular time because just as fast as the church was snatched out that is how fast Great Tribulation comes in.

And now understand this, you know after the Snatch there is no way to get out. I know that some people would rather talk about heaven than hell but we must understand that both exist. Now, we want talk to about the reality of heaven and as we talk about the reality of heaven I realized that in the chapter on the reality of hell I gave you only certain compartments of hell and all of this is biblically based. We shared in that chapter "The Reality of Hell", the different compartments of hell and all of that biblically based also; remember in Luke 16 that we covered the rich man and Lazarus and how the rich man and Lazarus died right around the same time and Lazarus lifted up his eyes in a place called Paradise. He lifted up his eyes, he was in Paradise that is a compartment of hell but it was a compartment of hell that did not experience the suffering; that did not experience any of the bad things that were on the other side. But when the rich man lifted up his eyes he found himself in hell in torment and he was in a place classified as the Bottomless Pit. And so now understand this, he was in a place where he was now going to experience the pain, the pressure, the burning and he was not going to be lifted out of that situation. Once he realized that he said some things probably some things that we would have said, because now he wanted to see his loved ones saved now that he was in hell and hell was a reality to him. We need to understand because there is not going to be any coming back to give a warning to your loved ones.

Do Love Ones Come Back To Visit After Death?

Any of you that have an Aunt Lucy or Uncle Sam, somebody that tries to come back and give you warnings--please know that it is not from God because once your relatives are gone that is it. I have proof right here in the bible. They are gone, they do not come back. And if somebody does come back believe me it is not her or him. I really want to deal with this very, very seriously because see some people really do believe that their love one came back and visited them. They believe that because it is so real; but now the devil will use any thing, any trick; anything to get to you because you are still here. He wants to really get to you but now he needs to use somebody; so what better person to use than Uncle Sam whom you really did love or Aunt Lucy whom you really did love, who could show up greater in your night hour to visit you and to be very persuasive. What that does is gets you so familiar with the underworld that you would want to go there. In Luke 16:23-24 "*And in hell he lift up his eyes, being in torments, and seeth Abraham afar off, and Lazarus in his bosom. 24: And he cried and said, Father Abraham, have mercy on me, and send Lazarus, that he may dip the tip of his finger in water, and cool my tongue; for I am tormented in this flame.*" (KJV)

Come on understand this, there was a real flame. Now we have to understand this, consider the things that we are engaging in this particular time and determine are they really worth that. Is it really worth going through that kind of torment, that kind of flame where the worm dies not, where it is just never ending. In verse 25: "*But Abraham said, Son, remember…*" who was he, he was a son. He was a son; he was not some person that was unsaved. Notice, Hosea 4:6 says this: "*My people are destroyed for lack of knowledge…*" Whose people, God's people are destroyed for the lack of knowledge and so now Luke 16:25 says, "*But Abraham said, Son, remember that thou in thy lifetime receivedst thy good things, and likewise Lazarus evil things: but now he is comforted, and thou art tormented. Verse 26: And beside all this, between us and you there is a great gulf fixed: so that they which would pass from hence to you cannot; neither can they pass to us, that would come from thence.*" (KJV) Abraham and all of those in Paradise have the love of God in their heart, if they could have passed from where they were to go on the other side just to give him some water they would have. But God made sure that there was a great distance that could not be accessed so that one side could not be accessed by the other. He made sure it was that way because He knew that we as his people have compassion. Luke 16:27: "*Then he said, I pray thee therefore, father, that thou wouldest send him to my father's house…*" Why, because they know that Lazarus died. Verse 28: "*For I have five brethren; that he may testify unto them, lest they also come into this place of torment, verse 29: Abraham saith unto him, They have Moses and the prophets; let them hear them."* (KJV) Who did he say – Moses and the prophets—all of them are dead; which means that their writings, only their writings are left behind. And so what he is literally saying is they have the writings of Moses and they have the writings of the prophets, let them get the writings because that is God's process.

If you do not get it the way God is delivering it right now, if Jesus comes back, this is still going to be the way that you are going to get it. You know, if Jesus comes back before you die, this is still the way you are going to get it. If you die before He comes back, it is too late. It may be too late for you if you wait.

What Happens When People Go To Hell – Where Do They Go?

What happens, where does a person actually go when once they actually go to hell? Let us take a look at this now. We talked about Tartarus; Tartarus was the prison for fallen angels. So every angel that fell right along with Lucifer, they are in Tartarus, the prison of fallen angels. Then there is another compartment of hell called Abaddon. The Bottomless Pit and now all of this is classified as the underworld. Every bit of this is classified as the underworld. So now understand this, the underworld is just as real as the heaven. Heaven is just as real as this earth. The only thing is that, in all 3 places you use something else to exist. Here on earth we can not exist without this physical body, this, what we have right now is called the earth suit. Your earth suit is the way you communicate with the earth, that communication is done through our five senses (sight, touch, smell, hearing and taste). When a person actually dies they take the earth suit off and the real person comes to the surface. Their spirit and their soul, it either goes to heaven or it goes to hell. Now there is also a place called Hades. Hades is the place of the grave where the body actually lays. And now understand this, Jehovah Witnesses believe that you go into Hades or you go into the grave and that is it. Well, they are going to have a rude awakening and some of them have already had a rude awakening because life goes on after the grave. But now the bible actually clearly indicates in Luke 16, that there is more after death. After you lay the body down there is more.

Remember, we are talking about the reality of heaven; I want to make sure that we are actually seeing ourselves in heaven and what actually takes place there. You as a person you are made of body, soul and spirit. When you shed off your body and your spirit and your soul goes to heaven or it goes to hell whichever place you chose. If you say well I do not want to go to hell, then you have to align yourself with the rules of going to heaven now. What happens to your body then? Your body is just still laying here at the funeral altar and we get to walk by your body and we get to see you as we remember you; why, because we are on earth, we remember you according to your state of being on earth. According to what you looked like on the earth, that is how we see you. In 1 Corinthians, Chapter 15, we can actually see what takes place. Now your spirit and your soul will experience either the joy of being in heaven or the pain of being in hell. But something happens to your body in this particular point. When you move from this earth your body goes into the grave or into Hades; when you go into that particular place and your body is just lying there. When they put you six feet under your body is lying in the place of the grave. But now when the Rapture comes what is literally going to happen is mentioned here *"In a moment, in the twinkling of an eye, at the last trump: for the trumpet shall sound and the dead shall be raised…"* (1 Corinthians 15:52 (KJV) -- what is going to happen at that particular point is that your spirit man, your spirit and your soul, is going to meet up with your body. It does not matter where you body is, it will meet up with your spirit man and your soul, whether your body is in the sea, whether your body is in the grave; wherever your body is your body just starts to meet up with you again because now remember it is still your body. That body still has your name on it. And so when your spirit and your soul meet your body again, what is literally going to happen, everything is going to come together but it will come back in a glorified way.

WHAT HAPPENS TO YOUR PHYSICAL BODY WHEN YOU DIE?

Remember when Jesus was raised from the dead He received a glorified body; but He still had the same body, he did not get a new body. This means that you have to watch what you do to your body because if you have messed it up by piercing here and putting big old circles in your ear and all of that, please understand it is going to be glorified that way. If you die you still have that big piercing in your tongue, that hole is still going to be in your tongue. I apologize I really do, I am not trying to be insensitive but you know what, I do not know what you put down to donate when you went there to get your license, I do not know what you put down but I am not donating anything. I am going to need my body when I come back. I believe that, I really do believe this; it is not going to grow back. If you take an alternator off your car and Jesus comes back, it is still going to be an alternator off of your car. That is me, it does not have to be you; you can operate with one kidney. Do not be donating with somebody, they are easy. I rather lay hands on somebody and get them healed and keep both of mine. If none of the body parts grow back you will need all of the body that you already have. The body is not going to be changed in terms of things growing back; the texture of it changes. It goes from corruptible to incorruptible; it goes from mortal to immortal we find that in 1 Cor 15:50-54 *50 Now this I say, brethren, that flesh and blood cannot inherit the kingdom of God; neither doth corruption inherit incorruption. 51 Behold, I shew you a mystery; We shall not all sleep, but we shall all be changed, 52 In a moment, in the twinkling of an eye, at the last trump: for the trumpet shall sound, and the dead shall be raised incorruptible, and we shall be changed. 53 For this corruptible must put on incorruption, and this mortal must put on immortality. 54 So when this corruptible shall have put on incorruption, and this mortal shall have put on immortality, then shall be brought to pass the saying that is written, Death is swallowed up in victory.* (KJV) the texture of it changes but the body itself does not change. You may be one that say "I do not believe that." Well let us see what happened to Jesus' body; was the hole still in His hand? Yes. He was operating off of a glorified body the hole was still in His hand that was proof that He went through that. So you put a hole in your body, it is still going to be there. You must take care of that body; you do not get another one. In Chapter 15 of 1 Corinthians, let us start at verse 50: *"Now this I say, brethren, that flesh and blood cannot inherit the kingdom of God; neither doth corruption inherit incorruption. verse 51: Behold, I shew you a mystery; We shall not all sleep, but we shall all be changed..."* We shall not all sleep, in other words we shall not all die but we shall all be changed; so every last one of us will have a glorified body. If you leave during the Great Snatch and you are snatched out of the earth while you are on your way up you are becoming glorified. But if your body lays in the earth, guess what, when it is snatched up out of here, out of that grave by the time you hook up with your spirit and your soul, that body will be glorified.

Go with me to 2 Cor 12:2-4 *2 I knew a man in Christ above fourteen years ago, (whether in the body, I cannot tell; or whether out of the body, I cannot tell: God knoweth;) such an one caught up to the third heaven. 3 And I knew such a man, (whether in the body, or out of the body, I cannot tell: God knoweth;) 4 How that he was caught up into paradise, and heard unspeakable words, which it is not lawful for a man to utter.* (KJV) Paul is caught up to the third heaven; Paul is saying I knew him, I knew that guy and when God took me to heaven I saw a person that I knew. I just could not tell whether he was in his body or out of his body. Do you realize that when you come out of that body, you are going to look like you? You are not going to look like Casper the friendly ghost I guarantee you. You are not going to look like anybody on ghost chasers, ghost busters; you are not going to look like that, you are going to look like you. So Paul says, "whether in the body... or... out of the body I cannot tell;" guess what if you go to hell you are going to look like you. This is exciting, Paul says, *"I cannot tell whether he was in the body or whether he was out of the body;"* is not that exciting? But God knows whether he was in the body or out of the body. Then he says, "such an one caught up to the third heaven." He is caught up where, to the third heaven; so if there is a third heaven that means that there is a second heaven and there is a first heaven. The first heaven is the one we see, the second one is where Satan lives, when he was with God he was in the third heaven and he did not do what he was supposed to do, therefore he was cast out of the third heaven and he was cast into the second heaven.

But then when Great Tribulation sets in, he is going to fall on the earth; where he is going to walk to and fro through the earth seeking whom he may devour. So if you are left here one of the people that you are going to rub shoulders with all of the time is Satan, himself, and there will be no God to stop him from doing what he wants to do to you. After that, during the millennial reign of Christ, he goes into the bottomless pit to be locked up for a thousand years.

Paul went beyond that place; Paul went to the third heaven and operating in the third heaven, while there he started to see people that he recognized; and so you will be recognized even though you are in heaven you will be recognized, you just will not be able to tell whether you are in the body or out of the body. Remember, we are talking about heaven and heaven is a real place and I hope to see you there because I am going to be there.

Let us look at Ephesians 1, starting with verse 15: *"Wherefore I also, after I heard of your faith in the Lord Jesus, and love unto all the saints, verse 16: Cease not to give thanks for you, making mention of you in my prayers; verse 17: That the God of our Lord Jesus Christ, the Father of glory, may give unto you the spirit of wisdom and revelation in the knowledge of him: verse 18: The eyes of your understanding being enlightened; that ye may know what is the hope of his calling, and what the riches of the glory of his inheritance in the saints, verse 19: And what is the exceeding greatness of his power to us-ward who believe, according to the working of his mighty power, verse 20: Which he wrought in Christ, when he raised him from the dead, and set him (where) at his own right hand (where) in the heavenly places, verse 21: Far above all principality, and power, and might, and dominion, and every name that is named..."*
(KJV) When you go to heaven you are far beyond any dominion, of any kind of a power. I really need you to see this you are far beyond any kind of power, any kind of evil power. If a person dies today they go to heaven, they surpass the first and the second heaven, they go to the third heaven if Great Tribulation has not happened yet; all of this the power, might, dominion, all of that operates here will not affect your travel. Understand this, right now if you are saved and you know that you are saved, let me help you out with this, you are saved from the power of sin, you are saved also from the penalty of sin. But you are not yet are not saved from the presence of sin and Satan can tempt you anytime he gets ready in certain areas according to the season he can tempt you in particular areas. But if you die tomorrow and you went to heaven (I believe God has given you long life) you go way pass principalities and powers because they do not exist in the third heaven; guess what, in the third heaven you are saved from the presence of sin; so not even the presence of sin has the ability to penetrate the third heaven. That is good news.

Maybe you do not try to imagine this but I try to imagine waking around and not ever being tempted, or having temptation around at all. Now what does that time look like; I really would like to know. You have got to understand this you have got to stay saved, remember, your salvation is a finished work, it is guaranteed, God will never leave you, but you can choose to leave Him. If you do not stay saved, this satanic power will have dominion over you while you are on earth. This demonic power will have dominion over you in any area, if you come out of the presence of God. We have to make sure that we stay in His presence; we walk under the shadow of His wing.

If Your Are Saved - There Is A Meeting In Heaven About You

Let us go to Job and take a look at a meeting that took place in heaven. I have got to show you that part in the word of God because meetings took place in heaven. Let me just take you right there, Job 1:6: *"Now there was a day when the sons of God..."* (KJV) Any time you see that word "sons of God" plural under the old covenant, it is really talking about the angels of God. "Now there was a day..." so there are days that angels get together with God to meet about you or me. When that meeting is about me I want it to be a favorable meeting; I want that meeting to go my way. Verse 6: *"Now there was a day when the sons of God came to present themselves before the LORD, and Satan came also among them."* Now here is what we have to understand because this meeting came into being called and Satan came also, remember he does not have access to the third heaven, therefore this was not a third heaven meeting, it was a second heaven meeting. See all of the angels that are in the earth, all of the angels that are in the heavens, all of the angels that are in the third heaven they all meet at a certain period of time in the second heaven. And Satan came also, he came to the meeting. Why would Satan be able to come to a meeting about you? God is God, you are here on the earth but you do represent God, so why would Satan have the ability to come into that meeting about you; see he knows when all of the angels are going to meet up with God, so he goes into that meeting about you. You want proof, let me show you. Job 1:6: *"Now there was a day when the sons of God came to present themselves before the LORD, and Satan came also among them."* Where? Among them. Verse 7: *"And the LORD said unto Satan, Whence comest thou?"* What are you doing here? Go to the book of Revelation and I will show you what he was doing there.

Satan was the accuser of the brethren, we find that in Revelation 12:10, read: *"And I heard a loud voice saying in heaven, Now is come salvation, and strength, and the kingdom of our God, and the power of his Christ: for the accuser of our brethren is cast down, which accused them before our God day and night."* (KJV) When did he have time to accuse in this particular period? He did it day and night or whenever the meeting was held? So he came into the meeting to accuse you before God, why, because he can not get to you except he can prove that he has rights. Go back to Job 1 to verse 7: *"And the LORD said unto Satan, Whence comest thou? Then Satan answered the LORD, and said, From going to and fro (what does to and fro mean: back and forward) in the earth, and from walking up and down in it."* (KJV) What does up and down mean: He was walking up and down from heaven to earth seeking whom he may devour. Peter talks to us about that in 1 Peter 5:8 *Be sober, be vigilant; because your adversary the devil, as a roaring lion, walketh about, seeking whom he may devour:* (KJV) Devour means to gulp entirely or to swallow. The devil is getting different looks at you to see whether or not he has rights. Look we really do think that we are getting away with sin but the bible says your sin will find you out.

Satan is walking to and fro through the earth; he is walking up and down in it, "let me see if I can say this to you better. This is what Satan says "Yeah, I think I can see you better from this standpoint." So now watch this that is what Satan does -- he goes up and "see if I can see you better; let me see if I can see through your window, see if that is your wife or your husband up in there." The very second that he catches you wrong, he rushes into the presence of God, waits for that meeting and says, "I caught them. I got them on video." And so Satan goes up and takes another look -- are you back in verse 7: "*And the LORD said unto Satan, Whence comest thou? Then Satan answered the LORD, and said, From going to and fro in the earth, and from walking up and down in it.* verse 8: *And the LORD said unto Satan, Hast thou considered my servant Job...*" God read the mind of Satan on why he was really there. God read his mind said, "Oh you are after Job, are you not? You do not see a way that you can get Job, do you? And so now watch this he does not see a way that he can get to you until after you step outside of how God operates. He does not even know that you are not God except by the way you operate; if you operate outside of God then he knows that it is not God. He does not know if you are male or female. Satan wants to know if you look anything like God, well, Satan sees an image and when he looks at the image he looks at you he says, "that is God" until you open your big mouth and you say something different than what God says. When you open your mouth and you say something different then what God says, he says, "that is not God; that is somebody that looks like God but it is not God." Therefore, we have to just keep saying what the word says. As long as you are saying what the word says he can not tell it is not God. He can not tell Father from Jesus, from the Holy Ghost, from you. He just can not tell. And when he catches you wrong he knows that he has rights, for instance, he knows that God is not down at the club, dancing, drinking and having a good time. He knows that God did not just tell that lie, you must understand this because I am telling you that there is a meeting that will take place in heaven and that meeting is all about you. Why, because he is the accuser of the brethren. Have you ever had anybody to accuse you of something? Does it feel horrible? Well Satan does that but he does it where it counts.

You and I may accuse somebody to a person that does not even matter, just anybody that will listen; Satan goes right into the presence of God because he wants to wipe you out. See Satan wants to completely and totally wipe you out; he wants that opportunity. You know what, God spoke this to me this morning: "Anything you hang a name on you have to prove that name", how many of you have named something and you reading this book believe that you got that name from God? You named something -- a child, church, a ministry, a business, or even you, if you put a name on anything, do you realize that God says that "when you name something you have to prove that name." Why, because now Satan has a right to challenge you on that name; he has right. So he goes to heaven and attends a meeting with God about you and say: "hey God, uh huh, so and so called their business this; so and so called their church this; so and so called this that; so and so called themselves a prophet." Satan does knows that he has rights to come and challenge you in that area.

God's Protective Hedge

God has a hedge around you every step you make, you can be sure that the hedge is around you no matter what you do, that hedge just never leaves you; no matter where you go that hedge is still on you, note that in Job 1:10 10 *Hast not thou made an hedge about him, and about his house, and about all that he hath on every side? thou hast blessed the work of his hands, and his substance is increased in the land.* (KJV) You shift that weight and that hedge is still on you; but now watch this, the very second that you do something different than representing that name (Jesus), the hedge says, "Warp;" you are no longer hedged in. And Job says it this way, "I was not in safety, yet trouble came. Job 3:25-26 *For the thing which I greatly feared is come upon me, and that which I was afraid of is come unto me. 26 I was not in safety, neither had I rest, neither was I quiet; yet trouble came.* (KJV)" The trouble really gets to you because you have not been hedged in, in that area or you have been tried for a space of time in that area. Why, because of name you hung on it or on yourself. Every name needs to gain a testimony. You know what, I think one of the worst things in the world that we can ever do is rename something to get out of the pressure of it. Do you understand what I mean? So in other words, you have a business and you rename it because you are under so much pressure under that business. That is the worst thing that we can do; you know why because we have never proved that name. We have to prove the things that we name in the second heaven also; we have to prove our God is God.

Heaven is a real place, your victory is there. Every victory that we need is all aligned in heaven. One example is that of people marrying people without finding out their purpose and destiny on the earth. You married that person without finding out what their destiny was going to be. This is very important because this person that you met, this person that you married; guess what, that name is heard in the second heaven. You might not be known on earth but guess where you are known in the second heaven and if you have named Christ out loud guess what, you are known in third heaven. So angels are ringing out your name up in the second heaven and third heaven you name is being sounded out. Glory to God, are you ready for something else, okay, you have a business and out of that business your giving has gone up before God. God announces the name of your business in heaven because that is part of your name. And Satan hears your name because remember there is a meeting going on and so in order for the angels to really get to you what you really need in the earth is a meeting that takes place in heaven on your business, on your church, your ministry, you, your family, whatever have a name. And you are wondering why you are tried; and you are wondering why is it that you are going through. You know why, because right here in the second heaven Satan is saying to his demons, "We have got to take them out because if we do not take them out they are going to be a testimony in the earth." And so what has to literally take place, you have got to endure your season. Job was tried but it was only for a season, we have already talked about that, Jesus was tried for a season. Once God announced that that He was His son in Matt 3:17 *And lo a voice from heaven, saying, This is my beloved Son, in whom I am well pleased.* (KJV) that had to be proven and Jesus was tested on that immediately in Matt 4:1-11 *Then was Jesus led up of the Spirit into the wilderness to be tempted of the devil. 2 And when he had fasted forty days and forty nights, he was afterward an hungred. 3 And when the tempter came to him, he said, If thou be the Son of God, command that these stones be made bread. 4 But he answered and said, It is written, Man shall not live by bread alone, but by every word that proceedeth out of the mouth of God. 5 Then the devil taketh him up into the holy city, and setteth him on a pinnacle of the temple, 6 And saith unto him, If thou be the Son of God, cast thyself down: for it is written, He shall give his angels charge concerning thee: and in their hands they shall bear thee up, lest at any time thou dash thy foot against a stone. 7 Jesus said unto him, It is written again, Thou shalt not tempt the Lord thy God. 8 Again, the devil taketh him up into an exceeding high mountain, and sheweth him all the kingdoms of the world, and the glory of them; 9 And saith unto him, All these things will I give thee, if thou wilt fall down and worship me. 10 Then saith Jesus unto him, Get thee hence, Satan: for it is written, Thou shalt worship the Lord thy God, and him only shalt thou serve. 11 Then the devil leaveth him, and, behold, angels came and ministered unto him.* (KJV) but after that season, the devil had to leave because he can only try you a season.

Giving Up Is Not An Option

Most of us give up on the brink of our miracle, the brink of our breakthrough but we give up and we say to God, "I am tired and can not do this any more". We are right on the brink of that miracle, right on the brink of what God is about to do for us most of us quit, most of us do, it is not just one of us, most of us quit right at the brink of what God is getting ready to do. There is going to be another meeting at the end of your season but once you give up and quit the test, quit the process there is no need for another meeting to take place, now all of the angels have to go on back. They have to go back to their assignment; why, because you quit, you gave up, frizzed out, faint, turned coward; that is what the bible says, in Luke 18:1 18:1 *ALSO [Jesus] told them a parable to the effect that they ought always to pray and not to turn coward (faint, lose heart, and give up).* (AMP). It says that when we quit we turn coward, we fainted, we quit. And let me tell you something, look when we understand what we have going on; when you understand that there is a meeting that is taking place in heaven on your behalf, or when I understand that there is a meeting that is taking place in heaven on my behalf, I need to find out what God said in that meeting. It is not difficult to find out what our God said in the meeting because He is going to say the same thing that this word says and so that meeting is taking place in heaven and we need to make sure that we understand what that meeting entails because when we understand that God and all of the angels of heaven are meeting on our behalf, and one of the things we have to do is to keep on saying what He is saying.

God says, "Look I made you more than an overcomer, more than a conqueror;" so I need to be saying that about myself. Can I talk to you about a reality of what I might experience on earth? I might be going through hell but I am more than a conqueror. Oh no, I can not quit now. This is what you have to say, "I can not quit now; I have come too far, I am in too deep now in the things of God." How many of you would at least say that you are in too deep. I mean look after all that you have been through, after all the fasting that you have done, after all the praying and the fire, and all of the sweating and the tears that you have done, you are going to quit now? You mean you are going to quit now, you are going to fizz out, faint on God now; all of the meetings that God called you in, you are going to do that now? Some of us faint while God is yet in the meeting. God is having a meeting on your behalf and one of the angels say to God, "God they quit." And the angels just wrap up all of their spiritual books and go on back to the third heaven, they say to each other let us just go on back to the third heaven and find out who really wants this gift that God is offering. When you realize that the main reason that we quit is because we get under pressure and one of the things that is under pressure is fear. You may want to reconsider quitting next time. Fear is usually the cause of our quitting, and if this is your testimony, do not quit because all of heaven is backing you.

On the next venture that you go through you must realize that you have all of heaven backing you. I am telling you I think about this, where in the world would I be if I had quit somewhere along the line. I have a million stories to tell you about moments I thought it would be more beneficial to quit then to keep on standing. If nothing else just the moment when as a man, I realized that I was going to have to raise five children by myself; if nothing else breaks me, that is a good reason to quit. But God held me up through that. I had 3 girls and I did not know how to comb their hair, therefore, they might have to suffer some wild hairdos for a moment until I learned how to braid their hair but, eventually I learned and the hairdos held up. In the beginning, they did not leave the house looking like Shirley Temple with the curls hanging beautifully but they held up. I had to also learn how to cut the boys hair, my finances at that time dictated that I cut their hair myself, therefore I had to practiced on my boys and that is why I am good at cutting hair today.

I want to encourage you because when you are at the point of giving up you are almost there. I mean this with all of my heart, if we would dare to hold on, I am telling you

God will send anybody, everybody if necessary to come by and encourage you if you just refuse to quit. I learned a lot in the area of not giving up. Realizing you can go through a storm but if you do not quit you will come out. I remember I heard Kenneth Copeland say one time, "God has guts enough to go in the mouth of the lion with you if you have guts enough to go." I said, "wait a minute, let me meditate upon that a bit; you mean God will go with me if I have guts enough to go; knowing this I will go as far as you can go. When you feel like you have gone as far as you possible can, God will have somebody to come by and encourage you and push you to the next level. I remember a time when I had no clue what me and the kids were going to do; things were so bad, that I really had no clue. I was at that time living with my parents, and one day I went into my parent's bedroom and I sobbed like a baby because I had all of these babies, they were not old children they were babies. My youngest, Nina at that time was about six and a half, all of the rest were younger than her; at that point I was totally discouraged. One of my girls Rhonda, who was at that time I think, maybe about 2 years old started singing a song. I have no clue where that song came from, I don't know when or where she learned the song, all I knew is that I was discouraged, I was at wits end. And she started to sing, "we are going to make it just be sure that you keep holding on." That was the first thing I ever heard her sing. I was encouraged, and I thought, "that has to be God." So then what do you do – you keep holding on, preacher you just got a word from the Lord. It was in song and it came from a little baby; you just got a word from the Lord. God is always giving us these kinds of words; it is just that we are not sensitive to the way He speaks.

We think discouraged when we buy into discouragement it is at that particular point that our meeting with God is on pause. We start saying "God remember me." God does remember, He is already at the meeting. But we continue asking "Lord Jesus I do not know what they are going to do to me" or "Jesus, do you have any clues what they are going to do". We act as if God had no idea what is going to happen and He need to find out Himself. God knows all things, right? But at this point you cause the meeting to be on pause. Why, because you have just paused things from earth and He can not go pass your pause in heaven on anything that you are not willing to do. Giving up is not an option! Do not fear! Do not give up because all of heaven in backing you.

Chapter 15
THE REALITY OF HELL

$\mathcal{W}$e have been actually talking about the Great Tribulation period. We have been talking about the Last Days. We have gotten into what takes place around the time of the Rapture. We are talking abut what is going to take place in the last days; we talked about the signs of the Last Days. We have been talking about the coming of Christ. We have talked about the Great Tribulation period and what takes place through that period of Tribulation and how there will be people that are going to want to die and not be able to die because death won't be permitted at least for about the space of 5 months.

We talked about how on the earth there will actually be that period when people are going to want to die but not be able to die. Whatever really takes place in our day and whatever decisions you make the time period that we are in, God is actually keeping record on all of this. Wouldn't it be wonderful to think about that everything that we do God will just forget about it? We like to say to God please God forget about that, I know that I did that but forget about it.

There is a time that God actually will cast your sin into the sea of forgetfulness and it never be remembered again but one of the things that we need to definitely remember is that whatever takes place, whatever we do in our body God has to reward us or penalized us for that particular work. There is coming a Judgment where we are going to have to give an account for that we do in the temple of God, our bodies.

If you and I are still on earth on this planet when the Rapture comes we will go up to heaven because we have accepted Jesus Christ as our Lord and Savior, we are living in heaven but there are people still on the earth because the earth is still in existence. Anybody that is left behind will go through a period called Great Tribulation. Understand this now, God's great, is not your great. So this is God's great; when God says great, it is great. When God says flood, the whole world floods out, not just one city, when God says a thing then it goes way beyond anything else that we really even imagine.

One of the things that took place in Noah's day when Noah was here, was that people were still planting crops, building houses, drinking wine, they were partying, they were doing the whole club thing, they were getting married, they were doing all of that. But God had sent all of them a message through Noah that it was going to rain; in other words, there is going to be a changing in time. Everybody was urged to get it right, right now, just get it together right now. The people had never seen a flood therefore; they made the decision not to really get it together, not to get ready.

We have never seen Rapture before; and because of that sometimes we make that decision not to pay attention to what the preacher is actually saying. If we don't engage in what is being said, the report of the Lord, then a lot of times the season changes on us and it may be too late. Everybody that is saved is rapture out (when the church is called home to heaven); this is called the Great Snatch. We are snatched out of the earth. Those that are left on the earth will go through Great Tribulation. I mentioned this before but it deserves repeating. Those left behind will go through Great Tribulation, which means that they will go through a period where people are going to want to die but they won't be able to die. They will go through a period where if they don't receive 666 that is classified as the mark of the beast, they will not be able to buy nor sell anything in the earth; but then, if you do receive the mark of the beast the 666, that means that you are locked out of heaven. You don't want to be locked out.

THE COMPARTMENTS OF HELL

What happens to you if you die before the rapture? What happens to you if you die, right now? We want to talk about the reality of Hell. It is wonderful to talk about that period of the rapture, isn't it? Age does not matter, you may be 15, 13, 17, 20, 40 or 90; whatever your age if the Rapture does not come first and you die before the Rapture, we have to understand that you have to go somewhere you can't stay here. If you don't stay here, then where do you go?

Now understanding this, we have to make some good decisions for ourselves, even as children we have to do that because remember this must be done at any age. For example if you are 13 years old or older you are no longer riding on your parent's relationship with God. You are on your own now and God classifies you as a responsible individual that can make a decision for yourself. You have the responsibility to declare Jesus as your Lord. You are the gatekeeper of your own life now. You make the spiritual decision for your life. It is either heaven or it is hell. Because after you leave the earth your spirit and your soul have to go somewhere. So, I want to talk about the reality of hell.

I realize a lot of times when we talk about this in church we only talk about Hell as a place; and that it is, it really is a place but there are several different compartments of Hell. One compartment of Hell is called Tartarus; compartment 2 is called Paradise; compartment 3 is called Hell or Hades; another compartment 4 of Hell is called Abyss or the bottomless pit; compartment 5 is called the Lake of Fire.

Many people have reasons for not receiving Jesus as their Lord and Savior. But no reason is sufficient to keep you out of hell. For instance, there are a lot of educated people who allow their education to cause them to believe that they don't need God; I personally know a lot of people like that, very educated and so they don't feel like they really need God, they feel like the weak people need God. But the reality is that sinners need God. And so that is the reason we come in relationship with God. We come in proper relationship with God and one of the benefits that you actually get is that you get to escape Hell. That is a wonderful benefit.

I am going to share with you later in this chapter from Luke 16 and show a few things because I want you to understand that hell is a real place. I want to share something with you from there and this is very important as we begin to understand this, because sometimes when we can't see a thing then sometimes we don't really believe it exists because we can't see it. You may say, how you know Hell exists, because the bible says so; how do you know that Heaven exists, because the bible says so. So when we really come into an understanding of this, we have to understand that every single thing that we do we are going to have to give an account for that. Every single thing that we do in this time period, we have to give an account. God has not created Hell for you; it was really created for the devil and his angels. But people do go there; and people go there because they have made certain wrong decisions on the earth and as a result they end up going into Hell.

Death And Judgment

Some people have made the wrong decision to hang around all of the wrong people. Young people sometimes feel invincible but please understand young people do die and when young people die they have to go somewhere. When older people die, they have to go somewhere. Understand this now, man is a spirit, he lives in a body and he has a soul. So when you refuse to pull it together then your spirit and your soul becomes contaminated with the sin that we actually get involved with. Then God cannot let you in Heaven. So you don't go any further than the Judgment Seat; 2 Cor 5:10 *For we must all appear before the judgment seat of Christ; that every one may receive the things done in his body, according to that he hath done, whether it be good or bad.* (KJV) you don't go any further than that. And so now understand this now, it is appointed unto man once to die, after death what happens? Judgment comes found in Heb 9:27 *And as it is appointed unto men once to die, but after this the judgment:*

(KJV) Now that Judgment is not to show you mercy, this is your trial because mercy and grace is for now, that exists right now not at the judgment. In other words, the bible says this, that we have an Advocate with the Father, Jesus Christ the Righteous. Now He makes intercession for you and I so that we don't have to go to Hell. So that we would make the right decisions; He gives us that space right now to repent of anything that we have done wrong; and most of the time we do know it is wrong.

WHERE ARE THE PEOPLE THAT HAVE ALREADY DIED?

So we want to make sure that whatever we do right now we want to make sure that we have everything right, there is nothing between my soul and my Savior as the old folks used to say, there is nothing between my soul and my Savior. You know at one point I didn't know what that meant but as I started growing in the Lord I learned what that really meant. You know, there is nothing, there is no sin, there is no dislike, there is no lack of love, there is no un-repentance, there is no thing like that between my soul and my Savior; my soul and my Savior are married together. As we are moving through the earth, as we are moving through this time when there is nothing between your soul and your Savior then that gives you a free passageway to Heaven, to be absent from the body is to be present with the Lord 2 Cor 5:8 *We are confident, I say, and willing rather to be absent from the body, and to be present with the Lord.* (KJV), I mean just immediately. So please don't think that by the time the home-going happen or by the time the funeral happen that we have come together so that we can now get you into Heaven; no, it is too late. By the time the funeral takes place, you are already in your place; you are already either in Heaven or you are in Hell.

In Luke 16:19 - 31: "*There was a certain rich man, which was clothed in purple and fine linen, and fared sumptuously every day: And there was a certain beggar named Lazarus, which was laid at his gate, full of sores, And desiring to be fed with the crumbs which fell from the rich man's table: moreover the dogs came and licked his sores. And it came to pass, that the beggar died, and was carried by the angels into Abraham's bosom: the rich man also died, and was buried; And in hell he lift up his eyes, being in torments, and seeth Abraham afar off, and Lazarus in his bosom. And he cried and said, Father Abraham, have mercy on me, and send Lazarus, that he may dip the tip of his finger in water, and cool my tongue; for I am tormented in this flame. But Abraham said, Son, remember that thou in thy lifetime receivedst thy good things, and likewise Lazarus evil things: but now he is comforted, and thou art tormented. And beside all this, between us and you there is a great gulf fixed: so that they which would pass from hence to you cannot; neither can they pass to us, that would come from thence. Then he said, I pray thee therefore, father, that thou wouldest send him to my father's house: For I have five brethren; that he may testify unto them, lest they also come into this place of torment. Abraham saith unto him, They have Moses and the prophets; let them hear them. And he said, Nay, father Abraham: but if one went unto them from the dead, they will repent. And he said unto him, If they hear not Moses and the prophets, neither will they be persuaded, though one rose from the dead."* (KJV) This is a good place to really talk about this because now what we actually have is the rich man, Lazarus who was poor, and Abraham. One of the things that I want you to understand is that at this place called Hell, this particular compartment was actually a place of torment on one side but then on the other side it was actually recognized as a place of comfort. This place of comfort is recognized as Paradise, well that is where the beggar went when he died he went to a place of comfort. According to the new Unger's Bible Dictionary Paradise is the place in Sheol, in which the spirits of the departed righteous are until the resurrection. There was also a place in Sheol for the wicked and this was the place of torment. Before Jesus' resurrection he mentioned paradise to one of the thieves that was on the cross with Him in Luke 23:43 43 *And Jesus said unto him, Verily I say unto thee, To day shalt thou be with me in paradise.* (KJV) this place was also called Abraham's Bosom

But when we really look at this and we really see this, the bible calls this rich man Lazarus' master and his master had a certain responsibility for him; now it was his master and his master refused to even let him eat from the crumbs that fell from his table. There is something interesting about this rich man because Abraham called him "Son." I mean really think about that, he was not somebody that was totally disconnected from God, he was a son. He was a son of Abraham, not a biological son but he was someone that was connected to Abraham. Knowing this in the world does he end up in Hell? How is it that someone that has made Jesus Christ Lord of their life end up in Hell? We expect people that are not saved to go to Hell. But now, you setting in church with me and I am setting in church with you, look we don't expect each other to go to Hell, right? Because we have made Jesus, Lord of our life. But there comes that time that we get to the place where we use our will to do what we want to do, when we want to do it, and how we want to do it but we need to know there are penalties on that.

I have to understand and you have to understand there are particular things I need a license for – I need a license to drive, I need a license to be married, I need a license to get sex; I need a license for that. I need a license to live with my wife. So if I get this without license, then what I am saying is God I realize what your order is but I don't want your order in my life right now. If I die under those conditions then it is either Heaven or Hell. God says look I don't want you coming up here living with Me like that and so you are forbidden access to live with Me in that condition. God understands that He has given you power to have victory over that. God understands that you do not have to be in that predicament because He has given you power over that. I want to apologize to you as a preacher and let you know that we have not told you all of the truth? Can I be the first one to apologize to you for all of the preachers, for all of the pastors, all of the set gifts, can I be the first one to apologize to you on their behalf and on my behalf that we have not told you all of the truth; because we sympathize with you where you are and we say, God understands that you are only human. The argument of being just a man is not going to go over because God knows what He put in you. You must understand that you can't live with a woman if you don't have a license to. So when you begin to lay down with somebody, you have got to understand this, when you begin to lay down with somebody God looks for a license. Otherwise you have violated the order of God. Do you realize that the beggar has a right to eat at his masters table because that was his master and right to eat at his table? But the man denied him rights, he had license to eat at his table that is my master or at the very least eat under the table because that is my master.

There is a biblical law that says, that if I am the servant to a man and this man is my master he is under obligation to make sure I at least eat, and if he does not he is in violation to the order of God. We can see God's order concerning servants in Lev 25:39-43 *39 If one of your countrymen becomes poor among you and sells himself to you, do not make him work as a slave. 40 He is to be treated as a hired worker or a temporary resident among you; he is to work for you until the Year of Jubilee. 41 Then he and his children are to be released, and he will go back to his own clan and to the property of his forefathers. 42 Because the Israelites are my servants, whom I brought out of Egypt, they must not be sold as slaves. 43 Do not rule over them ruthlessly, but fear your God. (NIV)*

The rich man violated the order of God because he would not feed his servant. Now, they both die – the beggar dies and then the rich man dies – the beggar goes to a place called Paradise; it was a compartment in Hell for the righteous. That compartment in Hell was arranged by God because Adam really messed things up for us. At that time nobody was able to go to Heaven, once Adam fouled it up, nobody could go to Heaven until after Jesus paid the price and so there was a compartment in Hell for the righteous and the wicked, everybody got to go to Hell at that particular time. Everybody went to Hell; it is just that some went to the upper compartment where they were going to be comforted. They were going to rest from all of their labors; they were going to rest in that particular compartment called paradise. The other side is where the rich man actually went, the side for the wicked and there was no rest for him, there was only torment and he says in this previous passage of Luke 16, look I am tormented in this flame. This flame indicates that Hell is a real burning place where the fire is not quenched and it never goes out and you are never burned completely up. So in other words when you go into a place called Hell you don't die, your spirit doesn't die.

On this earth your flesh dies but your spirit remains alive, your soul remains alive and you are in this place where you are living further. You are an eternal being. That means that you won't die, you won't ever die. Your spirit and your soul won't ever die; your spirit and your soul never die, it lives forever. Now, the word dying only means this, it means to cease to exist on this plain; that is all it means. You died as far as we are concerned, but as far as God is concerned you only passed from here to there (down), or here to there (up). See one or the other, you either go down or you go up but you pass off of the earth. The only reason that we have this body that we exist in is to keep us in communication with earth. Wherever you are right now your body is telling you what the temperature is in the place where you are. If you were on the outside of your body you would be neither hot nor cold, but because you are locked in your body, you know the temperature of the place. You know that because your body is actually giving you a signal, but that is only so that you can function here.

Sin Is Fun – Hell Is Torment

When you go to Hell you are under torment. And so, now your soul is understanding it is hot in here; it is a flaming heat in here, this is unbearable. Because then you are under the penalty. Verse 25 says this, *"But Abraham said, Son, remember that thou in thy lifetime receivedst thy good things, and likewise Lazarus evil things: but now he is comforted, and thou art tormented."* Verse 26: *"And beside all this, between us and you there is a great gulf fixed…"* (KJV) Nobody that was in Paradise could pass to the other side and nobody that was on the other side where they were being tormented could pass to the side of comfort. They could see over there but they could not enjoy there. Your decision that you make on this earth right now is what actually takes you there. This is good information when you are saved. When you are saved and you are walking right with God this is good information. Now when you are saved and you know that you are not right, whatever sin you are fellowshipping with this does not feel good you can ask the Lord Jesus deliver you and that is exactly what has to happen. There is a remedy. Because, all of us one day were headed to hell not one of us or some of us but all of us one day were headed to Hell.

I am telling you right now when I used to fornicate, adulterate, club and smoke and smoke weed all of that, I am sorry I was not born saved. I drank, created dances, all of that. You couldn't keep me off the dance floor wasn't a wall flower, none of that, I was on my way to Hell and loving it. I am telling you I was having a good time. I don't know what people were talking about (church folk) when they say, there is nothing in the world come on out of that world; oh, there was plenty in the world for me. I was having a good time, I was drinking everything I wanted to drink, hitting a joint every time I wanted to hit the joint, come on I was having a good time. You know going in the house where I was staying and paying nothing to stay there and fix me six hot dogs that I did not buy. I was on my way to Hell and loving it, enjoying myself; so much so wake up the next day, anybody got a joint? I don't have any lies to tell you, I smoked herb and loved it. You know I am telling you, I smoked and I loved it, I wasn't having a hard time in the world. I don't know where all the money came from to buy all the alcohol I was buying and the weed I was buying; I don't know where all that money came from, I wasn't working and I wasn't stealing. Nevertheless, I was on my way to Hell.

So the good time that I was having in the club became the distraction to keep me in that vehicle, to keep me in that way. I was being distracted greatly. Go down to the Club or somewhere like that just having a good time. Please understand that I had a good time – let's count the ways: I wasn't married, I had no responsibilities but I was on my way to Hell and loving it. I wanted to go back to the club the next day. That became my distraction; and when people wanted to witness to me about Jesus I didn't want to hear it; because I was having a good time. When the Evangelist came to tell me to come out of that world, there isn't anything in there for you, it not even fun; I did not relate, I couldn't relate because I was having a good time.

Some people who have gotten the opportunity to do what I was doing and having fun and loving it died in the process, where did they go? Straight to Hell because now they have to pay, they have to be penalized for all of that they did on earth and they rejected Christ. Take note of this, to not receive Him is to reject Him. Hell was created for the devil and all of his angels. If you make the decision that you are going to walk contrary to the word of God or live in conditions that is contrary to the word of God then what we are saying is, that we want the devil's order for our life. You don't want God's order; you want the devil's order. And, if you have the devil's order in your life then that means that you need to live with him. So you have a decision to make. We all have decisions to make – at any given time you can make the decision; many people say "but you know what, I think God has delayed His coming and because He has delayed His coming I think I might have a little more time to engage in areas that I want to engage in; look this is all about me".

Let take a look at 2 Peter 2:4 - 7: "*For if God spared not the angels that sinned, but cast them down to hell, and delivered them into chains of darkness, to be reserved unto judgment; And spared not the old world, but saved Noah the eighth person, a preacher of righteousness, bringing in the flood upon the world of the ungodly; And turning the cities of Sodom and Gomorrha into ashes condemned them with an overthrow, making them an ensample unto those that after should live ungodly; And delivered just Lot, vexed with the filthy conversation of the wicked:*" (KJV) Now wait a minute. If God did that to them, what about you and me in this day where He has given us power and ability to rise above our challenge? What is going to happen to us? See, there is a place that we must all go when we leave the earth and that is heaven or hell. We actually make the decision on where we want to go or where we desire to go in this particular time. We make the decision on that. So, if God did not spare the angels; He didn't spare them that refused His order; He is not going to spare you with your cute self, with your handsome self He is not going to spare you; because God does not look on the outer appearance.

Do you realize that some of the people think that God is going to overlook stuff and this where we as parents might have to apologize to our children, because some of us do not properly discipline our children and have given them an indication that God is going to overlook our stuff? God doesn't have any problem with disciplining us but He also doesn't have any problem spoiling us. He does not have any favorites to the point where He is going to allow some to sin and come into heaven and then there are the others that He is just going to cast away immediately. That is not how God functions; He is no respecter of persons. So we really need to make the decision; we need to come out of from wherever we are. We need to come out from whatever, our holdup or our hang-ups, we need to realize that Jesus actually died for those hang-ups and we need to accept what He did for us.

Let's go back to this place called Hell. Let's check out 1 Peter 3:17-20 *For it is better, if the will of God be so, that ye suffer for well doing, than for evil doing. 18 For Christ also hath once suffered for sins, the just for the unjust, that he might bring us to God, being put to death in the flesh, but quickened by the Spirit: 19 By which also he went and preached unto the spirits in prison; 20 Which sometime were disobedient, when once the longsuffering of God waited in the days of Noah, while the ark was a preparing, wherein few, that is, eight souls were saved by water.* (KJV) This word "prison" is actually translated Hell. This is the place of torment. So now, what spirits is in prison? They are the spirits that were actually in Hell.

Let's go back to this based on some of the scriptures that we have already read. Those that rejected the message of Noah they went to the place of torment in Hell.. Those that died had to go to hell also, but there were different compartments. Let's take a look at an example, Cain died, he went to Hell. His duration on earth was that he is a vagabond, a wandered; there was no way to get him back in proper alignment with God. He had to go to Hell; why, because he violated the order of God. And the same is true today, all of those that rejected Christ went to Hell, if they rejected Christ when they died they went to Hell. Cain went to a place of torment but now people like Abraham, who followed God's order as well as he knew, went to a place called Paradise. There were a lot of Old Testament saints that submitted to the order of God they went to a place called Paradise. At that time everybody either went to Paradise or Tartarus the place of torment; they went to that place to be tormented or comforted waiting the time that Jesus would pay the price for the saints to be with him in heaven. When He paid the price then they were released from that place to heaven with Him. Look at 1Peter 3:19 again: "*By which also he went and preached unto the spirits in prison;*" (KJV) He went and He preached to spirits that were in prison. Now go to Ephesians 4, let me show you this, so that it will be a little clearer to you. This is a scripture that we are probably familiar with but maybe not familiar with in this context. Ephesians 4 comes to life. Verse 8 says this, "*Wherefore he saith, When he ascended up on high, he led captivity captive...*" (KJV) Who was in captivity? those that were captivated in Hell on the Paradise side that is who He led. He led captivity captive; He led them out of that particular compartment of Hell, the Paradise. Everybody else is still there in that place of torment and the population is growing.

Look, I apologize if I have to be the one to tell you this. But if you have a loved one that was not saved, now only God knows that, but let's not try to judge this because I am telling you when we go to Heaven, we are going to be surprised who we see; and if you decide to go to Hell you are going to be surprised who you see. If you choose to go to hell you may have to say, "you preached the Hell out the church, what are you doing down here?" Preaching is just preaching it will not send you to heaven or hell; I am not minimizing that because I am a preacher, but what it really does bless you by the word that comes out my mouth even if I get no credit for it. So the only way that I am going to get credit for all of this is how I live when I am on earth. That determines where I go when I leave. Somebody can swing from the chandeliers and I mean raise the dead up in the church but if he or she lives like a fool when they leave earth, they are on their way to Hell; they preached a powerful message-- on their way to Hell. Remember what Paul said, 1 Corinthians 9:27: "*...lest... when I have preached to others, I myself (would) be a castaway.*" (KJV) Can I preach to each and every one of you and be cast away myself? Yes. I can sing like the angels and end up in Hell? Yes. I can witness to everybody, get a million people saved and don't live that life myself and end up in Hell? Yes.

Now I am going to take you to 1Corinthians 9 anyway and just show you. 1 Corinthians 9:27: "*But I keep under my body, and bring it into subjection...*" (KJV) He says, but I keep what? under my body. You know what that means; that means that I have the responsibility to bring this body under subjection, I can do that. As a matter of fact 1 Corinthians 10:13 says, there hath no temptation taken you. It won't even come except you have the power to defeat it. God won't let it come unless you have the power to defeat it. If it happens to you, or if it comes to you that means that you can defeat this. 1 Corinthians 10:13: "*there hath no temptation taken you but such as is common to man; but God is faithful... (he will not tempt you) above that ye are able; but will with the temptation... make a way to escape...*" (KJV) This lets us know what to do when temptations comes, we must look for the way of escape because that is what God grants to you in the moment that you are tempted. You are never tempted without a way of escape. You know on your way to the place of sin that God has already prepared a way out, you know because God is warning you all the way this is not a regular meeting, this is not a regular time; you are getting ready to sin and a red light goes off. Anybody that says, well I fell in sin; you didn't fall, you dived. No, you did not fall you really did dive into it because the Holy Ghost who is your Helper has rung the alarm on your way there. You mean He can sound the alarm and we can still end up in Hell? Yes, if we don't heed the alarm. Let's go back to Ephesians 4, because I really do need you to see what happened there Eph 4:8-14 *Wherefore he saith, When he ascended up on high, he led captivity captive, and gave gifts unto men. 9(Now that he ascended, what is it but that he also descended first into the lower parts of the earth? 10 He that descended is the same also that ascended up far above all heavens, that he might fill all things.) 11 And he gave some, apostles; and some, prophets; and some, evangelists; and some, pastors and teachers; 12 For the perfecting of the saints, for the work of the ministry, for the edifying of the body of Christ: 13 Till we all come in the unity of the faith, and of the knowledge of the Son of God, unto a perfect man, unto the measure of the stature of the fulness of Christ: 14 That we henceforth be no more children, tossed to and fro, and carried about with every wind of doctrine, by the sleight of men, and cunning craftiness, whereby they lie in wait to deceive; (KJV)*

Two things He did—He led captivity captive, this is at the place where He died for us, He died for you, He died for me, this is that place. He died for us. He paid the price for us. He paid the full price for us and He led captivity captive; He gave gifts to men. All of those that were in that compartment of Hell called paradise, He led them out and then He left gifts to the church. Why, because He is now on His way out of the earth. He is rapturing out of the earth and He is taking all of the Old Testament saints with Him and so therefore, He says to us, now where I used to prophesy I need you to prophesy. Where I used to be the Apostle here, I need you to be the apostle here. Where I used to be the Prophet, you are now the prophet. Where I used to be the Evangelist, now you are the evangelist. Where I used to be the Pastor, now you are the pastor. Where I used to be the Teacher, now you are the teacher. He left gifts to men. Let me tell you something, everybody in the church functions out of one of those arms. You may not be an apostle but you function in that apostolic arm of administration and the setting of order. You may not be a prophet but you function out of that prophetic arm through music ministry, through prophetic inspirations or prophetic utterances and different things like that; you function somewhere inside one of these offices that is true for everybody in the church. One of the five is where you function; you may not be the person in the office, you may be one that functions in one of the duties of that particular office. Everybody is affected by the gifts. Everybody has something in them that God can use.

RELEASE OF THE SAINTS IN PARADISE

Go with me to Psalms 40, because you need to see this and I believe that we need to really see this, now we have all these souls in Paradise that are locked in that compartment of Hell, can you imagine Ps 40:9 *I have preached righteousness in the great congregation: lo, I have not refrained my lips, O LORD, thou knowest.* (KJV), you have all of these souls that are in Paradise, remember the thief on the cross with Jesus, that asked Jesus to remember him, he went to Paradise but he didn't stay long. Why? Because when he said to Jesus, remember me when you come into your Kingdom. He knew that he was headed to hell, but he wanted to make sure that he ended up being with Jesus. The other thief on the cross was self-righteous said; if you really are who you say you are save yourself and us. But the other one said; remember me when you come into your Kingdom and as soon as that the thief died he went straight into Paradise; Why? Because Jesus said this day shall thou be with Me in Paradise. Jesus had to go to Hell then He comes into His Kingdom. He goes to Hell first; because He needs to pay a price for you and me. So that you don't have to go to Hell Jesus went on your behalf. So that you would not have to suffer in Hell Jesus went on your behalf. David talks about this in Ps 16:10 *For thou wilt not leave my soul in hell; neither wilt thou suffer thine Holy One to see corruption.* (KJV), what Holy One? You talking about that holy one, who committed adultery with Bath-sheba? This will just tear you up. How in the world was he going to say that, you will not suffer your Holy One to see corruption? That is two-fold: on one side of that he is talking about himself; on the other side of that he is talking about the Christ. So he will go into Hell but he won't be left there. When Jesus Christ goes to Hell He pays the price for you and I, what He did benefits us and then He goes back and preaches to the great congregation. Watch this, Psalms 40:9: *"I have preached righteousness in the great congregation: lo, I have not refrained my lips, O LORD, thou knowest."* Verse 10: *"I have not hid thy righteousness within my heart..."* (KJV) *He goes down in the midst of them; remember* (Eph 4:8 *Wherefore he saith, When he ascended up on high, he led captivity captive, and gave gifts unto men).* (KJV) of all of them and preaches to everybody that is there and the only ones that are able to follow Him up out of that are the ones that were in Paradise. He unlocks the gate because now remember they were held captive – Abraham and everybody else were in Paradise held captive against their will. You have got to realize the enemy had every right to hold them captive; why? Because of what Adam did. But God says, look you can not touch them; you can not bring them in torment because they lived for Me. Their likeness was of Me and so you can not torment them there, I don't have any way to stop you from bringing them into Hell.

How Does Satan Get The Right To Take People To Hell

So when you and I sin guess what happens? We are giving the devil right to bring us into Hell. We are giving him permission. How in the world does he get that permission? He has permission because we agreed with him because we don't have to obey God; we are not made to do that we can choose to follow the devil all the way to hell. We agreed with the devil because we don't have to follow the order of God, we can choose not to follow God's order if we want to do that. We agreed with the devil and when we agree with him he has every right to bring us where he is living. Therefore, we have to make sure this day, beginning with this day right here, we fall out of agreement with the devil. We are not going to Hell. If you are reading this book and this applies to you, make the decision not to go to hell and say to yourself "I am not going to Hell; I set my will right now I am not going to Hell; I submit my will to God; I submit myself to God and I am on my way to Heaven and I am glad about it".

Chapter 16
THE INTERCESSOR AFTER THE ORDER OF MELCHIZEDEK

*O*ver the pass ten years I have been raising up prophets and prophetic people, but now God has given me an additional assignment to train intercessors. Therefore, I want to make sure that I include this in this book. God has drilled in my heart over the years to really teach from where I live. I have been in a strange place because God has recently shifted me and this shift had caused me to add the training of intercessors to my current assignment. I am still going to raise up prophets and leaders because that is my God given assignment, but this shift has given me a passion to raise up intercessors. Some of the people that I am finding think that they are prophets but are really intercessor. They do not know where they really are. They would hear form God and really try to operate as a prophet but failed to get into the greater depth of the operation of the prophet and they find themselves backing out of that but still find themselves praying for folks that no one else wants to pray for. When it comes to making intercession for the people many of us have actually failed in the process. Therefore, God has given me the assignment to teach and train people after the order of Melchizedek.

WHO IS MELCHIZEDEK? ACCORDING TO UNGER'S BIBLE DICTIONARY MELCHIZEDEK

(mel-kiz'e-dek; "king of righteousness"). Was the king of Salem (i.e., Jerusalem) and "a priest of God Most High," who went out to congratulate Abraham on his victory over Chedorlaomer and his allies. He met him in the "valley of Shaveh (that is, the King's Valley)." Melchizedek brought bread and wine for the exhausted warriors and bestowed his blessing upon Abraham. In return Abraham gave to the royal priest a tenth of all the booty; this is found in Gen 14:17-20 17 *And the king of Sodom went out to meet him after his return from the slaughter of Chedorlaomer, and of the kings that were with him, at the valley of Shaveh, which is the king's dale.18 And Melchizedek king of Salem brought forth bread and wine: and he was the priest of the most high God. 19 And he blessed him, and said, Blessed be Abram of the most high God, possessor of heaven and earth: 20 And blessed be the most high God, which hath delivered thine enemies into thy hand. And he gave him tithes of all.* (KJV).

WHAT IS THE MELCHIZEDEK ORDER?

What is the order of Melchizedek? Unger's also states that the statement "According to the order of Melchizedek" if found in Ps 110:4 *The LORD hath sworn, and will not repent, Thou art a priest for ever after the order of Melchizedek.* (KJV) is explained to mean "manner," i.e., likeness in official dignity-a king and priest. The relation between Melchizedek and Christ as type and antitype is made in the epistle to the Hebrews to consist in the following particular: each was a priest (1) who is not of the Levitical tribe; (2) who is superior to Abraham; (3) whose beginning and end are unknown; (4) who is not only a priest, but also a king of righteousness and peace. "Without father," etc. (Heb 7:3 *Without father, without mother, without descent, having neither beginning of days, nor end of life; but made like unto the Son of God; abideth a priest continually.* (KJV), refers to priestly genealogies. Priests are ministers that represent the people or a person before God. We in the body of Christ are a royal priesthood.

I have been in a strange place for a while now and it has been difficult for me to know where I am, that was difficult place for me because I must know where I am at all times. Because you can never really talk from where you are not you can only talk about where you are now or where you have been. I have been training prophets, apostles and leaders for many years now and over the past several months it has been difficult for me to do those things that I have been doing for years. I am not a pretender, even though I use to be. It is difficult for me to pretend that I know where I am when I don't know. God has drilled in my heart to really speak from where I live. Over the past several months I been shifting and I needed to know exactly where I am. Have you ever gone to an unfamiliar place and God was not saying anything. You knew that something was going on inside and did not understand where your tabernacle moved to. Somehow God shifted my tabernacle and I did not know where I moved to. I know now where God shifted me now but when I shifted I had to identify where I was. Sometimes God on purpose does not tell you where you are because he wants to know that you are hungry enough to search for where you are.   God is not adding lazy people anymore. God wants to know that you are serious about finding out where you are and where you exist. God wants to know that you are willing to wake up in the middle of the night to find out, you are willing to go through whatever you need to go through to find out or you are willing to labor in prayer to find out. You ask God "where am I God, where did I shift to and did not know where I shifted, I need to know where I am?"

I realize that some of you that are reading this book has also shifted to another place and you do not know where are, you do not understand this new spiritual place where you exist today. Remember, this is the same place. Some of you have experiences that you know that is not your issue. You know you do not have a problem with that particular situation, you know that you do not have any struggles in that area. But you find yourself having difficulties getting rid of those particular situations.

If you are going to be an intercessor after the order of Melchizedek that means that you are going to have to come to a different place where there is no beginning to you or no end to you. But yet you are called to stand in the gap for somebody or for some situation. Somebody will totally be in trouble if you do not have their experience. Therefore, what we are going through is our engaging in things that we know do not have an issue in that situation and now for some strange reason you are finding it difficult to come out.

I have done a lot of training of prophets and prophetic people, but now my season has shifted and now as a prophet I have to raise up intercessors, but not regular intercessors, these are intercessors after the order of Melchizedek. God spoke to me some years ago and He said Rodney "I want you to go through the next Veil", the Holy of Holies and I saw myself and I saw myself getting ready to step through into the Holy of Holies and God says "Wait, know that you know that when you step through that next Veil you don't want to come back out."

The book of Hebrews talks about Jesus praying for us to order of Melchizedek. Heb 6:19-20 19 *Which hope we have as an anchor of the soul, both sure and stedfast, and which entereth into that within the veil; 20 Whither the forerunner is for us entered, even Jesus, made an high priest for ever after the order of Melchizedek.* (KJV). The order of Melchizedek has no beginning and no end Heb 7:3 3 *Without father, without mother, without descent, having neither beginning of days , nor end of life; but made like unto the Son of God; abideth a priest continually.* (KJV) The author of Hebrews talks so much about this intercessor that it is difficult to determine whether he is talking about Jesus or Melchizedek. Later, this chapter goes on to say that this is the same kind that you are. The objective is to bring us into the understanding that He has called us as an intercessor according to the order of Melchizedek which we can never be released from. We are expected to operate according to the order of Melchizedek. Therefore, we understand that we can never be released from that position. That scares a lot of people because too many people in the body of Christ are too fickle minded, we like to do things for a season. I crush that kind of attitude and attack it every time that hear it. We like to make statement like "I am only in this for a season" or "I am only going to be at this church for a season". Any place that you go and your objective is to only be there for a season you act like you are only there for a season. The endurance that you need you never get because you will not sign on the dotted line as if this is it. God wants us to step into everything that we step into as if this is it. If you are my assignment as an intercessor I can never ever look like I am only praying for you for a season

There is a problem when it comes down to intercessors because we have too many people that are intercessors are not worthy to be called an intercessor. If you an intercessor I should be able come to you and say pray 'for' me. I need to be able to go to any intercessor and say pray for me. Many of us do not really understand what that means because that word is a loose word now and we just say that loosely. We ask people to pray for us but we lack the understanding of what we have just said. Let me explain what that means. When you say pray for me I relinquish every ounce of me to the intercessor and now their objective is to pray for me. I have now made myself vulnerable to the intercessor because I passed the authority to pray for me to the intercessor. For this reason you have to be careful who you ask to pray for you because once you do that you can no longer pray for yourself because you have released that to the intercessor. Before you ask anyone to pray for you make sure that you know that they will not give up on you, no matter what they see, they will not give up on you. You have to be careful who you ask to pray for you, because that is not the same as asking someone to pray with you. When you ask someone to pray with you that request is different because praying with you does not relinquish your authority to pray for yourself now the both of you are in position to pray.

When I ask someone to pray for me I pass the authority on to the intercessor but I also pass to that person my experience. Let me help you with this. Some of us are going through some things in our bodies right now that does not belong to us because we agreed to pray for someone and we did not realize our responsibilities and now we have to live out their experience. Where the problems come up is the fact that we as intercessors forgot about the fact that we said that we would pray and now we are going through and we are stuck with this thing until we get back on the assignment.

Remember, what Paul said, though you have 10,000 instructors yet you have not many fathers found in 1 Cor 4:15 15 *For though ye have ten thousand instructors in Christ, yet have ye not many fathers: for in Christ Jesus I have begotten you through the gospel.* (KJV). In other words, you get saved before I ever knew, but when we come into this relationship I had to give birth to some things for you and so some things I go through is for you. Therefore, we need to cooperate with our man or woman of God because we struggle in childbirth because the baby's head will not turn and I cannot give birth until the person that I am giving birth for turns in the correct direction so the baby can be born. The baby cannot be born until its head in turned in the right direction.

The intercessor must become very familiar with what you go through because the intercessor prays for you. Remember, an intercessor does not pray with, an intercessor prays for. A pastor prays with but an intercessor is not a pastor. That is the reason we have to raise up in our churches a ministry of intercessors and we have to make sure that they are intercessors indeed. Intercessors are in the prophet's family but one of the reasons they do not know exactly where they are they are also in the pastor's family. Sometimes the intercessor does not know where they are. Having a prophetic experience is my praying for you from your vantage point. That is the best way for me to pray for you. If I am going to pray for you then I need to feel what you feel. An example of this is an experience that my wife and I had a while back. We were looking for a house and we visited a house that we wanted to see and immediately we both knew the situation of the owner. The house was in foreclosure and we were just looking at the house, but before he opened his mouth my wife and I both knew his situation he did not have to voice it. The house was in foreclosure because of a divorce and as soon as I came into his presence in my spirit I felt what he was feeling. I knew what was going on with him; we both felt what he felt. I can never pray for him until I can feel what he felt. When he opened his mouth and begins to confirm what was in our spirits

You must feel what they feel if you are going to intercede for a person, you cannot intercede for an alcoholic if you have never felt what they feel. You cannot even be compassionate for people if you have not felt what they feel. An intercessor must go into the very quarters of where they live. I remember hearing the testimony of a man that played the part of Jesus in a movie. He said that they had to take a long break because he was overcome with emotion. You cannot play that part without feeling that experience. This is where the prophet comes in again because prophets have vivid imaginations and they can imagine themselves there. I discipline myself to listen to people because if I listen long enough I can feel the pain that the person is feeling.

Let's take a look at Jesus our chief example setter in Isa 53:4-7 *Surely he hath borne our griefs, and carried our sorrows: yet we did esteem him stricken , smitten of God, and afflicted. 5 But he was wounded for our transgressions, he was bruised for our iniquities: the chastisement of our peace was upon him; and with his stripes we are healed. 6 All we like sheep have gone astray; we have turned every one to his own way; and the LORD hath laid on him the iniquity of us all. 7 He was oppressed, and he was afflicted, yet he opened not his mouth: he is brought as a lamb to the slaughter, and as a sheep before her shearers is dumb, so he openeth not his mouth.* (KJV) notice verse 4 surely he hath borne our griefs, and one of the toughest battles I have is when I preach somebody's funeral. I love to preach funerals. I would rather preach funerals than weddings. I get nervous when I preach weddings but nervousness goes out the window when I preach funerals, something happens when I preach a funeral; an anointing comes on me to do them. But the reason I have problems is because I am feeling what the family is feeling and I cannot breakdown at this moment because I am the center of attention and if I break down everybody else will break down. Every word that comes out of my mouth when I preach funerals comes out based on the fact that I feel what the grieving family feels. I almost want to get other people to do the weddings but you are not going to get a chance to do my funerals because I love to do those.

In order for you to pray as an intercessor you must be able to feel what the person feels. This is testing moment as to whether or not you can feel what people feel that you are called to intercede for. This is also a testing item as to whether or not you are ready for this next level of ministry. Our not being able to feel what people are feeling is the reason many people do not want to come to church it is also the reason that many of family members do not want to come to church with us is because we don't feel their pain we don't feel what they are feeling. Everybody is not going to follow you but somebody should once you begin to feel what they feel. Out of their pain you will be able to pray from their vantage point.

What I endured for a three year period I had to endure because I had to know what rejection feels like. I went recently through a three year period of rejection. Christian don't know what rejection feels like, many say they know what rejection feels like but they don't know what rejection feels like until they feel like everybody that sees their face is pointing at you, now that is rejection. Now what God actually sends to me is people that feel rejected, so that I can love them back into shape. I know how they feel and I am able to pray from their vantage point. I know how their feel because I am intimately acquainted with their grief, why, because I carry their sorrow. You have to carry something before you can pray for it. I know without a shadow of a doubt how somebody that carry rejection feels.

There is an anointing that is available for this, and you will not qualify for this next level of anointing until you can feel what somebody else feels. Do you want someone to give up on you? If not, that is the exact attitude that you have to take whenever you pray for someone else. Let's go back to verse 4 and 5 *Surely he hath borne our griefs, and carried our sorrows: yet we did esteem him stricken, smitten of God, and afflicted. 5 But he was wounded for our transgressions.* One of the things that an intercessor does not mind is being aligned with you where you live. Proud folks do not want that. If you are all messed up they do not want to be seen with you because they do not want people to believe that birds of feather flock together. This is how you know that you can really feel what they are feeling because you do not get a different felling when somebody sees you with them. For instance, if you are praying someone that is challenged with their sexuality, ask yourself, "can I hug them in public?" If not, you reject them and you can not pray for them why, because you feel funny and you start looking around because you don't want somebody else to think they you have some issue with your sexuality. But when you are an intercessor after the order of Melchizedek you do not care what people are saying as long as they are wrong. That person could be one step away from stepping into the body of Christ and getting changed or stepping away from it being loss forever. Then God is going to look at you when you get to heaven wanting to come in and say there is blood on your hands. Then you will be saying "God what do you mean, you know how I walked before you, you know how I stayed clean before you, and you know how I stayed away from sin". God will say but you also stayed away form those you could have won, God will say, look, I have placed on you the burden of an intercessor and you rejected it because you were more concerned about your reputation, than you were concerned about a soul that would be loss, you were concerned about you.

BEARING GRIEFS AND SORROWS

Jesus bore their griefs carried their sorrows, He was hung up on a cross between two transgressors, He was seen with drunks to the point where they called him a winebibber, He was around sinners to the point where they thought that He was in sin. All the way down to where we are now and they are still making up bad stories about Him, The Da Vinci Code if you will. Some of us are transgressors too because we gave our money to watch it, we nailed another nail in his hand, we knew what it was all about before we ever went to see the movie but we wanted to hear another point of view.

Verse 7 says 7 *He was oppressed, and he was afflicted, yet he opened not his mouth:* Jesus endured; He did not open His mouth. He endured what they said about him, he endured what they took him through. This is talked about in Heb 12:2-3 *2 Looking unto Jesus the author and finisher of our faith; who for the joy that was set before him endured the cross, despising the shame, and is set down at the right hand of the throne of God. 3 For consider him that endured such contradiction of sinners against himself, lest ye be wearied and faint in your minds.* (KJV) When Jesus was on the cross He did not lose heart, he saw His seed, which is you and I, Jews and Gentiles, bond and free people, He saw it all and He would not open His mouth. He could have called for a legion of angels but He did not open His mouth. You and I are going to have to do what Jesus did and go down into the spirit world and break the bondage that is on the lives of people. People are bound in the spirit and that is where we have to go to get the bondage broken. There are certain things that are manifested in the flesh realm but we are going to have to go down in the spirit world and break the bondage. We are trying to attack on the flesh level to break the bondage in the natural but we must break it in the spiritual world. You say how am I going to do that? Remember, you are praying for them and that is how you are going to be able to do that.

All of the hell that I went through for about three years I would not trade that for anything, not then; even now I would not trade it in for anything because now I can pray from the vantage point of the rejected and also those that are in bondage. Anybody that is bound by anything I am confident that I can get them free. Why, because I can pray from their vantage point. If you are called as an intercessor, learn the lesson from this point ask God to give you what he gave me, ask Him to let you experience that thing spiritually because if you don't experience it spiritually you will experience it naturally or physically and if you have to experience it naturally or physically you will never forget that lesson.

Why would God allow you to go through the hell that you are going through right now? Because God so desperately wants to win everybody on this earth that is bound, He wants to win everybody on this earth that is not saved and He does not mind doing it at your expense, because we go here at His expense, as a matter of fact it would please Him to do so we see that in Isa 53:10 10 *Yet it pleased the LORD to bruise him; he hath put him to grief: when thou shalt make his soul an offering for sin, he shall see his seed, he shall prolong his days, and the pleasure of the LORD shall prosper in his hand.* (KJV).

We are agreeing to pray for folks but we do not know how. We have a lot of situations that we are going to have to deal with in the church. Everybody that is bound do not want to be bound they want to come out they just don't know how. We have been a hypocritical church because we pretend like that we never have any problems. We have been hypocrites because we have been acting like we have it all together and we did not have it all together. And now that we have it together we hide behind the cross or hide behind the pulpit and still pretend like we never had a problem. We act like we do not know how they feel. There are big problems in the pulpit; there are big problems in the pew. The reason people are still locked up and bound is because there has been no word from the church that says that I can identify where you are.

One of the concepts that is used in network marketing is feel, felt, found. If you are going to bring them out you have to help them in their mindset. When you begin to intercede for someone you must have this process working for you. You have to be able to say to them "I know how you feel, I felt the same way myself and here is what I found God is a deliver and is able to bring you out of this", but we can't do this because we won't admit that we have ever had a problem.

Eph 6:10-13 *Finally, my brethren, be strong in the Lord, and in the power of his might. 11 Put on the whole armour of God, that ye may be able to stand against the wiles of the devil. 12 For we wrestle not against flesh and blood, but against principalities, against powers, against the rulers of the darkness of this world, against spiritual wickedness in high places. 13 Wherefore take unto you the whole armour of God, that ye may be able to withstand in the evil day, and having done all, to stand.* (KJV). We are interceding for a lot of people that do not understand the wiles of the Devil. They don't know how to stand against the trickery, traps and schemes of the devil. They can't see a scheme of the Devil if they tripped over it. We have to learn to be proactive. To be proactive only means that you have power over how you are going to respond. One of my favorite authors Steven Covey says between the stimuli and respond there lies your power to choose how you are going to react. You have to know how to respond to things before you ever lend you members to it. Look at verse 12 For we wrestle not against flesh and blood, so if you act in a way that is not Christian then it not you, it is the enemy, because you are flesh and blood. When I was a child one of things that we use to do is to put two dogs in each others face just pushing them at each other and when their teeth begins to show and they begin to growl at one another we would turn them loose and just stand back and watch. This is how the devil does us. Two demons will get one of us by the neck and the other demon will get the other by the neck and push them in each others face until the two people begin to fight and then they stand back and watch. Why, because you can not see the devil, you can't see his schemes and there is not one of us that did not see an argument coming on. We know that we are about to argue before it starts. You do get a chance to choose not to argue. What happens is that pride stood up and you could not back down and you have something to prove now. But take a look at what we wrestle against "principalities, against powers, against the rulers of the darkness of this world, against spiritual wickedness in high places". Notice that these go from level to level to level and the devil never has to use the highest level on us because we fall for the scheme.

The Battleground Is In the Second Heaven

The intercessor has to go to where the battle is, the battle is not in the first heaven, it is not in the third heaven but it is in the second heaven because that is where the devil fights us. The battle takes place in the second heaven because that is the meeting place. Satan binds people in the second heaven and you cannot see there unless you get wise to the devil's schemes. The intercessor lives in the second heaven. That is where they must fight. The battle takes place in the second heaven. If you understand this you can win every battle. Let's take a look at this in Job 1:6-7 *Now there was a day when the sons of God came to present themselves before the LORD, and Satan came also among them. 7 And the LORD said unto Satan, Whence comest thou? Then Satan answered the LORD, and said, From going to and fro in the earth, and from walking up and down in it.* (KJV). We discussed this in the chapter the world before Adam. Satan had already lost his throne in this passage, Satan throne was in the earth and he had lost it and now he is angry with you and I. Remember, Satan does not have access in the third heaven but you and I are seated there; we find that in Eph 2:6 *And hath raised us up together, and made us sit together in heavenly places in Christ Jesus*: (KJV). The intercessor operates in the second heaven but they are from the third heaven. Our affections are already set in heaven. That is in Col 3:1-2: *Since, then, you have been raised with Christ, set your hearts on things above, where Christ is seated at the right hand of God. 2 Set your minds on things above, not on earthly things.* (NIV) We are seated in the third heaven far above principalities, powers, rulers of the darkness of this world, and spiritual wickedness in high places. How is it that the devil gets to strong arm you and I? How is it that we get locked up in things then? It is because you and I have become intimately acquainted with the earth and understanding this everybody is bound by things that are in the earth and then we do not want to leave.

Remember the passage in Mark 12:20-25 *20 Now there were seven brethren: and the first took a wife, and dying left no seed. 21 And the second took her, and died, neither left he any seed: and the third likewise. 22 And the seven had her, and left no seed: last of all the woman died also. 23 In the resurrection therefore, when they shall rise, whose wife shall she be of them? for the seven had her to wife. 24 And Jesus answering said unto them, Do ye not therefore err, because ye know not the scriptures, neither the power of God? 25 For when they shall rise from the dead, they neither marry, nor are given in marriage; but are as the angels which are in heaven.* (KJV) Jesus is saying, you don't know what you are talking about because when we leave earth there will not be marriage in heaven. All of that is an earthly affection and God has no problem with us being married in the earth but when it is time to leave earth we must be willing to leave because there is none given in marriage neither is there any married. Enjoy your spouse while you have them now because there will not be marriage in heaven, remember, your affections are set in heaven not earth. Now if you are going to get anybody out of their bondage it is because your affections are already set in heaven. People are battling with things that are in the earth, there are no drugs in heaven, and there is no crime in heaven, no alcohol is in heaven all of that is here. Enjoy the anointing now because we will all have the same anointing in heaven and it is an anointing that is within us not an anointing upon us.

Now if you are going into the enemy's camp and get people out you do not have to be afraid of anything because you affections are set in heaven and your mentality is such that you realize that you have power and dominion over every principality and power over every name that has been named, you have authority over that. And when you began to have their experience you know that it is not yours and you realize that the only reason that you are experiencing this is so that you become intimately acquainted with their grief and pray from their point of view; in order to do that you need to feel what they are feeling. We have to go places that we may never have been before to be able to have the experience of the person that we are praying for. I am not saying that you need to be in sin, I am not saying that you need to practice their sin or bondage, remember Jesus became intimately aquatinted with where we are, He was in all points temped yet without sin. He experienced everything that we go through. He never sinned but He experienced what we have experienced.

In Job 1:6 the sons of God came to present themselves before the LORD and Satan came also among them, this was the second heaven because the devil does not have access to the third heaven. God came down to the second heaven to meet with them. The second heaven is where people are bound therefore, the intercessor lives and fights in the second heaven. The sons of God were the angels of the Lord and Satan came to the meeting because he wanted to accuse Job. This meeting in the second heaven was against Job. Satan wanted to count Job out because all eyes were on Job at this point and the devil wanted to bring him down. This is a good reason for you to pray for your pastor from his or her vantage point. You do not need to interview your pastor to do this. If you live in the second heaven you will know because you will feel what your pastor feels and will be able to pray for him or her from their vantage points. If you do not live in the second heaven you need to climb up there.

THE ISSACHAR INTERCESSOR

When it comes down to the relationships in your life someone that is in your life will be in your life forever, for the rest of your life they will be there. In Gen 49:14-15 Issachar is a strong ass couching down between two burdens: 15 *And he saw that rest was good, and the land that it was pleasant; and bowed his shoulder to bear, and became a servant unto tribute.* (KJV) Check out verse 14 Issachar bowed his shoulders to bare burdens, he carried two burdens. Intercessors bare burdens. We talked about the sons of Issachar but we have never talked about Issachar himself. His sons knew seasons and times and knew what Israel aught to do. We talked about Issachar from this prophetic point of view but we have never talked about Issachar as an intercessor. Intercessors bear burdens. When you bear someone's burdens you have to crouch down. Remember that old birthing position where you had to lift your heart about your head; your head had to be down between their legs. Unless prayer is going to cost you something people cannot come out. Unless you go down and lift someone's burdens up they can never get out. You have an awesome assignment of interceding for someone.

Remember I talked about earlier my wife and I feeling the pain of a person the we were seeking to buy a house from and immediately we felt the pain of that person. That person was our assignment. All of a sudden the house was not our main issue; we turn to the pain of the seller of the house and begin to try to help him. It was not by chance that we felt his pain, and we knew that he was our assignment. You do not always have to hear a testimony of the pain from the person that you are praying for. Once you feel that pain you can take that up to the first heaven, up to the second heaven, and on up to the third heaven and put that on the alter of God; and as you pass the second you let the devil know that he cannot have that person. We, in the church world, have become so calluos because we can just walk away from people in that kind of pain. How do you just walk away from people in that kind of pain and just leave them there.

I remember one time that I was praying for my brother, we used to be drinking partners until God delivered me. But my brother was still dirking alcohol all of the time.

God had delivered me from that and after that I hated people that were drunks because I could not stand to remember how I use to be, it reminded me of me. That was hypercritical but I did not think so at the time. Nevertheless my siblings and I were casting the devil out of my brother trying to help him. We didn't know what we were doing but we knew that we had to do something. We would throw him down and we were trying cast the devil out of him, but after we got through with that he would get up and say ha, ha, it didn't work and we would throw him down and try again. We were just practicing what we thought the bible said to do but nothing happened. Then one day I saw him walking down the street quite a ways from home stumbling and holding on to a fence trying to make it home and when I saw him in a split second something happen inside me and I yelled out "SATAN LOOSE HIM NOW!" And not many days after that he come out of that and he is still saved today. It had to come from somewhere other than us practicing. It had to be something else. At that moment I became intimately acquainted with where he was, this came out of my pain of trying to get out myself. I became acquainted with his grief and pain with where he was. This came of my pain of my trying to get out myself. I remembered what I use to be and I understood how he felt because I remember how I felt. I had to stop hiding and pretending that this had never happened to me. When I quit hiding I was able to help, I use to drink everything from beer to grain alcohol. We in the body of Christ have to stop hiding and pretending like nothing has ever happened to us so that we can help those that struggle with what God has delivered us from. We have to learn to bear each others burdens as Issachar intercessors.

THE ASSIGNMENT OF THE PROPHETIC INTERCESSOR

God wants to now train up a company of intercessor to accompany the company of prophets. Every intercessor should be accompanying a prophet. Every intercessor has to stay in their particular lane, some believe that they are prophets but are actually intercessors. As intercessors you have to identify exactly where you are, the intercessor is actually the forerunner of the prophet; the intercessor paves the way for the prophet to speak. The prophet cannot do what they are called to do effectively until the intercessor breaks the ground, after that the prophet is released to speak. The intercessor gets the first assignment and after that they say to the prophet now, it your turn. We, as prophet, have tried to do our assignment without the intercessor breaking the ground first and this has caused our job to be more difficult that it should be. This happens because some of us prophets have never pushed the intercessor forward. When the intercessor goes first the peoples hearts are ready to hear the voice of the prophet. Every senior prophet, the ones that are called to a company of prophets, needs to identify the chief intercessor that will walk along side of them. Every intercessor that is assigned to the senior prophet must be able to go through what the prophet goes through; they must be able to feel what the prophet feels. This intercessor must enter a session for the person that they are praying for. The intercessor breaks up the ground so the prophet can speak to that particular thing. The intercessor must be acquainted with their grief of the person that is being prayed for. This is why not everyone can do this, as an intercessor is to literally go where the battle is. The intercessor must understand where the spirit man of the persons being prayed for is locked up and they need help to get out.

Chapter 17

CHOKE THE DEVIL'S INFLUENCE AT THE ACCESS POINT

*L*et me make it perfectly clear that the devil does not have access to your spirit, he has to speak to you through your soul and your soul has to convince your spirit to obey it. Your body is going to obey your soul or your spirit. The one you feed the most is going to win. Take a look at this diagram so that we can identify the function of your physical body, soul and spirit.

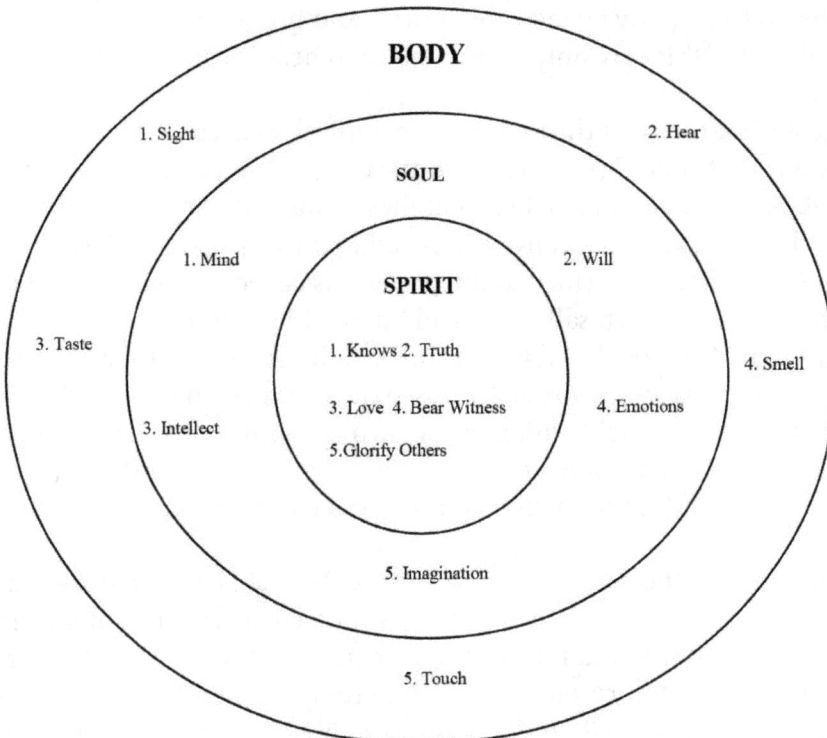

BODY

1. Sight   2. Hear

SOUL

1. Mind   2. Will

SPIRIT

1. Knows 2. Truth

3. Love 4. Bear Witness

5. Glorify Others

4. Emotions

3. Taste   4. Smell

3. Intellect

5. Imagination

5. Touch

As you can see from the diagram, your body communicates with the earth through the five senses. According to Wikipedia, the free encyclopedia the five senses are defined as follows:

1. **Sight or vision** is the ability of the brain and eye to detect electromagnetic waves within the visible range (light) interpreting the image as "sight." There is disagreement as to whether this constitutes one, two or three senses. Neuroanatomists generally regard it as two senses, given that different receptors are responsible for the perception of colour (the frequency of photons of light) and brightness (amplitude/intensity - number of photons of light). Some argue[citation needed] that stereopsis, the perception of depth, also constitutes a sense, but it is generally regarded as a cognitive (that is, post-sensory) function of brain to interpret sensory input and to derive new information. The inability to see is called blindness.

2. **Hearing or audition** is the sense of sound perception. Since sound is vibrations propagating through a medium such as air, the detection of these vibrations, that is the sense of the hearing, is a mechanical sense akin to a sense of touch, albeit a very specialized one. In humans, this perception is executed by tiny hair fibres in the inner ear which detect the motion of a membrane which vibrates in response to changes in the pressure exerted by atmospheric particles within a range of 20 to 22000 Hz, with substantial variation between individuals. Sound can also be detected as vibrations conducted through the body by tactition. Lower and higher frequencies than that can be heard are detected this way only. The inability to hear is called deafness.

3. **Taste or gustation** is one of the two main "chemical" senses. There are at least four types of tastes[4] that "buds" (receptors) on the tongue detect, and hence there are anatomists who argue[citation needed] that these constitute five or more different senses, given that each receptor conveys information to a slightly different region of the brain[citation needed]. The inability to taste is called ageusia. The four well-known receptors detect sweet, salt, sour, and bitter, although the receptors for sweet and bitter have not been conclusively identified. A fifth receptor, for a sensation called umami, was first theorised in 1908 and its existence confirmed in 2000[5]. The umami receptor detects the amino acid glutamate, a flavour commonly found in meat and in artificial flavourings such as monosodium glutamate. Note that taste is not the same as flavour; flavour includes the smell of a food as well as its taste.

4. **Smell or olfaction** is the other "chemical" sense. Unlike taste, there are hundreds of olfactory receptors, each binding to a particular molecular feature. Odour molecules possess a variety of features and thus excite specific receptors more or less strongly. This combination of excitatory signals from different receptors makes up what we perceive as the molecule's smell. In the brain, olfaction is processed by the olfactory system. Olfactory receptor neurons in the nose differ from most other neurons in that

they die and regenerate on a regular basis. The inability to smell is called anosmia.

5. **Touch**, also called tactition, mechanoreception or somatic sensation, is the sense of pressure perception, generally in the skin. There are a variety of nerve endings that respond to variations in pressure (e.g., firm, brushing, and sustained). The inability to feel anything or almost anything is called anesthesia. Paresthesia is a sensation of tingling, pricking, or numbness of a person's skin with no apparent long term physical effect.

These five senses are what we need to communicate with this physical world here on earth. Our body in its physical form is the house that our soul and spirit man inhabits while we are on the earth. It is the same body that we need when we go to heaven but it will be glorified and made to be immortal. It is through these five senses that we collect information about the physical world around us and send that information to our soul. Your physical body will respond to and act on information that it receives from the soul or from your spirit man. Your body is accustomed to obeying your soul more than your spirit man because our soul has been receiving food, that is information from our body every since we were born and we have been responding to that information. For instance, if your body sends your soul information through one of your five senses that you are in pain, the soul will tell the body what to do and you do that because your body needs to be directed by your soul or your spirit.

But your spirit man has been receiving spiritual food, that is information that we have only been able to understand since we have been saved, that is giving our lives to Jesus Christ, and also been fed by the word of God.

Your soul is happy to tell your body what to do and your body is happy to do what it is told. Remember, that Adam's body was just a lump of clay until God blew the breath of life into it. Gen 2:7 7 *And the LORD God formed man of the dust of the ground, and breathed into his nostrils the breath of life; and man became a living soul.* (KJV). Adam was just lying on the ground lifeless, without his spirit or soul until God breathed into him the breath of life. So, the body need to be told what to do. It has not life in it without the spirit and the soul.

Notice from the above diagram the attributes of the soul. The Wikipedia, the free encyclopedia defines these five attributes as follows:

1. Mind - Mind collectively refers to the aspects of intellect and consciousness manifested as combinations of thought, perception, memory, emotion, will and imagination; mind is the stream of consciousness. It includes all of the brain's conscious processes. This denotation sometimes includes, in certain contexts, the working of

the human unconscious or the conscious thoughts of animals. "Mind" is often used to refer especially to the thought processes of reason.

2. Will - The standard use of this term is as a distinction between internally motivated and caused events and external events. Jumping off a cliff would be an act of free will; accidentally falling or being pushed off a cliff would not be an act of free will.

3. Intellect - Intelligence (also called intellect) is an umbrella term used to describe a property of the mind that encompasses many related abilities, such as the capacities to reason, to plan, to solve problems, to think abstractly, to comprehend ideas, to use language, and to learn.

4. Emotions - An emotion is a mental and physiological state associated with a wide variety of feelings, thoughts, and behaviors. It is a prime determinant of the sense of subjective well-being and appears to play a central role in many human activities.

5. Imagination - Imagination is the ability to form mental images/sounds/feelings, or the ability to spontaneously generate images/sounds/feelings within one's own mind. It helps provide meaning to experience and understanding to knowledge; it is a fundamental facility through which people make sense of the world, and it also plays a key role in the learning process. A basic training for imagination is the listening to storytelling (narrative), in which the exactness of the chosen words is the fundamental factor to 'evoke worlds'.

Imagination is the faculty through which we encounter everything. The things that we touch, see and hear coalesce into a "picture" via our imagination. The way we understand things... the way that we 'make sense' of things is through our imagination. The ability to problem-solve... to see things from a different perspective... to empathize... all happen because we have this Technicolor, multi-channel, curious imagination. Imagination IS the ability to create perceptions: novel perceptions, fantastical perceptions, or hypothetical perceptions.

The soul is the part of you that the devil tries to use to get to you. He sends information from the body, the five senses to the soul and your mind, will and emotions get involved. It is at this point that your spirit needs to be giving the directions to your soul and your body. Now, when the devil speaks to your soul, your soul has to convince your body to obey it, however, your spirit should never obey your soul except when your soul has been disciplined to obey the word of God. We can see that in Rom 12:2 2 *And be not conformed to this world: but be ye transformed by the renewing of your mind, that ye may prove what is that good, and acceptable, and perfect, will of God.* (KJV) We must have renewed our minds before our spirit can yield to our soul. We must have our mind renewed, because our mind is conformed to this world and our soul will get us in trouble because it does not want to change. If we want our soul to change we must discipline our soul. How do we do that? One way to do that is by fasting, your soul loves natural food. It is use to eating whenever it let's your body know it is time to eat. If your soul does not want to change and conform to the word of God we simple threaten our soul with a fast. Fasting is a way to humble your soul and that is what is needed to get your soul to yield to your spirit man. Notice in Ps 35:13 3 But as for me, when they were sick, my clothing was sackcloth; I humbled my soul with fasting; (NASB) We simple say to our soul "if you do not corporate I am going on a fast" Make sure that you really mean that and will follow through with what you said.

On many occasions God would instruct His people to fast in order to be able to follow the Holy Spirit and not the soul. One such example is found in Lev 16:29 *This shall be a permanent statute for you: in the seventh month, on the tenth day of the month, you shall humble your souls .... (NASU).* The word humble in this pass means to afflict in the Hebrew. This was the time of annual Atonement for Israel, a time of fasting and the time of clensing for God's people. Remember, our soul is normally driven by our carnal nature and this has gone on since the time of our natural birth; therefore we must afflict our soul by fasting in order to get our soul to submit to our spirit man. Our carnal nature is called our flesh; this is not just our physical body, but our physical body is use to taking directions from our carnal flesh, but once we are born again in Christ we put on a different nature. We are in Christ and our spirit man wants to communicate with God but our flesh, or carnal nature is against the Spirit of God.

Paul talks about this in Gal 5:16-26 *16 But I say, walk by the Spirit, and you will not carry out the desire of the flesh. 17 For the flesh sets its desire against the Spirit, and the Spirit against the flesh; for these are in opposition to one another, so that you may not do the things that you please. 18 But if you are led by the Spirit, you are not under the Law. 19 Now the deeds of the flesh are evident, which are: immorality, impurity, sensuality, 20 idolatry, sorcery, enmities, strife, jealousy, outbursts of anger, disputes, dissensions, factions, 21 envying, drunkenness, carousing, and things like these, of which I forewarn you, just as I have forewarned you, that those who practice such things will not inherit the kingdom of God. 22 But the fruit of the Spirit is love, joy, peace, patience, kindness, goodness, faithfulness, 23 gentleness, self-control; against such things there is no law. 24 Now those who belong to Christ Jesus have crucified the flesh with its passions and desires. 25 If we live by the Spirit, let us also walk by the Spirit. 26 Let us not become boastful, challenging one another, envying one another.* (NASU). This is very important because we have not considered that our flesh, our carnal nature will be totally against following the Spirit of God, our soul more that likely will want to follow the deeds of the flesh rather than the fruit of the Spirit mentioned in verse 22. Therefore, if we are going to live by the Spirit and walk by the Spirit we must afflict our soul and bring it into subjection to our spirit man because as long as our carnal nature controls us we are in opposition to the Spirit of God and we will not follow the Spirit or God or the Word of God.

Many of us think that we can convince our carnal mind to cooperate with the Spirit of God, but we cannot do that, however, we can get or mind transformed to the mind of Christ as we mentioned before but the carnal mind is what it is. It is not subject to the law of God, neither can it be. Notice what Paul says about that convincing the carnal mind to change in Rom 8:7-8 *Because the carnal mind is enmity against God: for it is not subject to the law of God, neither indeed can be. 8 So then they that are in the flesh cannot please God.* (KJV). It is not possible for our flesh to please God. We must get our spirit man in the position directing our body and have our soul submit to the direction of our spirit man. Remember that every aspect of our soul supports me, myself and I. My will says I will to do this or that or I just want what I want. Likewise, my Intellect, my emotions, my mind and my imagination are all self centered. Only our spirit is God centered. We have to get our spirit man in the control seat of our physical body and we do that by fasting. This tells our flesh, our carnal nature that I no longer want you to control me. I want the Sprit of God to control me. You are my servant and I tell you what to do and I want you to obey the Spirit of God. If you do not want to do that I am going to fast until you do because this is the way that God has shown me in His word how to get my flesh under the control of my spirit man.

In order to deny the devil access you have to abandon your will, remember that the will operates in the soul. Your will is use to being in control and it will be difficult to make that change without disciplining your will. You must also feed your spirit with the word of God. The more word you have in your spirit man the stronger your spirit will be and with that strength your spirit man will be able to override the will's desire to follow your soul.

God speaks to your spirit not your soul, He speaks Spirit to spirit. If you have your spirit at a place starvation that it will not be the dominant factor in getting your body to obey it. For instance, when God calls you to get up at 4:00 AM to pray because He wants to talk to you, your soul will say no, you are too sleepy and you turn over and go back to sleep, but your spirit will say get up, get up God has something important to say to you. Your soul will argue with your spirit and probably win if you have not renewed your mind or if you have not fed your spirit constantly with the word of God. God wants His people to be led by His Spirit, but that will not happen unless our spirit man is the one giving directions to our body. When that happens we will surrender our will to our spirit man and we will not be lead by our feelings, emotions, intellect or our imagination all of which are attributes of our soul. When we surrender our will to the Spirit of God and allow ourselves to be lead by the Holy Spirit He will direct our path and lead us according to the will of God and the word of God. We see that in Ps 119:105 - *Your word is a lamp to my feet and a light for my path. 106 I have taken an oath and confirmed it, that I will follow your righteous laws.* (NIV) This is how we stop the devil from influencing our soul to overpower and spirit and led us away from the word of God. What about our spirit, how does it function? We find that in following passage John 14:15-28 *If ye love me, keep my commandments. 16 And I will pray the Father, and he shall give you another Comforter, that he may abide with you for ever; 17 Even the Spirit of truth; whom the world cannot receive, because it seeth him not, neither knoweth him: but ye know him; for he dwelleth with you, and shall be in you. 18 I will not leave you comfortless: I will come to you. 19 Yet a little while, and the world seeth me no more; but ye see me: because I live, ye shall live also. 20 At that day ye shall know that I am in my Father, and ye in me, and I in you. 21 He that hath my commandments, and keepeth them, he it is that loveth me: and he that loveth me shall be loved of my Father, and I will love him, and will manifest myself to him. 22 Judas saith unto him, not Iscariot, Lord, how is it that thou wilt manifest thyself unto us, and not unto the world? 23 Jesus answered and said unto him, If a man love me, he will keep my words: and my Father will love him, and we will come unto him, and make our abode with him. 24 He that loveth me not keepeth not my sayings: and the word which ye hear is not mine, but the Father's which sent me. 25 These things have I spoken unto you, being yet present with you. 26 But the Comforter, which is the Holy Ghost, whom the Father will send in my name, he shall teach you all things, and bring all things to your remembrance, whatsoever I have said unto you. 27 Peace I leave with you, my peace I give unto you: not as the world giveth, give I unto you. Let not your heart be troubled, neither let it be afraid.* (KJV).

This is wonderful because in this passage notice what Jesus is saying to us. If you love me keep my commandments. This means that we should want to keep His commandments and that means that we want to live by the word of God, that is, whatever commandments Jesus has given us to keep. That also means that we must be willing to surrender our will to the Holy Spirit and allow Him to lead, direct and order our everyday lives. The first thing that our spirit man is going to have is the Spirit of Truth and we are going to know Our spirit is going to know the Holy Spirit. The Holy Spirit is going to communicate with our spirit not our soul. The Holy Spirit is going to abide with us forever and He also dwells with us and is in us. This is how Jesus explained in the passage what is going to happen after He leaves. Until we are born again in Christ our souls leads us to whatever it wants to do. But once we are in Christ we are to be lead by the Holy Spirit, who will also comfort us when our soul wants to lead. It may be painful to give up our will if we have damaged emotions, but Jesus is saying here that "I will not leave you comfortless: I will come to you" He desired to heal those damaged emotions because damaged emotions cause us to make bad decisions.

The second thing, that thing that operates in our spirit is truth. Jesus has given us the spirit of truth and He will abide with us forever. Remember this from the above passage "*…that he may abide with you for ever; 17 Even the Spirit of truth…*" The world cannot do this but we can because Jesus has given us the Spirit of truth. The Holy Spirit knows the truth and He is the Spirit of truth, our soul can guide us with bad information but the Spirit of Truth will not.. For instance, our perceptions are sometimes based on the information that we get from our body or our soul, but the perception is wrong. We may think that certain people or a certain person does not like us based on facial expressions. Our soul will convince us that these people or this person has a problem, but our spirit will not do that, our spirit knows the truth because it is fed by the word of God and by the Spirit of Truth.

The third thing that our spirit will do is to love. Our spirit loves God. Our spirit is connected with God and only operates in love. Notice, If a man love me, he will keep my words: and my Father will love him, and we will come unto him, and make our abode with him. This is exciting, The Father loves us and is going to come unto us and make His abode with us. Remember, the functions of our soul and body, love is not a part of either of those, so guess what, love will not be a consideration when our soul gives directions to our body unless it has been transformed, as we mentioned previously. Love is not going to be a primary push for our soul or our body.

The forth thing that our spirit will do is bear witness. Notice this from the above passage Comforter, which is the Holy Ghost, whom the Father will send in my name, he shall teach you all things, and bring all things to your remembrance, whatsoever I have said unto you. The Holy Spirit will bear witness of what Jesus has said to us, He will bear witness of the word of God and our spirit will bear witness of what the Holy Spirit is giving us. Our soul is selfish and it wants us to be controlled by ourselves but the Holy Sprit will help us obey the word of God. For instance, Romans 8:28 is the word of God that states Rom 8:28 *And we know that all things work together for good to them that love God, to them who are the called according to his purpose.* (KJV), states that all things work together for our good, our spirit knows this and will lead our body to any situation that does not feel good to us and help us to stand through that particular situation, season, circumstance or storm. But our soul does not like pain and it will yell loud and clear NO!

TRANSLATIONS AND TERMINOLOGY

Apostle	Special messenger sent from God.
Blessed	Empowered by the anointing to prosper.
Christ	Greek – Christos, Hebrew – Messiah, English – The Anointing
Disciple	One disciplined, taught, instructed. One who accepts and helps to spread the teaching to another. The followers (disciples) of Jesus.
Egypt	The world system.
Enmity	Deep-rooted hatred or irrevocable hostility toward God.
Fervent	To burn, very hot, to glow, exhibiting deep, sincere emotions, prayers impassioned.
Gentile	A person or nation who did not know or have a relationship with God.
Gospel	Good news.
Grace	God's unmerited or unearned favor.
Hail	(RV) Greetings. If anyone comes to you and does not bring this doctrine (of Jesus Christ), do not receive him into the house or give him any greeting; for he who greets him shares his wicked works.
Hallowed	To be sanctified or set apart; to be praised; to be adored; Holy.
Horn of Salvation	The metaphor of horn(s) symbolized strength and honor. Horns being the chief source of attack and defense with animals, they are employed in scripture as emblems of the power of God and of Christ.
Holiness	Being of one mind with God.
Humble	Submission and cooperation with what God has said.
Jesus Christ	The Anointed One and His Anointing.

Kingdom of God	God's way of doing things.
Know	Intimately acquainted with God.
Lasciviousness	Wantonness, filthy, unbridled passions, uncleanness, greed, drunkenness, sexual lust, insolent pride, pride of the emancipation from the restraints of personal conscience or public opinion. Loss of sense of shame.
Mercy	Compassion and blessings that are an act of divine favor.
Might	Supernatural ability of God.
Propitiation	Atoning sacrifice.
Redound	To lead to an unusual or unplanned end, as if by an inevitable flow of consequences; become transferred or added; accrue (increase).
Saints	Consecrated people; separated to God.
Salvation	Safety, deliverance, ease, sound or soundness, forgiveness of sin, answers to prayer, joy and peace. In the New Testament, salvation is regarded almost exclusively as from the power and dominion of sin. Jesus Christ is the author of salvation. It is freely offered to all men but is conditioned upon repentance and faith in Christ.
Virtue	New Testament (Mark 5:30 and Luke 8:46); does not refer to moral character in the statement made by Jesus when the woman touched him in the hope of being healed. In this understanding, virtue means: A power. Properly translated in the Greek: dunamis (dynamite or dynamic) power.
Withal	(Pronounced "with all") With everything else, in addition or also (Hebrew), all together.
Zion	Strong Mountain, fortress of God, family of God.

ABOUT THE AUTHOR

*"Jeremiah 1:9-10 (KJV) **9 Then the LORD put forth his hand, and touched my mouth. And the LORD said unto me, Behold, I have put my words in thy mouth. 10 See, I have this day set thee over the nations and over the kingdoms, to root out, and to pull down, and to destroy, and to throw down, to build, and to plant.***

Bishop Rodney S. Walker I is a dynamic prophetic voice whose ministry is renowned as being a catalytic agent for understanding and maturing in the prophetic.

A native of Washington, D.C., Bishop Walker is the Founder and Senior Pastor of Heritage Church International, established in 1990 in Waldorf, Maryland. He serves as the General Overseer of Bishop R. S. Walker Ministries - formerly Another Touch of Glory Ministries - that covers national and international churches, para-church ministries and businesses.

He is spiritually covered by and accountable to Dr. Michael Freeman of Spirit of Faith Christian Center in Temple Hills, Maryland. He is also submitted to his Spiritual Father, Bishop Ralph L. Dennis of Kingdom Fellowship Covenant Ministries in Towson, Maryland.

In addition to being a graduate of the Jericho Christian Training College, Bishop Walker received his Doctor of Divinity degree from The Spirit of Truth Institute. Bishop R. S. Walker's training by versatile and equipped instructors, guidance from his Mentor, as well as submission to his Spiritual Father, has developed him into a well-balanced, grounded, and seasoned prophet.

On July 19, 1997, Bishop Walker was ordained Elder in the Office of Prophet by Kingdom Fellowship Covenant Ministries. In 1999, Bishop Walker founded the School of the Prophets. The School has locations in Waldorf and Baltimore, MD, Raleigh and Wilson, NC, Abuja, Nigeria, York, Pa, and has been hosted throughout the United States and beyond using online streaming. March 15, 2002, Bishop Walker completed the coursework for the Joint College of African-American Pentecostal Bishops Congress and July 3, 2009 was Ordained and Consecrated in the Office of Bishop by Kingdom Fellowship Covenant Ministries.

In addition to equipping and training in the prophetic, Bishop Walker has also assembled a body of Prophetic Presbyters who assist him in managing the great assignment God has set to his hands.

Bishop Walker is the author and publisher of over 10 books including: The Prophetic Prayer Journal, Raising Prophets of Character, Becoming a Proven Prophetic Voice, The 21st Century Prophet, The Renaissance Prophet, Foundations of Prophetic Maturity, and The Father/Son Encounter all of which prove to be phenomenal resources of the serious believer's library.

Among Bishop Walker's many accomplishments, is that of being a devoted husband to his lovely wife, Pastor Betty Walker, and a loving father to his eleven wonderful children.

Bishop Rodney S. Walker's ultimate goal is to fulfill all that God has purposed for his life and to effectively lead those placed in his prophetic and pastoral care. His love for God is evident in his preaching, teaching and zeal for ministry. You will experience the wind of the Spirit through this Man of God.

Order Form

Bishop RS Walker Ministries

2760 Crain Highway
Waldorf, MD 20601
301- 843-9267 or 877-200-8967 • Fax 240- 427-4606
www.bishoprswalker.com • e-mail: bishop@bishoprswalker.com

Name	
Title	Date
Church/Ministry	
Address	
City	State Zip
Daytime Phone	E-mail

Items Ordered:

Description	DVD	CD	Quantity	Total
Raising Prophets of Character Book				$14.95
School of the Prophets 15-week Course	$190.00		Discount	$110.00
Renaissance Prophet's Manual				$43.95
Foundations of Prophetic Maturity				$15.95
The Art of Tongues Book				$10.00
Raising Prophets of Character Prayer Devotional				$14.99
Creating Habits for a Functional Life				$14.99
The Father Son Encounter				$14.95
The Fundamentals of Faith (6-CDs)				$50.00
The Ministry of the Holy Spirit				$15.95

Shipping Information:
Add $4 for Priority Mail first item
$1 per additional item
MD add 6% sales tax

Method of Payment:
Please charge my: Discover   MasterCard   VISA   AMEX
Card Number: Expiration Date (Month/Year): / /
Signature (as shown on credit card):

Check or Money Order

Total price of items	
Add shipping charge	
Tax (if applicable)	
Total Amount Enclosed	

For Speaking Engagements contact: The Administrative Office of Bishop RS Walker
Ministries: (240) 573-3418 or admin@bishoprswalker.com

www.ingramcontent.com/pod-product-compliance
Lightning Source LLC
Chambersburg PA
CBHW080457110426
42742CB00017B/2921